Techne Theory

ALSO AVAILABLE FROM BLOOMSBURY:

Aesthetic Marx, edited by Samir Gandesha and Johan F. Hartle
Misanthropy, Andrew Gibson
Enduring Time, Lisa Baraitser
Eco-Aesthetics, Malcolm Miles
The Cultural Promise of the Aesthetic, Monique Roelofs
The Politics of Aesthetics, Jacques Rancière
Slow Philosophy, Michelle Boulous Walker
Reparative Aesthetics, Susan Best
The Curatorial, edited by Jean-Paul Martinon

Techne Theory

A New Language for Art

HENRY STATEN
University of Washington, USA

BLOOMSBURY ACADEMIC
LONDON • NEW YORK • OXFORD • NEW DELHI • SYDNEY

BLOOMSBURY ACADEMIC
Bloomsbury Publishing Plc
50 Bedford Square, London, WC1B 3DP, UK
1385 Broadway, New York, NY 10018, USA

BLOOMSBURY, BLOOMSBURY ACADEMIC and the Diana logo are trademarks of Bloomsbury Publishing Plc

First published in Great Britain 2019
Reprinted 2019

Cover design by Catherine Wood
Cover image © Petra Tischler / EyeEm / Getty Images

A catalogue record for this book is available from the British Library.

A catalog record for this book is available from the Library of Congress.

ISBN: HB: 978-1-4725-9289-7
PB: 978-1-4725-9290-3
ePDF: 978-1-4725-9292-7
eBook: 978-1-4725-9291-0

Typeset by Newgen KnowledgeWorks Pvt. Ltd., Chennai, India
Printed and bound in Great Britain

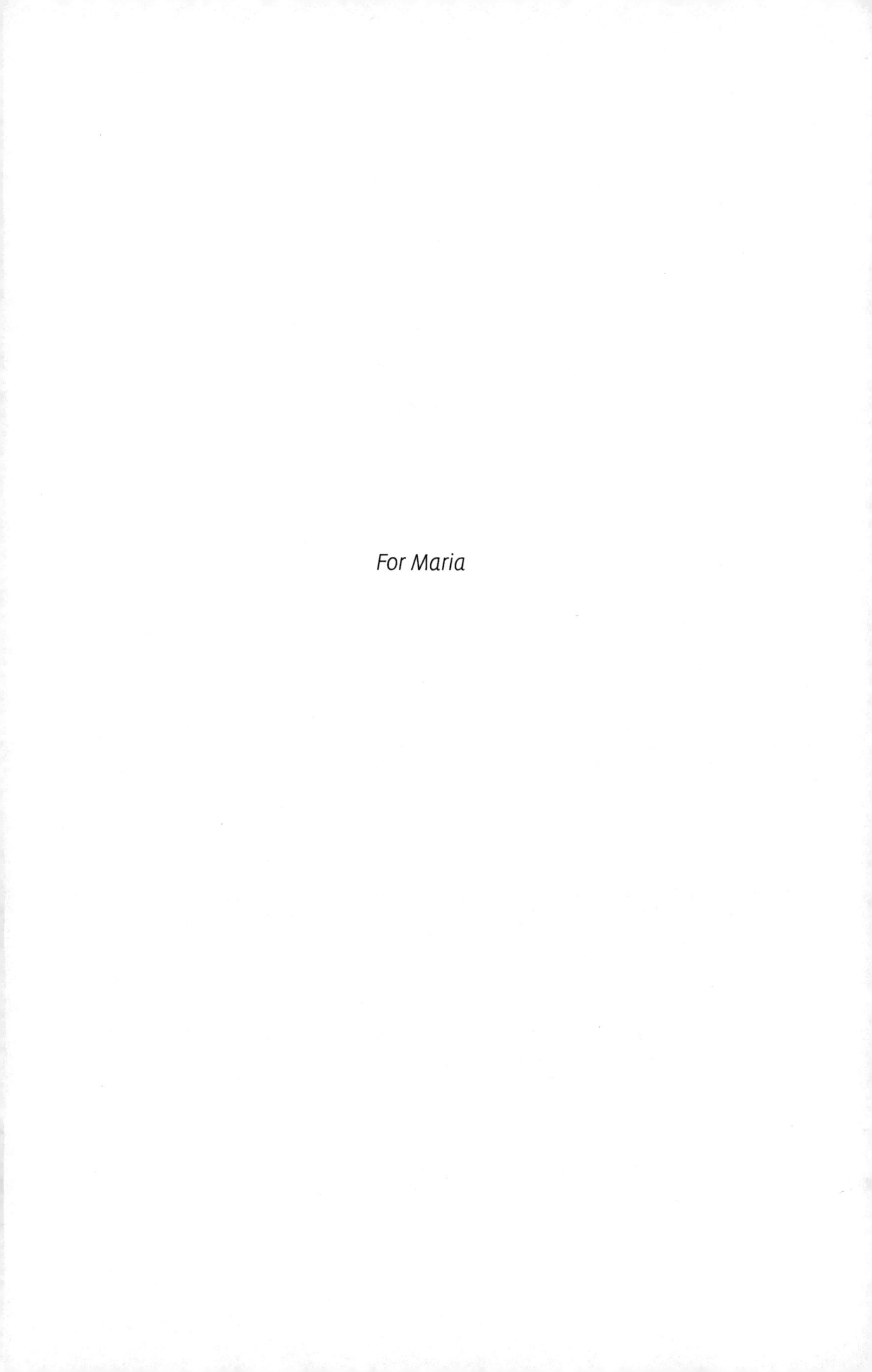

For Maria

CONTENTS

ACKNOWLEDGEMENTS

Two longtime friends, Charlie Altieri and Joe Marioni, have had an incalculable influence on the shape of the argument of this book. Charlie has offered decades of resistance to my ideas about techne, insisting that I properly address the *particulars* of making; Joe has given me an extended inside view into the hands-on aspect of an illustrious artisan's work, a view that has gone a long way towards helping me address Charlie's demand. The resistance to the techne standpoint of two other friends belonging to the 'Romantic-humanist' camp, Marshall Brown and Stanley Corngold, has also played a significant role. But one also needs some positive feedback to keep believing in what one is doing, and on this side I am warmly grateful to Derek Attridge for his receptiveness to my ideas and for helping me work them out in a series of dialogues that we published as a book a few years ago. I also owe special thanks to three people I've never (yet) met, who read the manuscript, comprising the present Chapters 2 and 3, out of which this book grew, and whose interest in the project emboldened me to continue it and to expand its scope. At the top of the list is Andy Clark, who generously read the manuscript after I sent it to him out of the blue, expressed his interest in seeing the work completed, and has continued to dialogue with me about it. Andy also put me onto the work of Edwin Hutchins, to whom I then sent that original manuscript, and whose warm response and critical remarks have meant a great deal to me. The third person to read it was Gary Tomlinson, to whom I sent it because I had been so impressed with his book on the evolution of the music faculty, and with whom I was delighted to discover a remarkable 'congeniality' of thought (in the old sense of the term). As the book developed, I sought, and received, the help on individual topics of a constellation of exceptional thinkers, without whom this book would be much more flawed than it is. On Plato, David Wolfsdorf and Christopher Janaway; on Aristotle, Joseph Dunne and Tom Angier; on language, once again Andy Clark; on Picasso, T. J. Clark; on radical painting, Michael Fried, Joseph Marioni and Joseph Staten (who also helped me with the introductory chapter); on Kafka, Stanley Corngold, who read an early version and, despite his skepticism about techne theory, was supportive of my approach; on universal design space, Daniel Dennett. I should also mention three colleagues who over the decades allowed me to tap their expertise on Aristotle, in conversation and correspondence: Nicholas White,

Marc Cohen and Leroy Searle. Finally, I'm grateful to Terrence Deacon for his receptiveness to my repeated inquiries and for having provided the final link in the chain of thought that this book develops. In my estimation, Deacon's thought is revising our fundamental understanding of nature in a way that constitutes a 'paradigm shift', and this book is intended to be in the spirit of that shift.

PART ONE
Fundamentals

CHAPTER ONE

The techne standpoint

Artists don't think about art the way non-artists do. Critics and audiences view art as finished products, to be appreciated and interpreted; an artist sees a work by another artist through the eyes of a fellow art-maker, as a *made thing*, and tries to discern how it was made, how its materials were worked. Experiencing other people's art is, for an artist, part of the endless quest to deepen her own knowledge of art-making – her own *techne*.

Non-artists' view of art – the passive, consumer's eye view – has spawned the pernicious concept of 'an abstract capitalized Art', as Raymond Williams called it.[1] Art with a capital A is the set of objects characterized by 'an ineffable quality' – a *je ne sais quois* or 'aura' – that does not 'obey pre-established rules', and which creates 'a space of secular spirituality institutionalized by the museum'.[2] Larry Shiner has chronicled the rise of this new definition of art in the eighteenth century, showing how the 'fine arts' were first elevated into a sublime new category raised above the mere crafts.[3] Before that time, there was no formal, hierarchical distinction – certainly not one expressible in money – between art and craft, as we see from the fact, cited by Shiner, that Leonardo was initially paid less for painting *The Virgin of the Rocks* than was Giacomo del Maino for carving the framework. Even in the eighteenth century, after the elite new classification of fine art had begun to take hold, fields such as mechanics, optics, watchmaking, surgery, engineering and landscape gardening could be included on the list of 'fine arts' (pp. 35, 81–2).

The emerging separation of a canonical set of fine arts from the rest of the crafts went hand in hand with a new, sublime conception of art-making and art-makers. In 1709 Dubos in his *Poets and Painters* still referred to his subjects as 'artisans', though he admitted he should have added the adjective 'illustrious'; and Batteux, who defined the canonical set of so-called 'fine' arts, nevertheless maintained in 1746 that even geniuses 'cannot properly create', they can only 'recognize where and how [something] is' (p. 114) – a prescient definition that I propose to validate in this book. But the Romantic breeze was beginning to blow, and would soon replace the notion of the illustrious artisan and the non-creator genius with that of the *genius creator.* Now techne, the skill and knowledge of the artisan, was depreciated as merely 'mechanical' activity, and our modern concept of Art and the Artist took centre stage.

Perhaps previous ages were less enlightened than we are, and had not yet recognized the metaphysical specialness of certain arts and those who make them. If so, this failure extends all the way back to the classical Greeks, for so long viewed as the supreme art-makers of the West, who lacked even a word for what we mean by Art. Their word was the one I have adopted, *techne*, and it included the arts of fishing, carpentry, generalship, mathematics – *all* forms of skilful attaining of a goal. Techne is just practical know-how of any kind whatever, no matter how sophisticated. The Romans translated techne as *ars*, with the same meaning, and the equivalent modern European words up to the eighteenth century – art, arte, Kunst – still meant the same. Techne, then, is the original – I want to say, the *proper* – sense of our word art.

In its original use, then, *art* refers not to artworks but to the skill and know-how by means of which artworks – and everything else – are made or organized. On this understanding of the word, museums do not contain 'art'; they contain works *of* art, things made *by* art. Because today most of the time, in most contexts, we hear 'art' as referring to art's products, the question 'what is art?' (asked as one looks at a painting, or Duchamp's urinal) has become an endlessly tantalizing riddle rooted in mystery. But you can't understand art by staring at art *products* and repeating 'Art! Art!' to yourself; it's the nature of their *making* that needs to be plumbed.

Even though the decisive turn towards the modern mystification of art was taken by the Romantic theory of genius, Romantic thought never entirely forgot about art in the traditional sense. Kant, who gave the Romantic theory its most influential form, tortuously reconciled the old value of art as maker's knowledge, derived from previous models of art-making, with the ascendant value of genius. But the last vestiges of regard for art as techne were erased in the modern notion, purportedly inspired by Duchamp, that art is basically conceptual. This step was the final metamorphosis of the idea of genius. The idea that the ineffable quality of artness was a product of a mysterious creative faculty in the artist spawned the notion that the troublesome process of struggling with materials and techniques could be skipped altogether; the artist could bestow the name of art on an object, any object whatever, and it became art.

Duchamp's opening up of the notion of art to admit 'anything whatever' was supposed to be counter-institutional, a step away from the monumentalization of the masterwork and its creator and towards the democratization of art. But it has not worked out that way; rather, the old, mystified value of the art object has not only survived but flourished, as the new kinds of objects defined as art are shown in the same exhibition spaces, with the same price tags, as the old ones. And the process of mystification at the level of theory, with its continued fetishization of the art object, goes on, now in combination with the evolution of the power of the art-market.

Among the most culturally pernicious effects of this mystification is what radical anthropological theorist Alfred Gell called the 'mismatch' between 'the spectator's internal awareness of his own powers as an agent' and the conception the spectator forms of 'the powers possessed by the artist'.[4] No doubt we should be impressed by another human being's know-how that exceeds our own; but the more the nature of a know-how is hidden behind a veil of mystification the more likely it is to stymie the spectator's sense of her own agency, and the more serviceable it becomes to the power interests to which art is so easily wed. By contrast, to the degree that the spectator learns *what art is* – productive know-how that human beings learn as they learn any other social practice, and which, like any other social practice, some people are better at than others, in large part (but not entirely) thanks to a combination of hard work and favourable circumstances – the visible work loses its aura of mystery, and the cowing of the spectator by the feeling of mismatch correspondingly diminishes.

But if art is techne, are 'artists' no better than plumbers? The question is badly out of focus and only seems momentous to the Art-mystified eye. From the techne standpoint, the mystery, and the fascination, is primarily in the *cunning* by means of which Art and all other systematic, goal-oriented, knowledge-based forms of human activity are carried out – the cunning that organizes materials, methods and the artisans' actions in the most effective way. When one shifts one's focus from the product to the *how* and *with what* of making, the differences between painters and plumbers do indeed become less intriguing than the similarities, because the real mystery of art's cunning is so much richer than anything having to do with the distinction between art and craft. Cunning is related to German *können*, which means both 'to know' and 'to be able to', and itself has had both meanings in the past; I mean to evoke both of them, as well as the sense of cunning as a 'crafty' kind of knowledge, one that can get around official obstacles. It takes a word like this to give a true sense of the suppleness and complexity of the kind of knowledge techne is – a know-how that is immensely far from 'merely mechanical', as the cliché since Kant has had it, a cliché today so deeply rooted that it seems like common sense.

The purpose of this book is to fight the fetishism of the art product by showing how much there is to know about the cunning behind the producing – the producing not only of what we think of as Art, but of everything that constitutes ordered human activity of all kinds, from language and the upright stance with which humans learn to walk, to poetry, rocket science, and shoelace-tying – all of human culture, in short. Obviously, there are deep differences among the technai, as there are among the kingdoms and phyla of the living world, but, like living things, technai all grow from the same root and have the same fundamental nature. They are systematic ways of organizing our world, the knowledge of which is universally inherited by human beings simply by virtue of being brought up in human societies. The crucial fact about techne, which makes it so unpalatable to Romantic-humanist ideas of Art, is that it is in the first instance a social-historical, not an individual-psychological, possession, a practical knowledge that before it migrates to an individual mind-body has been accumulated within and across cultures over generations, centuries, millennia. The individual's power to make anything, whether a craft artefact or a fine artwork, or to be the agent of any goal-oriented act, is *necessarily* and *always* derived or delegated from techne.

We are, however, so inured to the idea that 'fine art', as opposed to craft work, requires a special, indefinable intervention on the part of the artist, that the definition of art as techne strikes us as leaving out precisely the most essential thing about art. We think: of course in art of the traditional kind the artist must have a certain acquired art-making knowledge, which she uses to hack away at the marble, *but* presiding over this skilled hacking-away there must be something that critical analysis can never pin down, a specialness that cannot be the product of mere techne. To this way of thinking, it seems self-evident that techne can produce only conventional, generic, 'mechanical' work.

In the past fifty years this Romantic-humanist theory of Art was submitted to a radical challenge from structuralism and post-structuralism. In its most polemical 'death of the author' phase structuralism theorized that artworks are produced by mechanical combinatories of pre-existing elements, a notion that had great appeal at the time for many of us who were sick of aesthetic mystery. The work done by the structuralists on the theory of art was, however, primarily negative; they did not produce a convincing new account. Structuralist ideas and techne theory overlap on some points, but none of the structuralists (I include here Foucault, Barthes and even Derrida) ever came close to understanding art as techne. Instead, they paved the way to a general loss of interest (in departments of literature, and to a considerable degree in departments of art and music as well) in the specificity of the work of art, so that the study of art in the 1980s and 1990s, and to a considerable degree still today, has been dominated by larger questions of culture and the political. For anyone interested in the question of art 'as art', whether as product or as production, and not in leaving it behind, the death of the author left the question of how art is made shrouded in deeper darkness than before. The question of art, in any sense of the term, whether as Art or as techne, is a question of value: either of where value resides in the art object, or, in the techne view, the radically different question of how, out of the infinity of forms that can be mechanically generated, a particular individual in a particular concrete situation makes judgments of better and worse resulting in a work that is a candidate for appreciation as art by the relevant valuing community.[5] The structuralist combinatory generates an indiscriminate proliferation of forms;

but how does an individual artist make the judgments of value that select the good ones out of this wilderness? Indiscriminate combinatorial play does not produce a pleasurable carnival of forms; well before structuralism, Jorge Luis Borges saw that the mechanical combinatory produces only the nightmare vision of the Library of Babel.[6]

That *genius* cannot be the whole picture was recognized by Kant in those same pages in which he argued that 'beautiful art is possible only as a product of genius'.[7] Even conscientious readers of Kant have had trouble recognizing just how fundamental, how shocking, is the limitation Kant then places on the sovereignty of genius: that genius as such does not and cannot produce the *form* of the finished art work, but only 'rich *material* [*Stoff*] for products of art'; genius left to itself, in the absence of the 'slow and painstaking', mechanical pursuit of form, produces 'nothing but nonsense' (50; p. 197). I underline: Kant says that *genius is not the source of aesthetic form; genius as such produces nothing but nonsense.*[8]

Coming from the diametrically opposite position from Borges, Kant arrives at the same impasse. The 'productive' faculty, whether genius or the universal combinatory, cannot account for the crucial factor in art: the *form* of the individual work. Only techne, referred to here by Kant in terms of the faculty of taste, can bestow form:

> To give . . . form to the product of beautiful art . . . requires merely taste, to which the artist, after he has practiced and corrected it by means of various examples of art or nature, holds up his work, and after many, often laborious attempts to satisfy it, finds the form that contents him; hence this is not a matter of inspiration or a free swing of the mental powers, but a slow and indeed painstaking improvement, in order to let it become adequate to the thought and yet not detrimental to the freedom in the play of the mental powers. (48; p. 191)

Despite his flight into the ineffable, Kant remains close enough to the classical tradition of art theory to think of Kunst primarily not as the products of art but as that by which these products are made; and he has enough of a sense of art as techne to set his account of production by mere 'taste' and artistic labour against the more unhinged, more properly Romantic, notions of genius that were influential in Germany at the time. From the standpoint of techne theory, Kant's most radical and penetrating insight is the one concerning the *limitation* of the creative power of genius. An art object is given *value* by being given *form*, of whatever sort might be appropriate to the kind of art that it is; and an innate, natural faculty, no matter how 'creative' in some notional sense it might be, cannot be the effective origin of form in art. This insight points us towards the fundamental question that divides Romantic and humanistic accounts of art from techne-oriented or at least techne-compatible accounts. If form cannot be brought forth by an innate faculty, then, as V. N. Volosinov explained in his fundamental, and still today essential, critique of Romantic philosophy of language, all form comes from outside – from the social outside, where form-giving technai are historically developed, stored up, and transmitted to individuals who then put them into action.[9]

It is, however, incredibly difficult to eradicate the feeling that art to be Art must be traceable to a spontaneous moment of form-origination, a pristine *arkhe*, – the feeling that, without such a moment, art would be mere machinery. There must be the possibility of art's being made by an utterly spontaneous artist, entirely in the absence of a culturally acquired techne; otherwise, how would art ever get started in the first place, way back at the beginning of culture? And if spontaneous creation is possible at the historical origin, then a 'natural' creative faculty must exist, and *could* be the real explanation of the originality of our own artists, or at least our most significant ones. This Romantic myth of the spontaneous artist is so deeply rooted in our cultural Imaginary that it turns up in surprising places. Even Monroe Beardsley, co-author with William Wimsatt of 'The Intentional Fallacy' – probably the most important polemic against the idea that artistic value originates in authorial subjectivity – revealed years later a lingering attraction to the idea of the solitary 'Romantic artist'.

> Of course we cannot deny that the Romantic artist may be supplied electricity by an institution, that his paper or canvas has to be manufactured, that his very thoughts will be . . . to some extent 'moulded' by his acquired language and previous acculturation. But that is all beside the point, which is . . . that he can make a work of art, and validate it as such, by his own free originative power.[10]

From the techne standpoint, this is not entirely wrong; art can be produced by a solitary artist, outside the official 'art-world', as long as the production is techne-guided; but, on the techne conception, it makes no sense to say that the artist's 'previous acculturation' is 'beside the point'.

Another prominent philosopher of aesthetics, Jerrold Levinson, argues that there can be 'private, isolated art which is constituted as art in the mind of the artist', as, for example, 'a solitary Indian along the Amazon, who steals off from his non-artistic tribe to arrange coloured stones in a clearing, not outwardly investing them with special position in the world. Might not this also be art?' It's not entirely clear what Levinson is imagining here, but since our own artists work in solitude all the time, his example suggests that he's trying, like Beardsley, to define a more primordial act of creation than that of our artists. Since the Indian's tribe is 'non-artistic', the impulse to make art in the Amazonian must emerge from some faculty natural to human beings, one that doesn't require learning an artistic techne.[11]

The whole philosophical debate over the definition of 'art' arises from taking too seriously our vague modern usage of the signifier 'art', as though it actually referred to something real that we should be able to nail down conceptually. From the techne standpoint, by contrast, what we call art emerges not just from an 'art-world' in the modern sense but, precisely, from the whole process of acculturation into the web of technai that forms human cultures. To understand the evolution of art (and Art) as a techne, or as a whole variety of technai, we need to understand how it emerged from the complex matrix of such acculturation. The imagined Amazonian tribe, no matter how 'non-artistic', will necessarily have all kinds of know-how in which the people will be adept: they will make tools, weapons, clothes, and other artefacts, and they will participate in various other kinds of organized group activities, such as hunting, which require knowledge and training of novices by master-hunters. All these, as we learn from Plato, are ways of *giving form* to the world, and it's a mistake to try to understand art by isolating it as much as possible from this matrix, which already, even in the earliest stages of the evolution of human culture, appears to have included the making and wearing of ornaments that from our standpoint have no practical value. We now know that even the Neanderthals made ornaments (and perhaps paintings too, some think). No matter how hard we try to imagine our proto-artist as ignorant of all form that comes from 'outside', from the historically evolved forms of social practice, we find that there are already form-giving technai of multiple kinds of which we cannot imagine him ignorant. 'Proto-art' will already be everywhere in the technai with which the Amazonian is acquainted, beginning with the symmetries of the simplest tools – symmetries that, as recent archaeological investigations have shown, may well have initially arisen for reasons having nothing to do with aesthetic appreciation.[12]

Of course there is somewhere a beginning in biology of the ability to create form, as there is, somehow, of everything about human beings and our cultures. Art, however, is the product not of some innate formative urge but of a long process of cultural evolution by means of which the form-bestowing powers of human beings are initially called forth out of our genetic endowment, then developed and enhanced until they become what *we* call art; and the form-bestowing power is coded by the long process of cultural evolution into the tools and know-how of social practices, from which it is picked up (sometimes with uncanny aptitude) by individual practitioners, and without which they would be entirely helpless to bestow form. And there is no firm or sharp boundary between the practices we think of as Art and the rest of the panoply of technai.

Once we become attentive to the nature of techne, it quickly becomes apparent that all purposeful, goal-directed human action that has any degree of complexity is techne-guided. There is no human agency without techne. We can't even form a goal-directed *intention* without the intermediary of techne. As Plato already saw in the *Republic*, human society is fundamentally made up of assemblages of technai, and human beings are transformed from biological organisms to agents by virtue of the technai they in-corporate, take into their bodies (*corpus*, body) – brain, nervous system, tendons, muscles, and viscera.

A techne is socially developed, and as it is developed it is socially 'inscribed', established in the form of a practice henceforth available for transmission to new practitioners. Such practices are virtual machines or programs in which is encoded the know-how human societies discover over time. Techne is the accretion or sedimentation of myriad acts of trial and error and micro-discovery that come together over generations. These discoveries are in part etched into the forms of tools; but techne itself has a morphology, analogous to that of a tool, which incorporates, to an incomparably greater degree than tools do, the know-how that has been accumulated by generations of anonymous artisans, so that when we wield a techne we act better than we know because we let ourselves be guided by it into optimal (or optimality approximating) paths of activity that we don't have to discover on our own. It's easy to see that an electronic calculator incorporates a know-how that can far outrun that of its user; it's not quite as obvious that our very ability to push the right buttons on the calculator itself incorporates know-how that outruns us in an analogous way.

That is to say that cognition is not just something that occurs in the brain; it is, as Edwin Hutchins has taught us to say, 'distributed' among persons, our tools and instruments, and the technai by means of which persons get tools and instruments to work. In his seminal *Cognition in the Wild*, one of the landmark works of an exciting new cognitive science, Hutchins showed how this all works by a staggeringly detailed analysis of every element of navigation on a large naval vessel.[13] Hutchins's analysis impresses on our minds and imaginations the vastness of the web of know-how, dating back in its historical origins to the Babylonians, that is woven into the ship's charts, instruments, mathematical techniques, and distribution of roles among pilot, navigator, and so forth, such that remarkably little of the cognitive process represented in the entire operation is contained in the consciousness of any single individual involved. To take the lesson of Hutchins's book is to see culture with new eyes – to begin to see how all of culture is woven out of analogous webs of 'distributed cognition'.

We give ourselves the impression that we, as individuals, are the origin of marvellous acts of intelligence and creation only by occluding the true marvel, the cultural machinery that makes the doing possible. As though a child with a calculator thought he were performing complex multiplications by knowing which buttons to push. In a sense of course, the child *is* carrying out these multiplications, only, the skids have been immensely greased by the machine. But the fundamental greasing of the skids, which had to take place before the machine could be devised to do its work, was done by those who devised every aspect of the system of arithmetic, including such things as the system of numerals. Consider, for example, how much harder it is to do calculations with Roman numerals than with our customary Hindu-Arabic numerals. We aren't aware of how much smarter we are with the numerals we learned in school than we would have been with the Roman system; we indeed are that much smarter, but not because there's any more mental activity involved. Behind both systems is the development of techniques of inscription ('writing'), without which we would have to make all our calculations with our fingers. The principle is the same with shoelace-tying, symphony writing, or rocket science. Our own abilities piggyback on inherited, socially inscribed know-how that becomes woven into our neuromuscular substance by culture, in a way analogous to that in which biological structures embody know-how discovered by biological evolution – the way in which, as Daniel Dennett points out, a bird's wings embody knowledge of the principles of aerodynamics.[14]

Think of Beethoven in a Neolithic tribe, one that has not yet even invented flutes. What would all his vaunted genius come to? The reality can be summed up in a simple equation: genius minus techne equals ZERO. It's intriguing, given the nature of Beethoven's music, to consider what he would have been even without the pianoforte, which was invented not long before his time. Think of that explosive genius confined to the harpsichord. The pianoforte embodies culturally evolved know-how the way a bird's wings embody biologically evolved know-how.

Nietzsche was right when he rejected the idea that human action is motivated by a mental 'picture of the consequences' of an intended action, but he thought this meant our 'real' motive must therefore be our drives. Drives conceived as biological energy, however, are as incapable of producing *effectual* action as are mental pictures; only drives that have incorporated the neuromuscular competence to perform the correct series of moves involved in achieving a goal can motivate effectual action, and such competence is attainable only through techne, encoded knowledge of previously verified, reliable pathways to specific ends. The more skilled I am in a techne the more habitually and justly – habitually *because* justly – I will picture as successful the probable consequence of my act. In fact, if I'm truly skilled, like a professional musician, I can dispense altogether with the picturing and do the thing with unreflective confidence.[15]

Our mental picture of the intended consequence can indeed play a role at times, but, like drives, it can only play an *effectual* role if the pathways towards that result already belong to our neuromuscular competence – that is to say, if the mental picture itself functions as an organon 'instrument' of the techne. There is no boundary of essence between the technai of thinking and those of worldly action – both are given causal power from the same source.

A techne is a system of institutionalized traces of the grooves of effectuality that have been worn into the real by untold previous actors, grooves along which we inheritors can then to some degree coast. But only the *traces* of these grooves are available to us until we actually put our tools and methods to the test, and then we encounter rough spots, crossroads, and dead ends, and that is where the real cunning or craftiness of techne comes in, where we use it, or allow it to use us, to make our own original contributions, not only rediscovering the old grooves but making new ones. This is the mystery of what is called 'creation' or 'invention'. Batteux, as we saw, did not believe that *creation*, strictly speaking – absolute origination, out of nothing – is possible for human beings, only 'discovery' of what is there, and from the techne standpoint, Batteux was right. Creation is a form of discovery; but discovery of a peculiarly complex kind.

Let's say human beings have started to hold their shoes tight on their feet with string poked through holes drilled in the leather. Now someone gets the idea of tying the string in some way that will be easier to undo, and fiddles with the strings until she figures out the sequence of actions required to tie a functional shoelace knot. I want to say with Batteux that this is a process not of invention but of discovery. Reality has to be constituted in such a way that such knots are possible; the trick is to discover which of the many possibilities available to us are going to yield the precise sequence of actions that will do the trick. The grooves or channels in the nature of material reality are merely 'virtual', completely invisible and unmanifest (but which we might imagine as hidden in what Dennett calls 'Universal Design Space', the subject of my concluding chapter); and we have to find them. Think of having to discover the only way out of a cave that has never been explored before. The correct pathway is there, in a sense, and in another sense not there. It isn't there in the sense that all undiscovered pathways, correct and incorrect, are equally non-existent, because for material reality there are no correct or incorrect pathways. It's only in relation to a specific purpose, which in this case could be that of a human or an animal, that there's a correct way out of the cave. The correct way out is a pure, almost empty idealization until we actually discover it. But if it turns out in the end to exist, we automatically conceive it as having existed from the beginning.

Now think about the questing inventor of the releasable shoelace knot. There are pathways in the real here too, the specific patterns of finger-motion that, once they are found, will fluidly tie the correct knot; they are already 'there' before we find them, in some difficult sense of virtual thereness that I think we need to get comfortable with. These as-yet-undiscovered patterns in the real, these 'lines of causality' in the real, are potential pathways of human action, which become *lines of force* when they enable mere expenditure of human energy to become effectuality, effective-force, *Macht*.

Human need sets human purposes, and human purposes poke and prod an enigmatic materiality until they find the points at which it most readily gives way to these purposes. Flint has a cryptocrystalline structure that splits readily into flakes when struck; we may take the crystalline fracture-lines of flint as a paradigm of the lines of causality to which human beings must adapt themselves. If they strike against the flow of the fracture-lines in the real, their effort is dissipated or entirely wasted; if they strike with the lines, its effect is amplified. Formerly one used whatever sharpened bit of stone came to hand to tip an arrow; then the useful qualities of flint were discovered, and now it takes less work to make an arrowhead, and a better one; with this improvement in the techne of arrowhead-making, the techne of hunting flows into new, less resistant, lines of causality. But the lines of force that human societies slowly discover and learn to exploit are neither *intrinsic to* nature nor mere constructions of the human mind. They are the dialectical interface between human purposiveness and the matrix of causal systems given in nature; and techne is the logos of this dialectic.

Each techne is the historical residue of a long process of human effort that gives rise to a specific configuration of lines of force, resulting in part from how a given corner of the system of nature *is* in itself, and in part from the way the elements of that corner are chipped at, moved around, and reassembled by human beings. Lukacs identified this process with Marx's 'human metabolic interchange with nature' – the labour process. While Lukacs was mistaken in treating techne and the labour process as strictly synonymous, there are the closest relations between the two, and these relations are of fundamental importance for techne theory.[16]

Is solving an art-problem anything like finding a way out of the cave, or figuring out how to tie a shoelace-knot, or flake a piece of flintstone? Remarkably like, in fact. It's easy to see how sculptors or painters have to grapple with materiality, but even the writer must do so. Word-sounds, meanings, rhythms and syntactic structures are the material qualities that the writer shapes into pleasing ensembles. But the question of how to approach the 'fine arts' from the techne standpoint is too complex for quick elucidation; that is the burden of this book.

In principle, music would be the best example by which to show the role of techne in art, because it is so purely and evidently techne, and I will touch on it at various points; but I discuss extensively only painting and literature because this is where techne theory has the most work to do. The main barrier to understanding art as techne is the hunt for interpretive 'meaning', and music isn't haunted by the spectre of meaning as literature and painting are; hence, music scholars are already accustomed to analysing music in strictly formal terms. (Formalism, in the ordinary sense of the term, is not synonymous with the techne standpoint, but the two are closely correlated.)[17]

Finally, I apologize to those devotees of the other arts that are scanted in this book, especially filmmaking, which is probably the pre-eminent art form of our time (now largely in the form of TV series). Like music theorists, cinema theorists are already highly techne-focused. Yet in neither field, to my knowledge, has the subject of this book, the *general theory* of techne, been investigated.

NOTES

1 Raymond Williams, *Keywords: A Vocabulary of Culture and Society* (New York: Oxford University Press, 1976), p. 33. Cited by Shiner, p. 189.

2 Thierry de Duve, *Kant after Duchamp* (Cambridge, MA: MIT Press, 1996), p. 76.

3 Larry Shiner, *The Invention of Art: A Cultural History* (Chicago: University of Chicago Press, 2001).

4 Alfred Gell, 'Technology and Enchantment', in *Anthropology, Art, and Aesthetics*, ed. Jeremy Coote and Anthony Shelton (Oxford: Clarendon Press, 1992), pp. 53–4.

5 This formulation is influenced by the 'institutional theory of art' of George Dickie, known mainly from his *Art and the Aesthetic: An Institutional Analysis* (Ithaca, NY: Cornell University Press, 1974), but substantially revised and improved in *The Art Circle* (New York: Haven, 1984).

6 Borges is often treated straightforwardly as a 'postmodernist' master of the 'play of the signifier'. That his relation to this 'play' was in fact extremely tormented has been convincingly shown by the recent work of Díaz Pozueta. María Díaz Pozueta, *Image, Form, and Death: Borges's Anti-Intellectual Project*, dissertation, University of Washington (2007); 'From Idealism to Ideology in "Tlon, Uqbar, Orbis Tertius" and "Deutsches Requiem"', *CR: The New Centennial Review* (2007) 9.3: 209–28.

7 Immanuel Kant, *Critique of the Power of Judgment*, ed. Paul Guyer (Cambridge: Cambridge University Press, 2001), sec. 46, p. 186.

8 One recent commentator has been so impressed by Kant's stress on the technical process of form-imposition as to argue that it is Kant's true theory of art-making, with genius entering in only as the theory, that we use, as observers, to put out of mind the 'concept' of the art object and judge it as though it were nature (i.e. to judge it in a pure judgment of taste). See Bradley Murray, 'Kant on Genius and Aesthetics', *British Journal of Aesthetics* (April 2007) 47.2: 199–214. I don't think Murray's theory can be reconciled with everything Kant says, but it does underline the strikingness – once one gives them their due weight – of Kant's remarks on form-imposition.

9 V. N. Volosinov, *Marxism and the Theory of Language*, trans. L. Matejka and I. R. Titunik (New York: Seminar Press), pp. 83–98.

10 Monroe Beardsley, 'Is Art Essentially Institutional?', in *Culture and Art*, ed. Lars Aagard-Mogensen (Atlantic Highlands, NJ: Humanities Press, 1976), p. 196.

11 Jerrold Levinson, 'Defining Art Historically', *British Journal of Aesthetics* (Summer 1979) 19.3: 232–51; quotation from p. 233. I should stress that Levinson's primary emphasis is on the essentially constitutive role of the artwork's relation to the history of art, a notion that does not in itself conflict with techne theory. The notion of the Amazonian artist sorts oddly with this historical emphasis.

12 'Preconceptual action sequences are structured according to . . . material affordances, the energy required in working them, and the biomechanical limitations of the worker; and all these together can be enough to engender systematic patterns tending to produce material symmetries. From this vantage, thinking of the hominin mind dictating symmetries has it backwards; it is the body-stone interaction from which symmetries (and perhaps even the mind) emerge.' Gary Tomlinson, *A Million Years of Music: The Emergence of Human Modernity* (Brooklyn, NY: Zone Books, 2015), p. 68

13 Edwin Hutchins, *Cognition in the Wild* (Cambridge, MA: MIT Press, 1995).

14 Daniel Dennett, *Darwin's Dangerous Idea: Evolution and the Meanings of Life* (New York: Simon and Schuster, 1995), pp. 197–8. See also Ch. 12, below.

15 I develop this argument regarding Nietzsche in an essay, 'Towards a Will to Power Sociology', in *Nietzsche and Ethics*, ed. Gudrun Tevenar (Oxford: Peter Lang, 2007), pp. 137–70.

16 Georg Lukacs, *The Ontology of Social Being*, part 2, ch. 1: *Labour*, trans. David Fernbach (London: Merlin Press, 1980). I cannot overstate the influence this deep philosophical investigation of the labour process has had on my understanding of techne, even though in the end Lukacs's 'intellectualist' standpoint has kept me from making more than occasional reference to it.

17 For some superb examples of how to discuss music strictly from the techne standpoint, see the YouTube videos currently being made by the brilliant young musicologist-composer Samuel Andreyev. I link three of these videos. The first, and from the standpoint of this book, most intriguing: Andreyev's attempt to define the almost indefinable form of a song by the mysterious, unclassifiable composer Jandek (www.youtube.com/watch?v=CZ41cFeSYTg&t=5s); then a question-and-answer in which Andreyev explains the techne of listening to music, what an instrument is and other fundamental points (www.youtube.com/watch?v=ml5B1sQk_xI&t=34); and an analysis of Captain Beefheart's 'Frownland', the first piece on his groundbreaking 1969 album *Trout Mask Replica* (www.youtube.com/watch?v=-FhhB9teHqU).

CHAPTER TWO

Art and evolution

Creativity is a habit, and the best creativity is the result of good work habits. That's it in a nutshell.
– Twyla Tharp

Rainer Maria Rilke, who started out with certain airy notions about creation, learned how to be a real artist from Rodin. When Rilke asked him what he should do to improve as a poet, Rodin replied that 'one must work – nothing but work' – a reply that deeply impressed Rilke. Because he had been living with Rodin and watching him work, Rilke was able to hear in this simple repeated word 'work' the answer to the deep mystery of art-making. He knew that Rodin meant intensive, sustained labour informed by consummate craft-knowledge, which the artist is always seeking to develop further. Rodin 'gave no play to his imagination, and invented nothing', Rilke writes in the first of his two great essays on Rodin; 'Not for a moment did he disdain the difficult development of his craft.' And in the second essay he says that 'what matters with art objects . . . the most important thing, is that they be well made'.[1] In one of his letters on Cézanne, who had the same approach to art as Rodin, Rilke refers to art-labour as the realm of the 'well done', and attributes to it the power to raise his own work to the highest level. In the composition of poetry, he writes, it is necessary 'to stay within the "well done" ', because if you do so, 'it increases and surpasses you again and again'[2]

With these words Rilke sets the fundamental terms of our problematic. The artist is to keep *within* the well done until eventually the well done itself will *surpass the artist*. To understand this way of thinking is to step entirely outside the modern notion of artistic creation.

The realm of work that is 'well done', in Rilke's sense, is what the ancient Greeks called techne. Techne is the oldest concept of 'art' in the

Western tradition – or rather, it is the historical prototype out of which our notion of art grew. But techne for the Greeks was not just 'fine art' (a concept they lacked); it was know-how of any kind, practical, theoretical, 'artistic', or any other – paradigmatically, the kind of know-how that is the common possession of a profession. Hence, in the most resonant invocation of the notion of techne in Greek philosophy, in Plato's *Ion*, Socrates gives charioteering and fishing as examples of genuine technai, accusing poets of creating poetry *merely* by 'inspiration' or 'possession' – not by techne. For Socrates, a thing could not be well done unless the doer had learned a disciplined, principled know-how adapted to that kind of task; and he believed that poets possessed no such discipline.

Socrates's doctrine of sublime poetic inspiration was intended as an ironic dig at poet and rhapsode, yet it has in modernity been understood as the highest praise that could be awarded to a poet, and has been expanded to include the makers of the other 'fine arts'. The novice reader of the *Ion* today might thus have trouble understanding how, if fishing and charioteering count as technai, *not* being techne could, for Socrates, constitute a *negative* criticism of poetry. But why has Western culture, during the very period of its turn towards the scientific world explanation, pinned the highest artistic merit on 'inspiration' and 'genius', descendants of the notion of possession by spirits? There is good reason to believe that Rilke's sober, techne-oriented thinking – another version of which was articulated by T. S. Eliot in 'Tradition and the Individual Talent', perhaps the most famous literary-theoretical essay of modernity in the English-speaking world – represents the stance of most artists in most cultures in most periods of history, including our own; but the view of art among non-artists in the West continues to be dominated by the Romantic idea that a leap of creation takes place between the level of the well done, on the one hand, and that of truly outstanding artworks on the other, a leap that only a transcendent faculty – genius, inspiration, or imagination – could possibly bring about.

The creative faculty, on this view, *must*, logically, exist, in much the way God was posited as necessary by the ontological argument for his existence. According to the ontological argument, the concept of God is that of an absolutely perfect being, and in order to be perfect he must exist. The very concept of a non-existent perfect being is unintelligible. But, since the concept of a Perfect Being is in fact intelligible, this being must exist. Similarly, on the Romantic-humanist view, artistic creation brings forth what is by definition *new*, and self-evidently, the new can come only from a faculty endowed with the power to bring forth out of *itself* – out of its own mysterious, self-caused power of radical origination. Since the analytic intellect can only dissect what is already in being (murdering it in the process, according to Wordsworth), the fountain out of which the new flows must be inaccessible to it. According to this Romantic conception, then, Socrates was right, even if he misunderstood his own insight: if art is conceived as techne, it follows that the greatest achievements of art *are not produced by art*, but, rather, by an inexplicable newness-originating faculty in artists that controls the making at the highest level, or else by a transcendent power that takes possession of the artist.

If, by contrast, true art is persistence in the well done, as Rilke suggests, and if an analytical account of the well done is possible – as, in principle, should be the case, since there is no mystery-faculty involved – it would follow that this account, to the degree that it explained how the well done comes about, would also explain art's highest achievements.

Obviously, there's an impressive qualitative difference between great art and merely craftsman-like work; but if there is not a higher *essence* to the more impressive work, if there is no impermeable boundary between them, then there is no reason in principle why the 'higher' kind could not be explained in the same way as the lower, as the same thing pushed to another level, a product of *artistic labour* empowered by *techne*.

The concept of techne developed in this book is drawn primarily from such sources as Greek philosophy, Wittgenstein and Russian Formalism; but it coheres well with the new cognitive science that has in recent decades mounted a challenge not only to the old computationalist cognitivism, but to reductionist materialism in general, to a degree that promises to close the book on the Cartesian split once and for all. On a naturalistic view, the dominant notion used to be that all cognitive phenomena could be explained, rock-bottom, at the neurological level, and the neurological level itself understood as a sort of computer; but in recent decades the explosion of work in embodied, extended and distributed cognition has assembled a great deal of support for conceiving the human mind as not confined to the brain, and the brain itself as not explicable in computationalist terms. According to this viewpoint, which I consider to be entirely in line with the thinking of the later Wittgenstein, the mind is a shifting configuration of interactions between the entire psyche-soma and the surrounding world, involving our actions as much as our perceptions. Two of the major figures in this movement are the cognitive anthropologist Edwin Hutchins, whom I mentioned in Chapter 1, and the philosopher Andy Clark, who has written a long series of books synthesizing and interpreting the research in neurophysiology, robotics, AI, and other fields that supports the 'extended mind' hypothesis. The new science shifts the ground under the debates over the role of the artisan's mind in art-making in the most profound way, by reconceiving the concept of mind itself, and this shift speaks in favour of the techne standpoint.[3]

My approach in this book is related to the work in distributed cognition and extended mind, but articulates the problematic of agency in a different way, beginning from the philosophical articulation in Plato and Aristotle of the fundamental concepts of techne theory. At all points I try as much as possible to keep in touch with the phenomenology of art-making and art perception, and with the materiality of the art process.

Evolution of the work of art

There is a close analogy between the resistance of transcendent-faculty theorists to analytical explanations of art-making, on the one hand, and the resistance of 'creationists' to the biological theory of evolution, on the other. When creationists look at an organ like the human eye, it seems obvious to them that nothing so staggeringly complex, yet so beautifully well organized and well functioning, could emerge from a causal process that mindlessly makes tiny mechanical adjustments to a series of simpler pre-existing forms. Yet, when one learns the minute gradations by which it would be possible to get from a simple, light-sensitive cell to the self-adjusting lens of the human eye, the intellectual (if not the emotional) need to imagine a Designer evaporates (see ch. 6, *Origin of Species*). And if in biological evolution a miraculous final organization like the human eye is achieved without any intelligent design intention at all, why should it be so hard to imagine that the most impressive achievements of art can be attained by superbly intelligent, skilled designers, equipped with know-how that their cultures have developed over millennia, without need of an imponderable Extra Something to do the work?

The techne standpoint towards art is in the first instance that of the artist. When the craftsman-artist looks at a finished artwork, she sees behind it not a miracle but an organized, systematic production process, made up of very small, unmiraculous steps. The artist is typically, as Paul Valéry said of himself, 'much more attentive to the formation or fabrication of works than to the works themselves'.[4] From the techne standpoint, the 'works themselves' show up as the encoded trace of the skilled labour that made them, the index or record of a struggle with the medium involved, a series of techne-guided decisions made by the artist, that remain on view in the result.

Part of what makes this techne-logic seem so mysterious is that the solutions to art-problems emerge not only across the time of making of individual works, but across the larger timespan of an artist's career, and in the careers of the foregoing artists whose work this artist's corpus implies. Here again there is an important analogy with biological evolution, in which each mutation that contributes to a successful organic design is the solution to an adaptation-problem, and the solutions are preserved for further development by future generations.[5] To adopt the techne-standpoint towards the perception of the artwork is to learn to see the cunning of techne as articulated across this entire temporal span, within which any individual 'artist's intention' is an important, but limited factor.

There is no better example of what I have just described than the evolution of cubism out of the work of Cézanne. Cézanne laboured in solitude for many years, breaking up solids into little geometric planes to work out his new techniques of flat representation, and then in 1907 Picasso and Braque walked into the great Paris Cézanne retrospective and in a flash saw the possibility of the analytical cubist style. This possibility was in some sense 'there', in the late work of Cézanne, waiting (so to speak) to be evolved into the next phase of its evolution; and Picasso and Braque were both in a position to see the nature of that possibility. The great breakthrough of 'genius' that they accomplished was prepared stroke by painful stroke by old Cézanne; there was nothing transcendent about it. Cubism was a further unfolding of the pictorial logic that Cézanne had developed up to a certain point. Nothing dictated that the next stage had to happen, or that it had to take the particular form it took; Cubism was not the working out of an intrinsic teleology. But the fact that some of the early cubist paintings by Braque and Picasso are practically indistinguishable from each other in technique, and the fact that the importance of their accomplishment was immediately recognized by so many other painters, for whom it also seemed to open just the door at whose threshold they had already been standing, show that Cézanne had been sweating over a problem in the material practice of painting as that practice had been developing since Impressionism, and had worked out a way forward from it. When one looks at the most masterfully achieved of his later paintings one can see them as punctual objects, visual icons embodying a vision of reality that the artist had and which he allows us to share with him, or we can see them as the decodable trace of the painter's struggle with the possibilities of the painting techne. The latter way of viewing it in no way excludes the former, but to the degree that we devote our attention to it, it begins to shift the centre of gravity of our response to art.

The very word *techne* indicates that the change of perspective has in view a certain 'mechanical' or 'engineering' aspect of art-making. Yet, as I have already indicated, this recognition in no way overlooks the designing activity of the art-maker, who must continually make judgments of value in the shaping of the work. If it weren't for the form-discovering activity of the artifex, if the alphabet could be turned loose to generate texts on its own, the product would be a near-infinity of nonsense, a Library of Babel in which Roland Barthes's ecstatically text-shaping reader would be condemned to spend her whole life looking for one coherent sentence. And yet what drove Borges to the vision of his terrifying library was his awareness that the creative automatism responsible for this Babel *is*, in one limited, but essential, sense the force that makes all texts. Barthes and Foucault were not wrong, but their sudden, festive conclusions about textuality were as premature as were those of the 'humanists' who opposed them. An important place must be made, and can be made, within a fundamentally post-humanist theory of techne, for the agency of the artist.

Unlike biological evolution, art requires a designer. Two particular human beings made cubism happen, on purpose – two human beings who were highly skilled painters, and in a unique position, as a consequence of the evolution or their own work up to that point, to see the next step to which the way had been opened by Cézanne. In drawing the initial analogy between art-making and biological evolution I ignored this essential difference, not to evade, but to refocus it. If we keep insisting that the first question to be answered is 'But how do the changes *originate*, what makes them pop into being out of non-being?' we are doomed to remain stuck inside the ontological argument for the existence of a transcendent faculty, precisely the aporia that the analogy with evolution is designed to circumvent. But if this question can be deferred long enough to allow a full investigation of production by techne, one begins to find the fantasy of ex nihilo creation less compelling. When the real, historically elongated, process of well-done work-making has been elucidated, an account becomes possible of how what Rilke says actually happens – how the well-done comes to surpass the artist.

Production according to techne

Among modern theorists of art production, only the (misleadingly named) Russian Formalists – who in their earliest phase, according to Shklovsky, 'approached art as a production, spoke of it alone' – touched the authentic techne standpoint. As Boris Eichenbaum explained, art production was for them strictly understood in terms of the notion of *technique*, which they quickly came to see as more essential than that of 'form'. The 'formalism' of the Russians thus involved turning away from the reified form of the product (what the New Critics would later revere as a 'verbal icon') to the process through which, and the 'devices' by means of which, the product was formed – a process from which the Formalists excluded the biography or psychology of the author, focusing strictly on what Rudolf Steiner calls the 'general technology of literary production and the laws that govern it'.[6]

For the Russian group, thus – unlike for Heidegger, whose neo-Romantic account of techne is today, unfortunately, the most widely known – there was nothing to be feared in the concepts of production or technology, which they readily used as an analogy for the formal generative systems of literary authorship.[7] But the Formalist focus on the 'general technology' of production left open the vast puzzle on which I am focusing, of just how it was possible for an individual maker to serve as the vehicle of the productive 'system', in such a way as to result in all the particulars of a given work. Technai are embedded in pragmatic contexts, and manipulated by individual practitioners on the basis of tacit, intuitively deployed knowledge. This is what makes technai adaptable to the demands of ever-changing concrete situations. If techne theory is going to offer a way out of the perplexity that generates the humanist-structuralist split over the origin of the work of art, it has to provide a new way to conceive this process, and it must do so in a way that simultaneously does justice to the role of the artist-artisan, on the one hand, and the systematic, in a strong sense 'technological' aspect of techne, concerning which the Russians provided important insights, on the other.

Techne belongs to the realm of social practice. That means that the concept of techne unfolds in a conceptual space to which neither Formalism nor the structuralism that followed in its wake provided any clear access. Structuralism was concerned with signification and signifying systems, and attempted to reduce the entire realm of culture to the play of semiotic codes. But social practice cannot be understood all the way down as a signifying system. There is no denying that social practice is bathed in semiosis, beginning with natural language itself; I take it as axiomatic that all aspects of human culture are held in the matrix of language. Yet this absolute dependence of all aspects of culture on language is misunderstood if it's taken to imply that all aspects of culture are themselves language-like and can be exhaustively understood on the structuralist model of language. Language itself, after all, appears to have evolved out of structures of practice, the *chaines operatoires* theorized by Leroi-Gourhan that I discuss in Chapter 5, rather than the other way around. Structuralism opened up the vista of limitless semiosis, the prodigal proliferation of meanings by the uncentred generative machine of language, which meant also the limitlessness of interpretation, because the interpretation was just the continuation of the same limitless generativity that produced the text to be interpreted. There was no text-in-itself, a text was a site on which a swarm of heterogeneous codes momentarily converged on their way towards an unlimited number of new combinations, and whether these took place through the mediation of a poet or a critic or a reader was ultimately indifferent. It was all at bottom the fecundity of the semiotic hive.

If social practice were nothing but a signifying system, its products would be, like the sentences we speak, boundless inward in their semiotic atoms, boundless outward in their semiotic recombinations, without centre or anchor. But a social practice is not like that. As Wittgenstein says in the *Philosophical Investigations*, there has to be something in a social practice that is *not an interpretation* – a moment at which we grasp *how to go on in the right way.* Wittgenstein illustrates this notion with the example of a student who is being taught how to develop a mathematical series according to a formula. The student does it this way, then that way, then finally she does it right. Ah, I've got it, she thinks; and the teacher thinks, ah, she's got it. The pupil can't pit her 'interpretation' against the teacher's; the teacher knows how the thing is done and the pupil doesn't.[8]

Wittgenstein's point is not unique to math, it pertains to all human practices. Practices are transmitted from one human being to another in concrete scenes of instruction, and they inevitably involve the imparting of norms of correctness. To perceive the centrality to social practice of such scenes, in which an adept conveys to a neophyte the feel for what is a correct or an incorrect move in the given practice, is to open a perspective heterogeneous to either structuralism or the essentialism that structuralism opposed. A social practice is not like anything else in the world; it has neither a 'nature' nor an 'essence' in the way conceived by classical metaphysics, but neither is it a signifying system productive of nothing but infinite interpretability and infinite interpretation. In classical metaphysics, form, nature or essence is conceived on the model of separate, bounded, self-identical, persistent *things*, where 'thing' is paradigmatically, as one philosophical wit put it, an item of medium-sized dry goods – a table or chair; but a practice is a way of *doing* things that has evolved historically within a given culture and which must be physically transmitted across generations, primarily through example and instruction. Techne is the form not of any *product* of practice but of *the practice itself* that brings forth a product, and the *form of practice* cannot be thought on the model of medium-sized dry goods of any kind, whether a bed or a 'well-wrought urn' (we will see how this problem plays out in Plato). Indeed, it's only in recent decades, thanks to the work of thinkers and scientists like Daniel Dennett, Andy Clark, Edwin Hutchins and Rodney Brooks, that the conceptual resources have become available for thinking about the forms of practices, which, far from being unitary and self-identical, are decentred, distributed, perpetually adapting and changing forms, much like biological species. Evolutionary logic is behind all of this rethinking; what we are seeing is the final, fullest flowering of Darwin's great conceptual breakthrough.[9]

Yet, just as biologists, despite the fact that species do not, in classical metaphysical terms, exist, and just as linguists, despite the fact that languages, too, do not in this sense exist, still have to group the phenomena they study with the use of these concepts, so we need to demarcate technai 'in themselves', as though they were really existing, individuated entities of a sort – a very complex and puzzling sort.

In a certain, limited way, as long as we keep in mind the anti-metaphysical strictures I have just listed, it doesn't hurt to conceive technai (architecture, engineering, marketing, painting, carpentry, medicine . . .) as social 'structures': historically accumulated bodies of systematic practical knowledge, socially inscribed in texts, educational institutions, in the practices of communities of practitioners, and in the psyche-somas, mind-bodies, of the individual adepts who make up these communities. Unlike the structures of structuralism, however, the sole purpose of technai is to enable human beings to *do* things. The great impasse of structuralism was the antithesis it set up between social structure and human agency. Sometimes, when structuralists denied agency to individuals, as in the 'death of the author' they attributed it to structures instead; what they never did was to conceive of structures that are incorporated into the psyche-soma of subjects as the very medium of their action. But agency is the whole point of techne; indeed, techne is what enables human beings to be agents in any consequential sense of the term. An infant is transformed into a functioning member of a society – a *person* – by the technai it learns, including, prominently, language. The very concept of human agency would be inconceivable without techne.[10]

Hadamard's essay

My aim, then, is to do justice to the full, concrete phenomenon of creativity in an account of techne that is minimally speculative and maximally descriptive – as close to what Wittgenstein called a 'perspicuous representation' as possible. A perspicuous representation of creation does not aspire to mirror its true, hidden nature – it has none – but, if successful, allows us to conceive the emergence of the new in a way that is clear and full enough that one need no longer be gnawed by the feeling that there must be a transcendent Extra Something at the root.

So techne theory should be as untheoretical as possible. Yet we need ways of imagining the processes that go on out of sight, imagining them in a way that is as simple and transparent, and as close to the visible surface goings-on, as possible, because otherwise we almost inevitably fall back into conceiving these processes as terminally mysterious. Fortunately, a sturdy, yet simple, theoretical model of this sort exists, in Jacques Hadamard's great 1945 *Essay on the Psychology of Invention in the Mathematical Field.*[11] Hadamard, who himself made important contributions to mathematics, argues, on the basis of a wide overview and the testimonies of a multitude of innovators in many fields, from Paul Valéry to Albert Einstein, that invention is basically the same in all fields, and shows how the mystery of intuitive bringing forth can be analytically decomposed into a regular, comprehensible process, one that is readily translatable into the terms of techne theory.

The most striking result of Hadamard's study of the creative mental habits of mathematicians on its face appears to weigh against the theory of techne. Hadamard found that the mental operations by means of which mathematicians perform their largest-scale creative work tend to be extremely idiosyncratic and very far removed from anything that looks remotely mathematical. These operations almost always exclude not only words – an exclusion one might expect in mathematical reasoning – but even numbers and algebraic symbols; they are extremely vague 'signs' that function as no more than pointers towards, or reminders of, masses of material that themselves remain in what Hadamard calls the 'anteroom of consciousness'. Hadamard himself, for example, when he tried to grasp what he calls the 'physiognomy' of a sought-for solution, thought in terms of extremely vague images. For example, to prove the theorem 'the sequel of prime numbers is unlimited', he began by imagining a shapeless mass with a point rather remote from it, then a second point a little beyond the first, then a place between the mass and the first point; or, considering the sum of an infinite number of terms, he imagined 'a kind of ribbon, which is thicker or darker at the place corresponding to the possible important terms' (pp. 77–8). Other mathematicians testified to him that they used nonsense syllables or music; some used words, but only in the same way as the other signs, as vague pointers or reminders; and Albert Einstein, who called such signs 'physical entities that serve as elements in thought', said that among the elements he employed were some of 'muscular' type, presumably a structured set of twitches (pp. 142–3). These methods are a way of grasping, holding onto and manipulating the inventive thinker's largest-scale perceptions of how the mathematical system is articulated at the level of the new formula or set of equations that is just beginning to come into view. I stress that the most essential characteristic of all these methods, as Hadamard mentions repeatedly, is that they must remain *vague* if the overall 'physiognomy' of the solution, the synthesis of all the elements, is to be kept in sight. (This discovery, that the quality of *vagueness* is essential to the larger movements of creative thought, is a surprising, and momentous one, which has important consequences for conceiving how language works, as we will see in a later chapter.)

Since the problem of holding onto the physiognomy of a large ensemble of elements is common to intellectual work of many kinds, it seems likely that methods related to those discussed by Hadamard must be found in those fields as well. I can testify, for what it's worth, that, interrogating my own efforts to conceptualize the physiognomy of the theory of techne, I find that, indeed, I am using various kinds of devices like those Hadamard documents.

But if phenomena of this type are highly idiosyncratic, an individual factor that is ineliminable in any kind of inventive activity, they cannot be an intrinsic part of techne as such, which is by definition a social phenomenon. What place, then, can we assign them in the theory of techne?

The function of this idiosyncratic psychological factor must be distinguished from that which Romantic theory has assigned to the individual creative psyche. This creative source has been conceived as an absolute and essentially *simple* locus of origin of the new, a unitary and self-identical fountainhead. By contrast, the radically individual psychological techniques brought to light by Hadamard do not create the new; they enable the inventor to grasp and hold onto forms that emerge out of a complex, multistage process driven by the inventor's knowledge of techne – and, ultimately, as we will see, by a kind of intrinsic *dynamis* (both dynamism and potentiality) of the techne itself.

The crucial point is that the ad hoc mental operations of the individual thinker derive all their sense from their reference to something external to individual psychology, which in the case of mathematics Hadamard calls 'the architecture of the mathematical building'. As an architect recognizes that a building 'will be better poised by the addition of a new wing', a mathematician recognizes that a particular mathematical operation will be a 'harmonious way' of completing a mathematical architecture (p. 129). Hadamard calls the faculty that enables such a recognition 'the feeling for beauty'. The ordinary calculations of ordinary calculators, the research mathematician's ability to identify a significant problem in mathematics, the creative thinker's ability to deploy ad hoc mental techniques towards the solution of a problem and the ability to recognize the correct solution when it is found: all are regulated by the feeling for the beauty of the mathematical building.

The feeling for beauty might be thought even more mysterious and intuitive than the idiosyncratic sign structures by which physiognomies are grasped. But as I have already stressed, it is no part of my purpose to deny the presence of intuitive and individual factors in the creative process. Such factors could scarcely be absent in art-making, since they are present in *every* kind of human action, no matter how humble, as a result of the gap between the non-conscious operation of the sensing and processing mechanisms of the body, and the consciousness that operates on the basis of this processing; as Hadamard says, the real mystery is not how there can be creative thinking, but how there can be thinking at all. The purpose here is, rather, to show that there is a way of reconceiving the significance of these factors within a more lucid, and complete, account of the creation process than presently exists. The feeling for the beauty of an architectural techne-structure, whether physical, verbal or mathematical, to the degree that that feeling involves genuine understanding of what is being appreciated, involves informed perception of the constructive principles that produced that structure. The nature of the feeling *qua* affect might not be susceptible of analysis, but even if it were it would be of only psychological interest. Illumination regarding the process of invention is to be gained not from contemplation of the feeling for beauty but from analysis of the *relation* between this feeling on one side, and the constructive principles of techne on the other, that results in beautiful architectures.

Creation and the 'combination of ideas'

The centrepiece of Hadamard's analysis of the constructive process is not the individual, intuitive factor, but rather his elaboration of Poincaré's 'combination of ideas' model, which Hadamard argues can be used to simulate the creative power of the unconscious in all fields, 'be it in mathematics or anywhere else' (p. 29). Poincaré imagined the system of mathematics as made up of a set of 'ideas' that the mathematician struggling with a problem must combine and recombine until the combination that constitutes the solution is found. The analogy, borrowed from Epicurus, by means of which Poincaré develops this notion is reminiscent of Watson and Crick's struggles with their physical models of DNA, by means of which they made their contribution to the great discovery:

> [Poincaré] imagines that the ideas which are the future elements of our combinations are 'something like the hooked atoms of Epicurus. During the complete repose of the mind, these atoms are motionless; they are, so to speak, hooked to the wall; so this complete rest may be indefinitely

> prolonged without the atoms meeting, and consequently without any combination between them.' The act of studying a question consists of mobilizing ideas, not just any ones, but those from which we might reasonably expect the desired solution. It may happen that that work has no immediate result. 'We think we have done no good, because we have moved these elements a thousand different ways in seeking to assemble them and have found no satisfactory aggregate.' But, as a matter of fact, it seems as though these atoms are thus launched, so to speak, like so many projectiles and flash in various directions through space. 'After this shaking-up imposed upon them by our will, these atoms do not return to their primitive rest. They freely continue their dance.' Consequences can now be foreseen. 'The mobilized atoms undergo impacts which make them enter into combinations among themselves or with other atoms at rest, which they struck against in their course.' In those new combinations, in those indirect results of the original conscious work, lie the possibilities of apparently spontaneous inspiration. (Hadamard, p. 47)[12]

Watson and Crick juggled physical elements with their hands, whereas Poincaré's atoms are mental, moved by his thoughts alone; but this difference is insignificant. The idea-system itself is 'substrate neutral' – it can be manipulated mentally, on paper, in a computer, with plastic pieces, or any number of conceivable actualizations, and they will be the same manipulations, with the same system, subject to the same constraints and charged with the same systemic potentials.[13]

But calling them 'manipulations' misrepresents the relation between the thinker and the powers of the system. Once the investigator has set its elements in motion they 'freely continue their dance' in the 'unconscious' mind. The 'atoms' of the combinatory do not merely hook on to each other by means of physical contact, like boxcars coupling; Hadamard describes a kind of magnetic pull by means of which whole complexes of atoms are attracted into viable new 'physiognomies'.

> When I am engaged in trying to think anything out, the process of doing so appears to me to be this: The ideas that lie at any moment within my full consciousness seem to attract of their own accord the most appropriate out of a number of other ideas that are lying close at hand, but imperfectly within the range of my consciousness. There seems to be a presence-chamber in my mind where full consciousness holds court, and where two or three ideas are at the same time in audience, and an ante-chamber full of more or less allied ideas, which is situated just beyond the full ken of consciousness. Out of this ante-chamber the ideas most nearly allied to those in the presence-chamber appear to be summoned in a mechanically logical way, and to have their turn of audience. (Hadamard, p. 25)

The notion that the ideas are summoned into consciousness 'in a mechanically logical way' suggests some kind of systemic necessity or force that determines what will be summoned. But to what degree the thinker is the 'agent' by which the new physiognomy is constructed, and to what degree it comes together out of properties of the combinatorial system itself, is indeterminable and probably not a meaningful distinction, because it carries the notion of agency beyond its legitimate field of use. The mathematician is the only agent in sight, in the normal deployment of that concept. But discovering a new mathematical law is not like driving a car or killing a fly, so the mathematician isn't an agent in *that* sense – rather, in a sense that owes so much to the power of the techne itself, that thinkers from Aristotle to T. S. Eliot and the Russian Formalists have been tempted to attribute the primary agency to *it*. Heidegger mystified the notion of 'letting be' by posing it as antithetical to intentional agency, but the evident fact is that there is something of letting be in the skilled, intentional use of any techne, by any kind of *technites*, and rather than being antithetical to, it is the essence of, the highest kinds of such agency.[14]

Thus Hadamard notes that often, after a thinker has worked hard and long on a problem, usually after a period of rest or sleep, the answer will flash into his consciousness in a moment of 'inspiration' or 'illumination'. The fact that the dance of the atoms continues spontaneously after having been set in motion by the conscious manipulations of the thinker does not, however, speak to the *creativity* (in the Romantic sense, as radical origination) of the unconscious, but to the mind's ability to keep playing with the mathematical (or other) combinatory during sleep and related states.

As Hadamard notes, Paul Valéry's famous remarks on poetic inventiveness have a particularly close relation to Poincaré's account:

> It takes two to invent anything. The one makes up the combinations; the other chooses, recognizes what he wishes and what is important to him in the mass of things which the former has imparted to him. What we call genius is much less the work of the first one than the readiness of the second one to grasp the value of what has been laid before him and to choose it (p. 30).

'We see how beautifully the mathematician and the poet agree in that fundamental view of invention consisting of a choice,' Hadamard comments, a choice that in the case of the mathematician is 'imperatively governed by the sense of scientific beauty' (pp. 30–31).

The essential, and game-changing, significance of Poincaré and Valéry's model of invention is this: it shows how we can stop thinking of the origin of the new in terms of a simple moment of origin, a pristine *arkhe*, a single moment at which it first 'emerges' into being. If there is no such simple moment of origin, no corresponding power or faculty of origination need be posited. The new comes into being by a complex process that occurs in distinct stages, and the originating power is, correspondingly, 'distributed' across the process. (This, of course, was already the lesson of Darwinism, a lesson that has only been more and more sharply drawn by the modern reinterpretation of evolution in terms of genetics.)

The Romantic-humanist view of artistic or intellectual 'originality' has always understood this originality as the power to produce what is *both* new *and* aesthetically or intellectually valuable, without analytically distinguishing between these two values. Hadamard's model makes it evident that the new and the aesthetically valuable have quite distinct natures, such that 'newness' per se emerges in the first phase of creation, but does not, merely qua new, have any intellectual or aesthetic value or significance (as Kant already implies when he says that genius as such produces nothing but nonsense). The new emerges via a quasi-mechanical process that Hadamard assigns to the 'creative' unconscious, but which can also be carried out consciously and methodically, as has been done by modern artists and writers who have explored various forms of 'aleatory' creation. This first-phase process generates 'the very numerous possible combinations, among which the useful ones are to be found' in a way that happens 'to a certain extent, at random'. The unconscious, or the generative method that replaces it, functions here as a machine that produces the new randomly and in excessive quantity, like nature producing excess offspring to kill off so that better designed combinations can thrive. A creative agency – be it a species, an individual, or a collective of individuals – is, as Dennett explains, a kind of 'search engine' that combs a specific possibility-space looking for useful bits (see Chapter 12).

Value is bestowed on a selection of these new elements in the second stage, when the maker or inventor consciously or unconsciously picks out the potentially valuable new elements from the rest and arranges them in the proper configuration. *This is the real work of invention.* It 'consists precisely in not mating useless combinations and in examining only those which are useful and which are only a small minority. Invention is discernment, choice' (Hadamard, pp. 29–30).

Hadamard says that it is this second movement that properly constitutes 'creation', and Valéry says that 'genius' lies mainly here; but their continued use of the old Romantic honorifics should not obscure for us the dimensions of the paradigm shift that has taken place. The most important moment in the creative process is now the *recognition* of the value of specific combinations (an aspect of the creative process that modernist experiments with collage and found art and so forth bring out in a particularly transparent way). The Hadamard–Valéry account posits the intuition of the inventor not as a power of 'bringing forth', like childbirth, but as a kind of extraordinary perceptual keenness, an 'esthetic' ability to see what is, so to speak, 'implied' by the mathematical or verbal combinatory, but which no one has seen or felt before – a sense, comparable to the perception of physiognomy, for the beauty of a whole 'gestalt' of which an inventive thinker picks up intimations.

Unlike the ordinary recognition of physiognomy, however, this kind involves picking up intimations from the scattered features of a face one has *never seen before*, yet which will be recognized when it finally takes shape (i.e. when the dance of the atoms falls into the sought-for configuration and emerges into consciousness in the 'aha!' moment). The *technites* feels intuitively that there is a way in which these features can be put together according to a hitherto-unknown ordering principle, and the intuitive power that is capable of such perception is impressive indeed; but more fundamental than the intuition is that which makes the intuition *possible*: the properties of the techne of mathematics (or whichever techne is in question) itself. That this is so in mathematics is evident from the fact that fundamental mathematical discoveries can be made independently by different investigators, at the same or different times, the most famous being the simultaneous discovery of the calculus by Newton and Leibniz. In poetry, by contrast, intuitions of form of any considerable magnitude that are not made by one *technites* will never be made by another (*Hamlet* would have remained forever unwritten if Shakespeare hadn't done it), but that difference can be attributed to the fact that the possibilities of recombination are so vastly more numerous and open in the system of poetry, not because the basic dynamics of the system are of a fundamentally different type. It remains the case that the discovery of the new is a perception of *something about the system of the elements itself*, as this system has been configured by previous generations into a beautiful architecture of some sort. The inventive thinker feels a kind of potential stirring in this already existing architecture.[15]

The crucial fact about the Hadamard–Valéry model is that *techne is on both sides of the equation*. The model of the combinatory pictures the internal functioning of the techne itself independently of the individual psyche in which it is instantiated; and the aesthetic sensibility that works the combinatory and selects its most 'beautiful' results for further elaboration is the educated taste of someone who has served an apprenticeship *in that same techne*.

NOTES

1 Rainer Maria Rilke, *Auguste Rodin*, trans. Daniel Slager (Brooklyn: Archipelago Books, 2004), p. 54.

2 Letter of 28 June 1907. Rainer Maria Rilke, *Letters on Cézanne*, ed. Clara Rilke, trans. Joel Agee (New York: International Publishing, 1985), p. 8. Rilke cites Cézanne himself as having once shouted at a visitor, 'Travailler sans le souci de personne et devenir fort –' (*Letters on Cézanne*, p. 38).

3 A number of experiments have shown that the system of vision, for example, rather than forming elaborate internal representations of the visual field (as was posited by the old, mentalistic psychology of perception) makes merely schematic representations that must then be continually supplemented by

perceptual-actional samplings of the world. In more complex, culturally coded actions, cognition is encoded or 'distributed', as Hutchins says, onto the technai and tools that a culture develops over a long period of time. To give just two examples of why this is so: because (as Hutchins exhaustively demonstrated in the case of modern navigation) the knowledge encoded in tools has been socially accumulated and in large part bypasses the cognition of the one who wields it; and because skill is trained as much into the muscles and nerve pathways as it is into the brain.

4 Paul Valéry, *The Art of Poetry*, trans. Denise Folliott (Princeton, NJ: Princeton University Press, 1958), p. 69.

5 As critics of 'adaptationism' in evolutionary theory have pointed out, the solution to an adaptation-problem in a biological species might well originate at an earlier time than that of its utilization as an adaptation, as a by-product of some other process, and not as a result of natural selection. There are important parallels to this insight in the evolution of technai.

6 Boris Eichenbaum, 'Theory of the Formal Method', in *Russian Formalist Criticism: Four Essays*, trans. Lee T. Lemon and Marion Reis (Lincoln: University of Nebraska Press, 1965). Shklovsky's remark cited in Rudolf Steiner, *Russian Formalism: A Metapoetics* (Ithaca: Cornell University Press, 1986), p. 65.

7 Heidegger manifestly misrepresented the ancient Greek concept of techne, as I show in detail in an article, 'The Origin of the Work of Art in Material Practice', *New Literary History* (Winter 2012) 43.1.

8 Ludwig Wittgenstein, *Philosophische Untersuchungen/Philosophical Investigations*, trans. G. E. M. Anscombe, P. M. S. Hacker, and Joachim Schulte (Malden, MA: Wiley-Blackwell, 2009), remarks 143–6, 198–202. Henceforth cited as '*PI*'.

9 I should mention also the bracing critique of the notion of a 'social practice' of Stephen Turner, who denies that there is any persistent 'sameness' in social practices. Instead, he says, 'what we have are private habits, with a variegated causal structure, that arise in response to public things', with 'nothing non-individual' beyond the 'overt manifestations' of the resulting behaviour of individuals. Stephen Turner, *The Social Theory of Practice* (Chicago: University of Chicago Press, 1994), quotation from p. 105. That private habits have a variegated causal structure seems highly likely; yet there does appear to be something 'non-individual' in social practices. As ground-breaking work by Swedish researchers has shown, social practices pattern our neural pathways in ways that can be mapped by brain imaging techniques. Practice coordinates neural networks so that the brain can perform cognitive activities such as grouping the sounds of a language into meaningful phonemes, or, among jazz musicians, responding to unanticipated deviations in rhythmic structure, and these networks show distinctive patterns across the brains of different individuals. See A. Roepsdorff, J. Niewöhner and S. Beck, 'Enculturing Brains through Patterned Practices', *Neural Networks* (2010) 23: 1051–9. But such brain patterns, clearly, must be as loosely structured and variable as the patterns they detect in the world. The brain can function in such a flexible way because it operates according to probabilistic, rather than strictly deterministic,

principles. See Andy Clark, *Surfing Uncertainty: Prediction, Action, and the Embodied Mind* (Oxford: Oxford University Press, 2016).

10 Foucault and his followers developed a curious theory of negative empowerment of human agents by oppressive structures which call forth their agency in the form of resistance. Even someone like Anthony Giddens, who made an important attempt to accept the lessons of structuralism while going beyond the structuralist impasse over agency, went no farther than to posit a dialectical relation between structure and human action. Never in any of these debates does the concept of techne come into view.

11 Jacques Hadamard, *An Essay on the Psychology of Invention in the Mathematical Field* (New York: Dover, 1945).

12 To get the full flavour of Poincaré's analogy, one should read Epicurus, or better yet Lucretius's *On the Nature of Things*, which expounds the system of Epicurus in inspired verse. This system lies at the origin of all modern atomisms and associationisms, including the 'combinatory' model of structuralism. The privilege that Hadamard grants to the mechanism of 'combination of ideas' injects him, perhaps unwittingly, into the old debate between Romanticism and its bête noir, the 'associationist' psychology that developed in the eighteenth century out of British empiricism. The strongest, most influential Romantic concept of creation, in fact, emerged from Coleridge's reaction against associationism's explanation of all human thought process in terms of 'combination of ideas'. In the most famous chapter of his *Biographia Literaria*, he argued that there is a truly creative, transcendent human faculty, the Secondary Imagination, that does not merely recombine the elements of the old but melts or smelts them down in order to recast their form in a truly *original* way. This power, he claimed, is the 'reflex' in the human mind of the 'Infinite I AM', the divine 'Primary Imagination' that continually refreshes what we today might call the Being of being. Coleridge's distinction seeped into the French literary tradition (it was echoed, notably, by Baudelaire, who cited Catherine Crowe's 1848 *The Night Side of Nature* as his source), but Hadamard does not show any awareness of the historical resonance of his argument. Nor does he have any use for the dualist opposition of mechanical and creative faculties. He disperses the elements of this opposition across an account that decisively leaves behind the terms of the Romantic/associationist debate, in favour of a focus on the dynamics of interaction between human intentionality and the techne of mathematics.

13 The notion that we can understand how the mind works with signs by looking at the way we work with signs on paper, developed by Wittgenstein in the *PI*, has been given extensive empirical support in recent decades by work on extended mind and distributed cognition. In the past it has been thought that the physical embodiments of our symbols are merely conveniences, while the reality that they represent – the meaning – has a separate, ideal existence. But as Andy Clark shows, the human brain is actually not very good at dealing with abstraction; it is built to interact with the world through the nerves and muscles. As Clark says, 'The squishy matter is great . . . at recognizing patterns, at perception, and at controlling physical actions, but it is not so well designed . . . for complex planning and long, intricate, derivations of consequences. It is, to put it bluntly, bad at logic and good at Frisbee.' (Andy Clark, *Natural Born Cyborgs: Minds, Technologies, and the Future of Human Intelligence* [Oxford: Oxford University Press, 2003], p. 5). Clark and Daniel Dennett argue that 'mental representation' is almost entirely a matter of skilfully (i.e. 'technefully') manipulating 'thought-objects' – physical tokens that can 'fold in' complex regularities and present them as simple objects that thought can manipulate. Even chimpanzees have been shown to be able to take advantage of this kind of symbolic boost to their powers of abstraction. In the key experiment cited by Clark, they learned to deploy the notions of 'sameness', 'difference', 'higher-order sameness' and 'higher-order difference' by using plastic markers of one colour to designate pairs of identical objects (such as two shoes or two cups) and markers of another colour to indicate pairs of different objects (such as a shoe and a cup). (We might think of Watson and Crick's models alongside these chimpanzee tokens.) Once the chimps had learned these distinctions using the objects, they were able to make them in the absence of the objects as well, as though the original physical object had been *aufgehoben* into a thought-object (Clark, 'The Roots of Norm-Hungriness', in *Philosophy of Mental Representation*, ed. Hugh Clapin [New York: Oxford University Press], 2002, pp. 41–2).

14 Krzystof Ziarek, commenting on Heidegger, helpfully glosses 'letting be' as an 'action in the middle voice' or 'aphesis', and defines it as a 'letting or allowing, but in an active rather than passive sense . . . of accomplishing something by actively letting it come to be rather than by producing or manipulating it'. *The Force of Art* (Stanford, CA: Stanford University Press, 2004), p. 50.

15 Poincaré apparently had the rare ability to consciously observe the functioning of his 'unconscious' combinatorial work. Hadamard cites Poincaré's account of one evening when he 'drank black coffee and could not sleep'. This put him into a state in which 'Ideas rose in crowds; I felt them collide until pairs interlocked, so to speak, making a stable combination.' In Poincaré's view, in such states 'it seems as though one is present at his own unconscious work, made partially perceptible to the over-excited consciousness, yet without having changed its nature' (pp. 14–15).

CHAPTER THREE

The artist's touch

Genius doesn't lie in not being derivative, but in making right choices instead of wrong ones.
– Ned Rorem

Paul Valéry's notion that the functions of production and of critical judgment together constitute the creative faculty, and could be carried out by two different persons, is strongly validated by the paradigmatic poem of modernism, T. S. Eliot's *The Waste Land*. As is well known, Eliot's original production that became 'The Waste Land', which bore the name 'He Do the Police in Different Voices', was much longer than the poem that resulted from Erza Pound's intervention, and was, in Eliot's own judgment – a judgment that has never been seriously challenged – a formless mess. In despair, Eliot gave it to Pound, who cut out half of it, rearranged some, added hardly anything, and amazed Eliot, and subsequently the world, with the result. Reading the facsimile of the original is a startling experience; there are passages so bad it's hard to imagine Eliot could not independently recognize their badness. He did, fortunately, recognize that the whole thing was formless, and seek help from just the right source. 'The Waste Land' is permanently ensconced in the modern canon, a work of genius if anything is, but who or what is the genius responsible for it as a successful aesthetic form?

Valéry says that the work of the first person, the producer, is to bring forth 'combinations', and the critical faculty's only power is the ability to recognize and choose the more valuable combinations among the mass of worthless or less valuable ones. The combinations in question are ensembles of the constitutive elements of the art in question (words, in the case of poetry), ensembles that, if they are to possess value for the critical faculty to recognize, must be 'proto-forms' of art, not yet art, but already worked over by it. That is, these proto-forms, which constitute the 'raw material' out of which the critical faculty must shape its finished forms, have already been formed according to the principles of the techne in question. On this account, then, the productive, 'creative' faculty itself is not a natural faculty that brings forth independently of prior models and conventions, but a preliminary stage of the operation of techne. In order to produce such proto-forms, the spontaneous productive faculty of the maker must have undergone rigorous apprenticeship in that art.

In this preliminary stage, a skilled artist generates or identifies combinations that are more than nonsense but which have only potential value, which the second faculty has to 'grasp' and 'choose' in order to actualize its potential. Let us say, in the example of *The Waste Land*, that the combination in question is a line of verse, which is on its face reasonably well formed as a line. This line, then, becomes a combinatory unit that has to be integrated into a passage of verse, and if the passage as a whole works, the line, which remains the same words in the same order as before, has moved up one level towards the realization of its potential value as a form. The final level of integration of combinations is the whole, finished poem.

This way of conceiving things implies that what the critical faculty recognizes in recognizing the value of a combinatory element is its potential for functioning within a larger form, which implies that the artisan must have an anticipatory intuition of this larger form. This 'intuition' is most often of a very vague type, an anticipatory fumbling around, but it is on the basis of this anticipation that the critical faculty recognizes the (proto-)value of the combinations which it selects from the mass of proto-forms. This is what Pound did for *The Waste Land*. Calling the recognizing and choosing agency a 'critical' faculty makes it sound like some straightforward action of analytical intellect; but it has to be considerably more than that, since its ability to pick this and not that involves some sense of the larger form that has not yet come into sight.

The artist's touch

Now let us focus sharply on the question that for techne theory takes the place of the question of origin at the centre of the matter: just how does an individual maker or practitioner, guided by techne, choose the *correct* or *superior* move at a particular moment in the process of making or performing a particular work? The moment of choice, when the artisan must judge that this is the right thing to do, and do so, most of the time, without thinking about it, is the white-hot core of the entire question of 'art', the phenomenon that seems most impervious to an analytical account. The completed work of art is made up of an ensemble of such choices, and the entire theory of techne depends on its ability to generate a persuasive account of their nature.

I will call the feel for the correct execution of a move in a techne work-process the *intuition* or *sense* of the *techne-limit*, and I want now to draw some vignettes of the phenomenology of this kind of intuition.

When the master painter trained in the art of painting makes a stroke on canvas with a paint brush, her hand feels with sure knowledge that precisely here the limit of the stroke has been reached. The form produced need not be classically well formed; it depends on the kind of painting that is being done. I am not talking only about 'academic' painting, but about any kind of painting that has any claim on the attention of the student of the art of painting. The painting with which I am most intimately familiar, in fact, and which I will discuss in a later chapter, is that of the New York painter Joseph Marioni, who paints quasi-monochromes with a house painter's roller. But whether the form is smooth or irregular, open or closed, mimetic or expressive, the productive force driving the painter's hand must not stop short of, and must not overpass, the limit that marks it as sufficient to accomplish its aesthetic purpose, defined according to the particular thread of a techne-tradition within which the artisan is working. Within techne of whatever kind, the hand must feel precisely the right moment at which to pull itself back, because this is where the movement is rightly circumscribed. The Romantic view is that the individual artist decides, by some transcendent power of origination, that this mark is correct; on the present account, the artist decides that the mark is correct because she sees (or 'feels') that it *is* correct, according to the presiding techne-standard. Even such an idiosyncratic, 'Romantic', creator as the filmmaker David Lynch speaks in these terms, of feeling on the one hand and correctness on the other. Correctness is *that which the feeling feels*.

> It's an intuitive thing. The film talks to you, the story talks to you, so it's a little bit of action and reaction, you're experimenting as you go, to get the thing to feel correct . . . So you work and work until it *is* correct.[1]

A parallel process occurs across the arts, when someone plucks a guitar string, executes a gesture of the hand in dance or chooses this word, rather than any other, as the correct one with which to end a line of iambic pentameter.

Now let us expand the field of view to include the reader, viewer or audience, to see how the sense of the limit operates on the side of criticism.

Let's take as a paradigm of techne-intuition on the part of both artist and audience the culminating moment of a movement by which a skilled modern dancer slowly extends his arm and then, as it begins to reach its full extension, slowly opens out his fist until his fingers too are *almost* fully extended, but then just short of full extension of the fingers, at just the right moment, slowly begins to pull them back in, and then slowly pull back his arm as well.[2] (This description is based on something I saw Balanchine's company do many years ago, which stuck indelibly in my mind.) Such a movement might be done with a skill that the knowledgeable eye recognizes as the clumsy attempt of a beginner, or as competently executed by a well-trained dancer, or as genuine artistry, executed so exquisitely that it takes one's breath away.

The moment in which this movement is executed is only one in an unbroken succession of moments, each of which, though less striking than the culminating moment, needs to have been as masterfully shaped. The analysis of the moment on which I am focusing applies equally to every other moment of the performance. But it is at such culminating moments that one becomes most intensely aware of the artistry of the performer. Now, what is our relation to the dancer's intuition at the crucial moment on which we are focusing?

Suppose that we perceive the performance as less than masterful. Let us say the dancer is a bit histrionic and overdoes the gesture a bit. We recognize that this one is trying a bit too hard for effect, and are not pleased. The techne-limit, so exquisitely intuited by the first dancer, has in this case been overpassed.

We see from these two cases that, even though we, as mere onlookers, are not capable of filling in, with the gesture of our own arm, the outline of the form defined by the techne-limit that we have seen demonstrated by the master dancer, we are capable of recognizing the limit itself, when it is demonstrated for us by the master – but also when it *fails* to be demonstrated, and is visible only in its violation. And this can be so in a medium, modern dance, in which the techne-limits are of a kind that is not standardized, a medium that, like most modern art, places a premium on the originality, the individuality of the performance. In one sense, only the dancer, guided by the choreographer, can decide where the limit is, and the most prized gesture is the one that goes farthest beyond what we could have imagined; yet for it to give us the pleasure we are looking for we must be able, the very first time we see it, to recognize its rightness. It is of the very essence of the cultural phenomenon of art that the audience must be able to say 'that is well done'. And how is that possible, if we could not have imagined what is done until it has been done?

One way to think about this is that the artist 'legislates' what is right, that she lays down the law of the limit. Formerly it was there, now I plant the flag of my genius *here*, and lo! the aesthetic line is redrawn. This way of thinking corresponds to our sense of surprise, our feeling that this that we are beholding is beyond all our previous conceptions. That sense of surprise is an undeniable, and highly valued, phenomenon; something has to be conceded to the notion of the artist as legislating, if only as an expressive figure. Yet, as in the case of our slightly histrionic dancer, the artist might innovate, yet do so in a way that fails to convince us. What then constitutes the legislative move in art? The art that surprises and convinces, legislates; but it must convince in order to legislate; and what makes it convincing? If we answer: it convinces because it has legislated, we are arguing in the circle of the 'ontological argument' for an originating faculty.

This argument also exaggerates the degree to which art surprises us, in all but the most extreme cases – and perhaps even in these. Even the most extreme cases – *The Waste Land*, serial composition, monochrome painting, Captain Beefheart's *Trout Mask Replica* – seem *utterly* surprising only to those who are not well informed about the line of development leading up to them.

If an audience is able to judge that an artwork or art-performance of a radically new kind has value, this judgment implies a proleptic intuition of the form that is judged, based on a sense, however inchoate, of the techne-limit. Sometimes, in fact, one has the sensation that this is just what one was aesthetically hungry for – 'Yes, yes – that's it!' – as though somehow the new forms one now has before one's eyes or ears had been *implied* by the previously existing forms (if only negatively, by failing to give us what we need, as when punk rock was implied by the insipid pop music of the seventies), but one had not on one's own been able to grasp the implication. Perhaps this is how Picasso and Braque felt at the Cé.zanne retrospective. But an audience will be unable to recognize the value of a radically new form of art if the 'taste' of this audience – that is, its intuition of the limit appropriate to a specific line of techne – has not been tutored right up to its brink. Hence in avant-garde art only those who have already been developing a taste for the new forms can *immediately* respond with intelligent appreciation when the next leap occurs: Pound reading Eliot, or Eliot reading Joyce, are paradigmatic examples. Pound and Eliot were both artists themselves, of course; but in relation to someone else's work they were just extraordinarily sophisticated members of the audience. And they were not the only ones at that level of sophistication; *The Waste Land* aroused much negative reaction on its first appearance, but there was also a widespread shock of recognition in an audience that was hungry for the new kinds of poetic effects that Eliot created.

Intuiting the techne-limit

The case of *The Waste Land* strikingly confirms many of the principles I have been articulating here. It validates in a surprisingly literal way Valéry's notion that 'it takes two to invent anything', one to generate the new combinations and another to 'grasp the value' of the ones that are worth preserving and developing further, since in this case the largest scale act of selection was actually performed by a different person (Pound) than the one who generated the combinations (Eliot). What I want to emphasize at this point, however, is not this division of labour, but the condition that makes this division of labour possible: the existence of a techne-limit of which Pound and Eliot, and the readers who then confirmed the rightness of their choices, had a shared intuition.

There can be many reasons why a word or line is wrong in a given poem. It might be simply a matter of knowing when not to lay on any more details. When Pound read the following lines about the typist's carbuncular boyfriend, for example, he wrote that they were 'probaly [*sic*] over the mark', and Eliot took them out:

Bestows one final patronising kiss,
And gropes his way, finding the stairs unlit;
And at the corner where the stable is,
Delays only to urinate, and spit.[3]

Pound's remark that the last two lines are 'over the mark' has particular resonance in the present context, evoking the notion of a limit that Eliot has overstepped, as one might miss a stop sign on the street, but then see it when one's attention is called to it. Pound did this by appealing to a standard both he and Eliot acknowledged. The poet works by putting words together in a way that is up to this standard, and if they aren't up to it, then they must go. This standard might be 'intuitive' and 'ineffable', but it is learnable, teachable, shareable; it belongs to techne. Pound and Eliot knew it and shared it by virtue of the fact that they were adepts in what at that time was a somewhat esoteric poetics that set this standard; but today any smart undergraduate who receives competent instruction can enter the club of Modernism and make shrewd remarks about the structure and meaning of *The Waste Land*. That is the nature of a techne-limit: it is not an eternal aesthetic form, but a system of judgments that evolves along a historically determinate line; or rather, a system of judgments that, like all evolutions, continually branches into new lines of descent.

The fact that the process of generation and that of selection were, in the instance of the overall reshaping of the poem, divided between two distinct persons should not obscure the fact that there is no essential difference in the nature of the revisions that Eliot made on his own, and the changes that Pound induced him to make. They are both expressions of the same techne-knowledge, as is also our own ability to see why the changes were necessary, and why the revised version is better. Here, for example, is a change Eliot himself made to line 104. Originally he had: 'And other tales, from the old stumps and bloody ends of time', which he changed to 'And other withered stumps of time'. The first version is so plodding that one wonders how the poet of *Prufrock and Other Observations* could have allowed it to get this far in his composition process; and today any young poet in a poetry workshop would be able to point out what is wrong with it, and to explain why the revised version is better.

Pound and Eliot followed very different paths through the literary canon (as well as through everything else) to get to their mature techne intuitions, yet they developed closely allied senses of what constituted the best kind of poetry at their moment in literary and intellectual history. So did a substantial number of other adepts of poetry, who immediately recognized the rightness of what Eliot-Pound had accomplished in *The Waste Land*. This avant-garde readership was still small relative to the mass audience; but it constituted a base for further propagation of the techne-intuitions that were evolving in their experience of literature, and which had been capable of recognizing the physiognomy of *The Waste Land*. Readers or viewers at the next lower level of awareness (lower, that is, on this particular scale of measurement, which is not the only one, but the one I am tracing at the moment) could feel enough of a positive response to moments or features of the work to keep them open to learning more about it, while yet initially finding the whole opaque; the more enthusiastic response of more advanced members of the audience encouraged them to remain open, to devote more study and attention, and slowly to develop a genuinely felt appreciation of the new work's achievement. Its achievement, that is to say, as defined or 'constructed' by the response of the first group of responders; yet not constructed arbitrarily, because this response was itself determined by preconstituted techne-limits that they were knowledgeable enough to be able to perceive.

There is, thus, no getting away from the element of 'subjectivity', the art-intuition, which is there both in the artist's touch and in the audience's response. It is irreducible in techne of any sort, because it reflects the fact that human beings are doing this, and everything human beings do requires judgment of an intuitive sort, mathematics and automobile repair (even when done with computers) as well as fine art. But, as the example of mathematics shows, some intuitions are extremely disciplined and rigorous. It takes skill to make art, and, as Twyla Tharp says, 'no one is born with that skill. It is developed through exercise, through repetition, through a blend of learning and reflection.'[4] And no one can comment on the resultant art in a significant way who does not attain the corresponding critical discipline.

Techne-knowledge precedes and guides the maker, not in the form of a mental representation but as incorporated in the strongest sense, as inscribed in the entire psyche-soma that has been trained in the rigors of a techne, and when the critic traces the outline of the form of the work, what she traces, in the strongest form of criticism, is not the product of an interior, *geistig* act of origination but the techne-cunning that guided the crafter's stroke, the knowledge of a 'rightness' on the basis of which the crafter herself judged when her own stroke was right. This is the historical order of precedence (first the techne, then the stroke) and also the logical and methodological order.

In order to choose, I must as maker be able to intuit with great precision just what contribution each given choice would make to the emerging form, how it would interact with all the other selections that have some apparent potential to form an ensemble with it. And in order to do this I must be able to judge of each candidate for selection how well it fills the outline of the limit that is prepared for it by the architecture of the ensemble as I, guided by my techne, have shaped it up to this point – to judge whether it spills over the edges of this limit in some way or merely falls short of it. I am looking, say, for the right word with which to modify 'stumps'; I consider this word and that word, and one is too weak, one too emphatic, another too colloquial, another too formal, another has some unwanted connotation. Then I find the one that fits without residue into this slot: 'withered'.

'Slot' is a very strong word in this context, because it suggests a definiteness of outline of what has not yet been chosen, and thus that the artist's power of choosing is constrained in what might be considered too mechanical a way. Yet such a feeling of constraint is crucial to the experience of the most highly wrought art. When Flaubert spoke of *le mot juste* he meant precisely this, that there is a word that is the best suited to be used just *here*, and that the conditions for its being the right word are set and ineluctable, and the artist must submit to them. In the modernist tradition of critical reflection on art, it is the ability to satisfy the conditions of this kind of constraint – to *feel* its *correctness* – rather than the capacity to originate ex nihilo, that defines the greatest artist; and it is the definition of the greatest artist in these terms that makes possible the rediscovery of the fundamental kinship of 'art' with techne-in-general.

But the kind of defined space in question, when it is a question of invention, is of a sort unlike any physical slot. We might imagine it as a multidimensional space – loosely analogical to the multidimensional spaces of modern physics – with boundaries at the edges of each of its dimensions. I only know of the existence of these boundaries because I can feel each word I try bumping up against them: the boundary of emphasis, of formal register, of sound, and so forth, all of these together forming the (multidimensional) 'outline' of the boundary of the form. This outline remains strictly indeterminate until it is actually filled, but it nevertheless has determinative force, serving as a kind of 'attractor' of candidates for selection (in a magnetic, not statistical, sense of 'attractor', though the statistical sense is probably relevant as well), and when it is filled, the choice is confirmed as correct (or not) by the techne-intuition of both artist and audience. In each art there will be, at each moment of actualization of the techne by an artist in the making of a work, such an outline of the next move projected by the totality of conditions set for that outline by the ensemble of elements of the work as that ensemble has been organized up to that moment, and by the sense of the emerging physiognomy that is sharply or dimly intuited. And behind this immediate ensemble and this emerging physiognomy will be the conditions set by the organization of the ensemble of elements of the artist's own earlier work, as this itself is nested within the organization of the ensemble of works by those preceding artists who have defined the techne by the agency of which the present artist's own previous body of work has been produced. Techne, conceived as the totality of all these conditions, marks off the limit of the force with which the guitar string is plucked, of the tone and volume of the speaker's eloquent voice raised at a crucial moment in her speech, and so on endlessly. And the way the expert artist learned how to feel when the move is right is, simply, or not so simply, by being trained into the practice, by seeing exemplars of correct joining, and by going through an apprenticeship in which the ability to judge correctly of one's moves is matured.

Techne-in-general

In the next two chapters I trace the way in which the fundamental concepts of techne theory were forged by Plato and Aristotle. In the process, I will lean heavily on the Greek vocabulary, not as a philological nicety but because one *thinks* differently, and better, with the Greek words – *techne*, *ergon*, *dynamis* and *organon* in particular – than with their modern analogues.

The fundamental advantage of translating our modern concept of *art* back into the conceptual field of the ancient Greek concept *techne* is that the Greek concept had not yet been channelled into the narrow confines of the 'aesthetic' and of Romantic conceptions of artistic inspiration. It was still in immediate, living contact, in everyday usage, with the full range of meanings out of which the later concept of art would grow.

We cannot attain clarity about the nature of the specific technai that are pre-eminently dignified with the name of art in our culture without first clarifying the nature of techne-in-general as it is displayed in the panorama of knowledgeable, skilled action of all kinds that every culture presents, going back to the primitive beginnings of human society. If the theory of techne is going to provide an adequate account of how the well done surpasses the artist, it must be as multifaceted and multileveled a concept as the phenomenon it seeks to explain.

Art in the modern sense is, of course, defined precisely by its separation from the fundamentally need-driven purposefulness of the labour process; yet the artist too must push and prod material reality, transforming the technai of the common workman into a form suitable for the needs of Art. The Athenians of the fifth century BC were uncomfortably aware of this proximity of some of their highly valued art to labour; hence, on the one hand, they already had their art-superstars in painting and sculpture, but on the other hand there remained a residual sense that these arts were *banausos* – mechanical, base, ignoble, because still redolent of physical labour, and therefore, in a slave-based society, improper for a freeman, a 'gentleman'. Only poetry, which involves no sweat-producing action of the muscles, and was ascribed to the afflatus of the gods, had already been lifted entirely free of this stigma. But the *Ion* attunes us to the fact that there is another, more fundamental dimension of purposeful, productive human activity that breaches the distinction between physical and intellectual work. The work of the farmer and fisherman and that of the mathematician and philosopher – the lowest physical work and the highest intellectual work – are alike *techne*. If poetry is not techne, then, according to Socrates, so much the worse for poetry.

NOTES

1 Interview with Charlie Rose, 12 January 2000, about the twelve-minute mark (www.youtube.com/watch?v=NcJ-DVq25-Q, accessed 13 April 2018).

2 For the purposes of exposition, I am simplifying this example to the single criterion of the precisely right extension of the arm, a criterion which itself is being reduced to its temporal dimension. Obviously the masterfulness of the gesture will depend on much more than this; every muscle must exhibit exactly the right degree of tension, the rest of the body must be held in exactly the right relation to the arm, and so forth. But each element into which the whole can be analysed can itself be conceptualized as an instance of an intuition of a limit.

3 T. S. Eliot, *The Waste Land; A Facsimile and Transcript of the Original Drafts Including the Annotations of Ezra Pound* (New York: Harcourt Brace Jovanovich, 1971), p. 47.

4 Twyla Tharp, *The Creative Habit: Learn It and Use It for Life* (New York: Simon and Schuster, 2003), p. 9.

PART TWO

Greek Origins

CHAPTER FOUR

How Plato (despite himself) invented techne theory

The fundamentals of the techne perspective begin to take shape in what David Wolfsdorf has called the 'reflection on techne' of the early and some of the middle period Platonic dialogues.[1] In these dialogues we see Socrates feeling around in his inherited thought-mass to begin defining concepts like form, function and techne. I find attractive the notion that Socrates was indeed, as ancient tradition holds, a stonemason by profession, because he displays an instinctive sense for the interaction of the artisan's actions with his materials, a sense that at times comes into conflict with the doctrine of metaphysical ('Platonic') Form. Whether the tradition is true or not, it seems clear that Socrates is responsible for the pragmatic aspect of Plato's discourse on techne, and I will often use his name in connection with it.

It's hard for us to grasp the techne perspective because of the overload of concepts with which our thinking is already programmed; for that reason, tracking the emergence into linguistic articulation by Socrates of the fundamental concepts of techne theory out of a practically virgin conceptual ground can help reshape our own thinking at the root. The techne standpoint cannot be grasped as an intellectual formula; it is itself a techne, and requires this kind of grassroots retraining of mental habits that in the contemporary thinking of non-artists (and some artists too) throws up automatic defences against thinking of art as techne.

The notion of techne that Socrates inherits has its earliest beginnings in Greek myth. In contrast with the Hebrew account of human origins, which takes the existence of the technai for granted, the Greek myths depict a naked, fragile, helpless humanity delivered from the brutality of its natural state only by the fundamental arts of culture, from the knowledge of fire to metalworking to language. The original model of techne, which apparently provides the etymology of the word techne itself, is carpentry; but by the time Aeschylus, or whoever wrote the *Prometheus Bound*, has Prometheus list the technai with which he has endowed humanity, they encompass 'virtually every aspect of intellectual activity'.

> From straightforward craft production to arithmos [number], to writing . . . The breadth of the list has led many commentators to describe Prometheus's gift as human culture itself . . . And the principle human resource is knowledge. 'Techne no longer means this or that particular ability, but in general human practical intelligence.'[2]

In the spirit of this generalization, Socrates in the *Cratylus* (414b) identifies the etymology of techne as *hexin nou*, to possess *nous* 'understanding, mind'.

The primary function of nous-bearing techne is to organize materials, objects and situations into coherent, well-formed things or states of affairs. The practitioner of any techne 'arranges everything according to a certain order (taxis), and forces one part to suit and fit with another, until he has combined the whole into a regular and well-ordered (tetagmenon) thing'. According to this account, not only artisans like shipbuilders and carpenters produce form, ordered dispositions of parts (taxis and tetagmenon have the same root as 'syntax'), but also, for example, trainers and doctors, because they 'bring order and system into the body (kosmousi, suntattousin)'; and also the good man who chooses his words carefully, because he, like all the artisans in the narrow sense, 'works with the purpose of giving a certain form (eidos) to whatever he is working on' (*Gorgias* 503d–504a). As these remarks show, Socrates thinks of techne not just as the making of artefacts but as knowledge-based action of any sort, on any aspect of the world, that organizes it to the point that it has a recognizable *eidos* 'form' infused with order-giving nous, 'mind', 'intelligence'. On this account, however, Homer and the other poets have no knowledge of techne because they create in a state of 'enthusiasm', divine inspiration, a state in which they are bereft of *nous*, literally 'out of their minds', *ekphron* (*Ion* 534b). Poetry, therefore, brings disorder rather than order to the soul.[3]

The concept of eidos is central to Platonic metaphysics and has had an immense influence on Western thought down to the present. This word and its synonym, *idea*, are derived from *eidenai*, 'to see', and thus refer in their base sense to the visible aspect of a thing, its typical outline by means of which we visually perceive what kind of object it is. However, because the form of the individual percept is also the form of the kind to which it belongs (we perceive the 'form' of Fido as that of the species, 'dog'), eidos in the Hippocratic texts of the fifth century BCE had already developed the more abstract sense of 'type' or 'kind', a sense in which Socrates often uses it. This sense of form as a 'universal' is abstract, thus 'ideal' in the sense that it has intellectual rather than physical existence, and also 'ideal' in the sense that it is, qua form, without flaw, as well as immune to contingency. But, since natural kinds are immanent to physical beings, this sense of form remains intimately related to the visual appearance of particulars. The final stage of evolution of Plato's concept of eidos, by contrast, separates it entirely from the sensible particulars in which it is instantiated. This is separately existing, eternal, changeless Form, the famous 'Platonic Idea' or 'Form'. Since the Forms are perceivable only by the intellect, the original reference of eidos/idea to visible form becomes enigmatic, and much scholarly effort has been expended in trying to figure out how particular physical objects could draw their own sensible forms from these separate, eternal, metaphysical Forms.

Plato never attains clarity about the relation among the various ways, beyond visual aspect, that he uses the notion of form. At one end of his spectrum of usage, forms are 'natural kinds', immanent to the beings of which they are the forms, in the middle they are abstract, intellectual entities of indefinite metaphysical status, and at the other end, they are entirely disembodied, absolutely real Ideas.

What is of central interest in the present context is the relation of these three senses of form to a fourth, much less familiar sense, the conception of form broached in the passage cited above from the *Gorgias*. As Wolfsdorf has noted with respect to this passage, 'the use of the concept *eidos* here and the related concepts *kosmos* (design) and *taxis* (order) are remarkable', because there is no 'theorization of universals' involved; 'Rather, *eidos* is understood as the idealized *ergon* [work or product] of a craftsman' (p. 117). Subsequently in Plato's work, then, 'the concepts of organized structure and order that emerge through reference to *techne* are . . . elaborated as Form' (p. 119), and the original Socratic understanding is abstracted away.[4] But artisanal form, as Socrates conceives it, is not the visual image of a thing, nor yet again the idealization of such an image into either a 'universal' concept, a transcendent Form, or the production of a divine demiourgos; it is the configuration or arrangement of component elements of something, a structure or structuration that is produced by the ordering power of techne, in immediate interaction with tools and materials. This techne-understanding of form is not only conceptually distinct from, but ultimately incompatible with, the general idealizing trend of Platonic thought, and in the space of this difference Socrates lays the original groundwork for techne theory.

Techne and *physis*

Ever since Aristotle, the key knock on Plato's notion of ideal, separate Forms has been that they are so utterly separate from individuated material beings that it's inconceivable how the latter could draw their own forms from, or, in the usual term, 'participate' in them. There is, obviously, no such problem about artisanal form, which emerges from an interaction, in view of some practical end, between the motions of the artisan's body and the physical properties of the objects or states of affairs on which the artisan works.

Socrates focuses on such an interaction, involving the simple action of cutting some unspecified material, in the following passage from the *Cratylus*:

> If we make the cut in whatever way *we* choose and with whatever tool *we* choose, we will not succeed in cutting. But if in each case we choose to cut in accord with the *physis* 'nature' of cutting and being cut and with the natural tool for cutting, we'll succeed and cut correctly. If we try to cut contrary to *physis,* however, we'll be in error and accomplish nothing. (*Cratylus* 386e–387a)

This passage explains that the actions of the artisan-maker are determined by the ineluctable material properties of the appropriate cutting tool ('the natural tool for cutting') and those of that which is cut ('the nature . . . of being cut'), properties that emerge into the light of knowledge from the way they constrain a techne-guided artisanal action. It is implicit in Socrates's explanation of this process that weighing and measuring – which he consistently treats as essential elements of techne, a mark of its rationality – would not by themselves yield a sufficient measure of the correctness of apprehension of the real by the technites. No doubt the artisan would weigh and measure and otherwise intellectually judge the qualities of tool and material, but the objective validity of these weighings and measurings is finally proven by the success of the given techne-action that they subserve.[5]

Socrates introduces the argument about cutting here, as elsewhere in his appeals to techne, in order to oppose Protagorean relativism. Artisanal means are not relative to individual perception; when artisans deal with things, they cannot be concerned with individual variations in perception and opinion that do not correspond to the needs of the task at hand. Of course there can be dissenting artisans who turn out to have a better idea of how to accomplish the same goal, but such dissent is itself subject to the test of success, and success depends on the correspondence of the new means to the nature of the material being formed. If they do not so correspond, as Socrates points out, they are simply and indisputably *in error*, as proven by the fact that we will 'accomplish nothing' of the artisanal purpose involved: the drawer will stick, the arrow won't fly straight, the lines won't scan. Relative to techne, though not absolutely, things can be meaningfully said to have, *in themselves* (*kath'auta*) what Socrates identifies variously as an *ousia* 'being' or 'essence', or a *physis* 'nature', of their own. This being or physis corresponds to correct techne-procedure; and Socrates concludes from this, surprisingly, that the *actions* constituting such correct procedure, since they are performed 'in relation to things', must also themselves be actually existing beings, *onton* (386e). I call this surprising because actions are temporally extended, a form of (Heraclitean) change, whereas the pull of Platonic ontology is towards (Parmenidean) timeless being, an idealization of the notion of an enduring physical object.

But even though Socrates momentarily proposes the ontological dignity of actions in this way, he does not acknowledge and try to deal with the problem of their temporal character. Temporally extended action in accord with techne carries the ordering power of nous 'intellect', by means of which it gives form to its materials. In order to transmit form in this way, techne action itself must be ordered and have form. And since form on Plato's understanding is static and unchanging, he apparently conceives the form that makes techne-guided action into a 'being' with 'presence', a static and unchanging interior architecture, such that every correct action by an artisan will be an instantiation of the form that every other artisan of that kind, in a similar situation, would reproduce. In this way techne-actions, although they are obviously processes, forms of becoming, are assimilated in Socrates's thinking to the static, Parmenidean conception of being, and the rigidity of ideal form is intruded into action itself. Thus Socrates at once presents a pragmatic account of artisanal responsiveness to the empirical qualities of tool and material, and attempts to recapture the vagaries of practical experience in ideal form (by treating action as a 'being').[6]

The concepts of physis 'nature', ousia 'being, essence', and eidos 'form, species' are all designed in accord with the purpose of anchoring the flux of natural becoming and transient perception in something fixed, something accessible only to pure intellect. At the limit of this trend in Plato's thought is the doctrine of separate Forms that only the psyche freed from the body by death can know (*Phaedo* 65–6). But, as Socrates admits in the *Parmenides*, it's far from clear how even natural kinds, let alone actions, can be thought of in terms of ideal Form; and in the *Cratylus*, as we just saw, he presents a flickering glimpse of physis – the specific nature or essence of a thing – emerging into the light of knowledge at the interface between artisanal process and materiality. On this alternate account, which is never allowed fully to unfold, the nature of things is not directly accessible by the intellect, only by the mediation of a complex, embodied, techne-guided interaction with the physical world.

In this connection, it's worth mentioning that, according to Gerald Else, Socrates's remarks about cutting in the *Cratylus* represent the first use of the term *physis* in the Platonic corpus.[7] This is striking, because it suggests that the very notion of 'nature' in the Platonic texts originally emerges out of the reflection on techne. Since, as Socrates elsewhere recognizes, techne is born from human needs and purposes (*Rep* 1, 341ff), a nature known by means of techne would in a sense be pros hemas 'in relation to us'; but not in Protagoras's 'relativistic' sense of the phrase (against which Socrates makes the *Cratylus* argument about cutting); in a way, rather, that modern investigations of the sociology of science are still trying to understand, and which for Socrates remains no more than an intuition grounded in practical experience.[8]

Looking towards the form

Platonic-Socratic form, in itself, is impervious to change or development in response to empirical conditions. Such form cannot be an ad hoc contrivance, arrived at, say, by an accidental initial discovery followed by adjustments made in response to the exigencies of use, by means of which the most efficient form is patched together. An empirical artefact can be put together this way in the Platonic dialogues; but its *form* by definition cannot. Platonic form as such, in any of its non-techne senses, is by definition always already optimally organized, presumably prior to any of the artisanal experiences that lead to the making of an actual instantiation of the form. This is the presupposition that, as Wolfsdorf says, Plato 'smuggles' into his concept of artefactual form (pp. 120–21).

Thus Socrates asks how a carpenter knows what form to give a weaver's shuttle, one made to replace another that broke while he was making it, and answers that the carpenter knows it by 'looking (blepon) toward' the eidos of shuttle. The eidos, the form of shuttle distinct from any of its instantiations, is *auto he estin kerkis*, the really existing shuttle, 'the shuttle itself that is'. Any particular shuttle can break, but the carpenter does not look at the broken one for his model, he looks towards the eidos to see it as it is in its pristine perfection that no physical contingency can affect.[9]

The distinction intended by Socrates here seems to be between the empirical shuttle that can be physically looked at and its categorical or perhaps transcendent form, but the point is obscure because his wording suggests that the rejected shuttle is inadequate as a model for the new one not because it is an empirical particular but because it is *broken*. Another thing that points towards an empirical focus is that, even though he refers to 'the eidos of shuttle', he is talking not about a single, universal form shared by all shuttles but about a specific subtype of shuttle, each type determined by its relation to the nature of the material it is designed to weave:

> whenever he has to make a shuttle for a light or a thick garment, or for one of linen or of wool or of any kind whatsoever, all of them must contain that specific eidos of shuttle that is naturally most *kalos* 'optimally formed' for each, and this is the physis 'nature' that must be given to each?
>
> . . . And the same applies to all other instruments. The artisan must discover the physis of tool that is naturally fitted for each purpose and embody that in the material of which he makes it, not in accordance with his own will, but in accordance with its physis. He must, it appears, know how to embody in the iron the type of borer naturally adapted to the nature of each kind of work.
>
> . . . And he must embody in the wood the type of shuttle fitted by nature for each kind of weaving. (*Cratylus* 389b–c)

Here, as Julia Annas says, Socrates describes artefactual form in terms of the 'functional principles' that the artisan must embody in wood if an artefact is to be correctly adapted to its purpose.[10] The key question concerns exactly *how* the artisan would 'discover the instrument naturally fitted for each purpose'. The notion broached here, that the artisan must consider what task the tool is for, and the appropriate material for the task, together with the earlier description of the nature of cutting and being cut, point towards a process of piecemeal empirical discovery of functional principles and of the best way to embody them in the proper material. But the notion of looking towards the eidos suggests something more like direct intellectual apprehension of the completed form, preadapted to the material circumstances of any specific making.

The same ambiguity is present in Socrates's conception of the technai that use these tools. The notion that technai, like tools, are preadapted to circumstances is implied at *Rep* 1, 342, where Socrates, giving precision to Thrasymachus's comment that the artisan qua artisan never errs, ascribes this intrinsic infallibility not to the artisan but to the techne itself. Each techne in itself, *en aute te techne*, is without 'deficiency or error (*hamartia*)', 'correct', 'without either fault or impurity', 'as long as it remains that very techne that it is'. Socrates does not explicitly say here that technai possess form and being, but we have seen that in the *Cratylus* he extends this recognition to techne-guided actions, and here technai are accorded the essential qualities of form: unity, self-identity and perfection. How did they get these qualities? Socrates does not think they are perfect because they were actually a gift of the gods. As the Hippocratic writings show, the Greeks knew quite well that technai have been developed by human culture and can start out very flawed but slowly, by reasoning over trial and error, 'rise from deep ignorance to approximately perfect accuracy', as the fifth-century Hippocratic treatise 'On Ancient Medicine' says.[11] Socrates's remark that the medical techne has 'now been *heurumene*', 'discovered' and *pareskeuasthe*, 'prepared' can be interpreted along these lines (*Rep* 341e).[12] But acknowledgement of such an evolution still leaves open the question of the nature or form of the techne that evolves. Does the eidos of a techne in some way pre-exist the empirical process by which it is discovered – as mathematical theorems in some way might? Is that why each techne is in itself perfect? Or is its excellence of form acquired by an intellect-illuminated, but empirical, process of discovery?

Because Socrates can take for granted the empirical existence in his own time of 'perfected' technai and their artefacts, he can fudge the question of the origin of their forms by treating these forms in a way parallel to those of living things, as already existing in perfected form, and as empirically graspable in the species of beings that instantiate them. 'Looking toward the form' can then be done by physically inspecting an unbroken physical shuttle of the correct type, because such a shuttle, despite being a mere empirical individual, correctly instantiates the form and can thus serve as a reminder of that form. This being the case, in principle the carpenter need not even look at an actual shuttle. All that is needed is to consult a mental image of the correct form of shuttle that the carpenter has acquired from previous such inspections. And this mental image, although acquired from experience of actual shuttles, can easily be conceived or misconceived as the image of a transcendent Form. But Socrates neither here nor elsewhere actually says that artefacts are resemblances of separate, eternal Forms (although *Rep* 10 confuses the issue, as we will see). He leaves the matter in a conceptual twilight that is never elucidated.

The ambiguity of Socrates's account appears to reflect the confused mixture of these two ways of thinking about artefactual form. But the unambiguously functional thread of his account entails that there can be no *metaphysically* separate Form of a shuttle or bore, because by definition such a form would be functionless and could not have been determined, qua form, in relation to the physis of specific artisanal materials or to a techne designed to fill a physical need.

The doctrine of use

Thus the opening in Socrates's reflection on techne towards a completely naturalistic account of artefactual form is limited by the impermeability to empirical determination of what he conceives as the forms *themselves*, their inability to change and evolve. But the opening is there, and, despite the characterization of techne itself as perfect in *Rep* 1, Socrates pushes this opening further in *Rep* 10.

The bond between artefactual form and earthly reality is tightened in the *Republic* beginning with Socrates's explanation in *Rep* 1 that techne originates in response to the *deficiencies* of earthly beings, the fact that they are *not* by nature already perfect. Thus, for example, 'because our bodies are deficient rather than self-sufficient, the techne of medicine has now been discovered' (341e). And when the discussion turns to the concept of *ergon* 'function' near the end of Book 1, the forms of tools are said to be determined by the need to optimize the efficiency of the corresponding artisan's practice. But this pragmatic trend appears to be interrupted at the beginning of Book 10, where Socrates develops the so-called imitation of an imitation argument: the couch maker, Socrates says here, does not make *ho esti kline*, 'the couch that is'; rather, he 'looks toward the *idea* "form"' of couch and makes something resembling it. Socrates's words here initially echo the account of shuttle-making in the *Cratylus* (with *idea* used in place of *eidos*), but, whereas the *Cratylus* unpacks the notion of looking towards the form in functional terms, Socrates now invokes instead what looks like the doctrine of separate Forms: he claims that the form, 'the couch that is', is made by a god.[13]

At first glance, Socrates seems here to have decided in favour of a straight 'idealist' interpretation of artefactual form (i.e. as a separate, transcendent

Form). However, as various interpreters have pointed out, the notion that artefactual forms are made by a divine artificer is not entertained anywhere else in Plato; and, besides, the notion that artefacts have eternal, changeless Forms makes no sense.[14] The claim about the divine couchmaker seems to be another of Socrates's opportunistic, occasion-driven arguments. Whereas in the *Cratylus* reference to 'looking toward the form' he was explaining the fit between the natures of material and instrument, here he is illustrating the notion of 'imitation in general', and his motivation is, apparently, rhetorical: he is trying, as Stephen Halliwell says, to give 'a symmetrical shape' to his painting-based argument (p. 114) about the nature of imitation. This requirement of symmetry generates the notion of three parallel artisans, the first of whom, a god, creates the really existing original which then serves as a model for the second maker, a human artisan, whose own product then is copied by the third 'maker', the painter, who is not, in fact, a true maker, because he does not make a real thing but only a simulacrum. But within the terms of this schema Socrates leaves conceptual wiggle room. He never says that the artisan's work is an 'imitation'; rather, he says that the maker of couch or table makes something *hoion* 'similar to' the really existing form, but not 'completely' or 'perfectly' (teleos) (597a) like it. Thus, while imitation is pure semblance, a phantom, void of reality, artefacts merely fall short of *complete* identity with the form. This of course makes sense without invocation of a transcendent Form. An artefact is superior to a mere mimeme because it has mass, three dimensions and functionality; but it is, on Plato's account, inferior to its (ideal) form, because the artefact is both imperfect and breakable.[15] But the only ideality that Socrates ascribes to the artisanal form conceived by the divine maker is that of being *one* instead of *many* (341d). The artisanal form is what we call a 'type' that can be instantiated in any number of 'tokens' or particulars. Such types are only as unbreakable and enduring as the lifespan of their last existing token, or their last physical or mental inscription. In saying that the form is 'one in nature', then, Socrates asserts something with which we can agree, yet without consenting to the notion that it exists in some separate, eternal realm.

There is no doing intellectual work without this kind of idealization; even the master of deconstruction, Jacques Derrida, speaking of the sign type-sign token distinction (in his critique of speech-act theory), conceded that one cannot deconstruct the notion of the sign-type past a 'certain minimum of idealization'.[16] The notion of minimal idealization is a useful one to introduce here because it allows us think beyond the starkness of the ideal/empirical opposition. The separate Platonic Forms represent the maximum of idealization; yet we idealize, without leaving the realm of empeiria, anytime we generalize beyond the immediacy of sense-impressions. The generic concept of a couch is necessarily 'ideal' in this sense. But it is *minimally* ideal, and Socrates's passing suggestion that its ideal or abstract nature points to a divine maker, to the degree that it might suggest the maximal ideality of the separate Forms, is badly misleading. We should be guided, instead, by his remark that the god made the artisanal form *physei*, natural or 'in nature'.

That Socrates has not, in the 'imitation of an imitation' argument, abandoned his functional account of form is conclusively shown by the brand new explanation of what is lacking in mimesis that follows shortly after. Socrates abruptly abandons the notion that the value of an artisan's product is measured by its proximity to a divine model, introducing in its place the measure of knowledge of the product's *function*:

> Does the painter, then, know the proper quality of reins and bit? Or does not even the maker, the cobbler and the smith, know that, but only the man who understands the use of these things, the horseman? . . . and shall we not say that there are some three arts concerned with everything, the user's art, the maker's, and the imitator's . . . Now do not the *arete* 'excellence', the *kallos* 'beauty, optimality of form', the *orthotes* 'correctness' of every implement, living thing, and action refer solely to the use for which each is made or by nature adapted? . . . it quite necessarily follows, then, that the user of anything is the one who knows most of it by *empeiria* 'experience', and that he reports to the maker the good or bad effects in use of the thing he uses. As, for example, the flute-player reports to the flute-maker which flutes respond and serve rightly in flute-playing, and will order the kind that must be made, and the other will obey and serve him . . . The one, then, possessing knowledge, reports about the goodness or the badness of the flutes, and the other, believing, will make them . . . Then in respect of the same implement the maker will have right belief about its excellence and defects from association with the man who knows and being compelled to listen to him, but the user will have true knowledge. (*Rep* 601c–602a)

The notion of the divine artist who makes the idea of couch, which Socrates so rapidly abandons, has completely obscured for a long tradition of interpretation the significance of the improved account that he replaces it with. In this revised triad, the user-artisan is silently slipped into the place at the top of the artisanal hierarchy that in the 'imitation of an imitation' argument was occupied by the form-making god – who is now entirely forgotten. And Socrates categorically declares that the *sole determinant* of the optimal form of an implement (form that has the qualities of arête, kallos and orthotes – excellence, optimality and correctness) is how it actually performs when used by an artisan, and that knowledge of this correct form comes *only* by the empeiria 'experience' of such a user. The privilege Socrates here gives to the notions of use and experience sharply manifests the divergence of the notion of artisanal form from those of visual, universal or metaphysical form.[17] We saw earlier how in the *Gorgias*, as Wolfsdorf says, '*eidos* is understood as the idealized *ergon* [work or product] of a craftsman' (p. 117). This idealization is now strictly defined not as transworldly perfection but as functional optimality: arête, kallos and orthotes, defined in relation to use. And Socrates lists *praxis*, 'action', along with organisms and artefacts as things that can have optimal, functionally defined form, giving a new sense to the suggestion in the *Cratylus* that techne-actions are *onton* 'beings'.

Regarding this passage Christopher Janaway objects that 'many things do not have the kinds of expert users who have superior understanding of excellences and deficiencies', citing as examples the couches and tables of which Socrates speaks earlier; and Janaway adds that even an expert user might know little about how a thing is made, so that it might take a 'designer or producer' to point out how a thing should be improved (p. 141). Janaway's objection makes us notice that Socrates has in fact now *dropped* couches and tables in favour of reins and flutes, and that this switch must be motivated by the fact that the latter, but not the former, have expert users. But this motivation is, as Janaway notes, confused by Socrates's notion that only a user-artisan separate from the maker can have the expert knowledge requisite for *kalos* making. The central issue, implied but not identified by Socrates, is not which artisan has the knowledge but what kind of knowledge is necessary (regardless of who possesses it).

According to the *Gorgias* account I cited at the beginning of this chapter, eidos is the orderly disposition of a complex of elements by rational, techne-guided action (what Aristotle will call action 'in accord with *logos*'), action that itself, according to *Rep* 601, has kalos 'fine, well-constituted, optimal' form. It follows that where there is no techne to guide it, there is no such thing as kalos use. The use of a thing that is not the *organon* 'instrument' of a techne – flopping on a couch, setting a cup on a table – is not techne-guided and thus possesses at best the rudiments of form.

This conclusion follows from the explanation of ergon – in the sense of 'function' – that Socrates gives in *Rep* 1, 352. Each kind of thing has its own ergon, Socrates says, and this is defined as 'that which one can do only with it', but more definitively as that which one can do with it 'in the most *kalos* "fine" or "optimal" way'. When Thrasymachus does not understand this definition of ergon from the example of horses (which are here treated in purely instrumental terms, as implements for human use), Socrates switches first to that of ears and eyes, and then to his prime exhibit: a pruning knife. One can use a dirk or an ordinary knife to trim vine leaves, Socrates says, but nothing will do the job as well as a pruning knife because it alone is *epi touto ergasthenti*, 'wrought for this', fashioned for the purpose of pruning. He does not use the word *eidos* here, but being epi touto ergasthenti clearly means that the tool is given what in the *Cratylus* is called the 'appropriate (prosekon) eidos' (390b), the one that has been properly ordered by the techne of knife-making to perform the task of pruning. Only with such a tool can this work be done in the most kalos 'well-formed, optimal' way.

What emerges from all this is that form for Socrates does not only follow function, it follows in the final instance from the imperative of *optimization* of function. Techne has only one need, one 'advantage', one imperative: to be *malista telean*, 'as perfect as possible' (*Rep* 1, 341a). This is the ultimate source of that intrinsic fineness of form that Plato 'smuggles' into his metaphysical notion of form – at least along the axis of the reflection on techne. Whatever the case may be with the eternal Forms, the imperative of optimization is intrinsic to the worldly nature of techne, which is by definition a need-driven pursuit of better and better ways to accomplish human purposes, perhaps driven at a physiological level by the principle of minimization of energy expenditure that appears to have contributed much to the evolution of the architecture of the brain-body.[18] Socrates's entire inquiry into techne is normed by the telos of optimality of form in the thing made, the action by means of which it is made, and the action that is subsequently performed with the thing made, so that the entirely worldly imperative of *functional optimality* reverberates across every level of his reflection on techne; and optimality of form is determined by the requirements of *use*, a user's need to perform the task at hand in the most optimal way.

That is why no action that is not optimally techne-guided can possess truly kalos form. Techne-guided action can only be kalos if it is supplied with a tool that has been skilfully 'fashioned for the purpose' and itself possesses optimal form; and such form encodes the empeiria that has, by trial and error, adjusted the tool's outlines most smoothly to the contours of the task for which it is designed.

Adjustment of this kind endows the tool with a kind of potential energy that only skilful use (itself honed by empeiria) can release. The concepts of potential energy, and of potentiality in general, which Aristotle would make central to his metaphysics, begin to be unlocked by Socrates from the Greek word-concept *dynamis*, 'ability or power to do'. Socrates sometimes uses *dynamis* interchangeably with ergon to mean what we translate as function, but dynamis is an essential terminological variant because it brings out the 'work power' aspect of tools and technai in a way that is not quite as salient in 'ergon' (because ergon ambiguously means both active doing and static product), and which is not at all hearable in the English word 'function'. And of course, because of the persistence in our own language of derivatives of dynamis like *dynamic* and *dynamite*, the dynamism (I can think of no better word here) of *dynamis* persists for our own ears.

Dynamis/ergon, the power to optimize action that is deposited or encoded in tool-form/design, can be released only by the techne of use corresponding to this form. As Socrates says at 374d, 'no . . . organon will make a man be an artisan or an athlete by his taking it in hand unless he has acquired the requisite episteme [i.e. techne] and has had sufficient practice'.[19]

By the logic of Socrates's argument, only the artefacts that are designed for expert use would have form in the *optimal* sense of form – the only sense that ultimately matters for Plato-Socrates. A table is, so to speak, passive in use, because the ordering dynamis of a using techne (the expert use by means of which the form of a tool that is 'shaped for the purpose' is honed) does not pass through it; by contrast, even so humble an organon as a broom would have this power in some minimal degree. A couch is an ergon only in the passive sense, as a work or product of techne, but an *organon* 'tool, instrument' both *is* an ergon of techne in this sense (as 'product'), and itself *possesses* an ergon in the sense of dynamis 'function, work-power', a power with which it is endowed by its design, and which is actualized by the ergon 'work activity' of an artisan skilled in the applicable techne. Casual use skims over the surface of the form of the object it uses, revealing its virtues and deficiencies only accidentally, whereas knowing how to use a tool expertly, or at least knowing how an expert would use it (as a designer or maker separate from the user would have to know), explores the contours of the physis of all aspects of the artisanal process and brings them into the light of systematic, though in considerable part tacit, 'embodied' knowledge – knowledge encoded in the forms of techne and tool, and then encoded in the body of the artisan by 'sufficient practice'.

Socrates's reflections on techne in their full complexity thus paint a far more complex picture of tool-making than the notion of 'looking toward the form' can suggest, even when we interpret this notion in terms of grasping 'functional principles'. Between the tool-maker and the form stands the tool-user's experience of testing preliminary forms through a process of trial and error, a process that reveals functional principles not as direct objects of knowledge but in their practical consequences, through qualities or deficiencies of the tool's performance. I have pieced together key moments from the Platonic dialogues at which Socrates evokes aspects of techne that we are today in a better position to understand and to value. We can today appreciate that in order to understand 'the nature of cutting and of being cut, and the natural tool for the job' (*Cratylus* 386e), the artisan must grasp the qualities of materials, artefacts, tools, and actions by a 'feel' for form that involves not just sense perception and mental exertion working together, but also tactile, proprioceptive, and other kinds of perceptual and cognitive capacities that work on embodied cognition is currently exploring. But the ability to do all this presupposes that the artisan's body has incorporated the know-how of the relevant techne, which is the primary facilitator of the artisan's action; and current scientific and philosophical work on extended, embodied, and distributed cognition has not yet sufficiently recognized the role that techne plays. Perhaps there is still something to be learned about this from Socrates.

It should not be surprising if Socrates turns out to be an ally of the post-Cartesian worldview that has been evolving from Heidegger, Ryle, and Wittgenstein to Andy Clark, Edwin Hutchins and Terrence Deacon. Socratic *nous* is not 'mind' as what Wittgenstein called 'a kind of queer medium'[20] – a thinking substance essentially equivalent to individual human consciousness – it is, like Heraclitus's *logos*, the impersonal principle of order-making that is responsible for all ordered things, from the cosmic scale to the work of the technai. In the *Phaedo* Socrates says that as a young man he learned from Anaxagoras to call by the name of *nous* the cosmic principle that 'would direct everything and arrange each thing in the way that was best' (97c). In the artisan's imperative to shape a well-organized form, thus, Socrates perceives a modalization of a universal imperative that is intrinsic to all existing things that can be called *beings* – those that have an intelligible and nameable eidos.

The fundamental technai – such as carpentry, farming, shipbuilding, metalworking – are thus rationality, nous or logos, in its original, untheorized form, practical rationality that arises in response to the needs of survival by directing and arranging things in the way that is best. For Socrates, techne, as bearer of nous, is the first incarnation of the rational logos; according to the *Phaedrus*, even language itself (also called 'logos') does not have full rational ordering until it is submitted to the rigor of the techne of dialectic (269–70). He is not concerned with how much or little the artisan's consciousness might be involved in the ordering process, only with whether the ordering is guided by logos-according techne, the agent or bearer of nous.

That is why, in the case of the ecstatic poet of the *Ion*, what Socrates criticizes is not the absence of lucid intentional consciousness in the process of poem-making, but the absence in the poet's ordering activity of the guiding principles of an appropriate techne. We should take Socrates literally when he says to the rhapsode Ion that 'to each of the technai the god has given the ability to know (gignoskein) a specific *ergon*, "work, function"', a remark that strictly speaking assigns the know-how not to the poet but to the techne itself (537c). Cognitive power is in the first instance contained in the techne, and the artisan knows how only by delegation from it. The notion that the techne itself in a sense 'knows how' is strengthened in *Rep* 342, where Socrates says that techne itself never errs, and makes technai the subjects of active verbs: they 'seek out what is advantageous' for those beings that they 'rule over', as medicine for example 'rules over' the body.

From the perspective of the modern concept of mind (roughly Cartesian), or of the notion that cognition happens in the brain, we might be inclined to think that Socrates is speaking figuratively when he makes techne a cognitive agent; but from the 'extended mind' perspective we are today in a position to make good literal sense of Socrates's words. In this perspective, techne can be understood as part of an artisan-techne-world circuit that functions as an integrated cognitive system. Technai obviously do not possess consciousness, but they don't need to in order to function cognitively, because cognition is a function of the entire system, which requires the operation *in some way* of the conscious intentionality of the artisan, but not that it should be in charge of everything at every moment. Consciousness operates in a supervisory role, and so, like other kinds of supervisors, is only dimly aware, and sometimes quite unaware, of what is going on when it isn't looking; when it is looking, it might have only a vague, and even a false, understanding of what it is doing. Since the range of what it can see at any given time is quite limited, most of what is going on, most of the time, necessarily takes place out of its sight.

This invisible work is done by a series of 'unconscious' cognitive workers, ranging from the neurons of the brain, through the tendon networks of the hands, to the tools the hands grasp, and above all, to the decisive element in cognition and indeed in the existence of culture and consciousness: the technai that contain the nous that runs the entire system.[21]

This is not to say that Plato or Socrates thought in terms of anything like what we call extended mind. The intellectual framework within which they worked is too radically different from ours for any such equation to be meaningful. Yet Socrates's discourse on techne shows that he had a keen understanding of how artisans actually work, and of the nature of techne know-how, and our own understanding must somehow converge with his.

NOTES

1 David Wolfsdorf, *Trials of Reason: Plato and the Crafting of Philosophy* (New York: Oxford University Press, 2008).

2 David Roochnik, *Of Art and Wisdom: Plato's Understanding of Techne* (University Park: Pennsylvania State University Press, 1996), pp. 40–41. Roochnik cites Thomas Kübe, *Techne und Arete* (Berlin: De Gruyter, 1969), pp. 36–7.

3 Given the difficulty of reconciling what Socrates says here about poetry and poets with what he says in the *Phaedrus* and the *Protagoras*, this would seem to be one of those places in the dialogues at which he argues in an opportunistic way, addressed more to persuading his interlocutor than to stating a worked-out position. If Socrates really believed poetry to be the direct utterance of the god, merely channelled by the poet and then the rhapsode, this would imply that the nous, and the eidos, instead of being delegated by the techne-giving gods to the art of poetry, would be divinely infused into the poem through the agency of the poet. But in that case, there would be no reason to ban poetry from the optimally constituted state.

4 Thus, when in the presumably later *Timaeus* he develops in detail the model of divine ordering suggested in the *Phaedo*, he calls the cosmos-organizing Mind the Demiourgos, while 'Platonizing' the messy reality of earthly making into a world-originating, purely logico-geometric craft that underlies the organization of worldly forms, specifically that of the human body. In this account, all connections to the practical aspects of techne that Socrates investigates in the earlier dialogues are gone.

5 On the relation between weighing/measuring and techne in the Socratic reflection on techne, see Tom Angier, *Techne in Aristotle's Ethics: Crafting the Moral Life* (London: Continuum, 2010), p. 22.

6 In the following chapter I examine how Aristotle, who often unpacks concepts left undeveloped by Plato, develops the notion of the form of action in the *Poetics*, and that of the transmission of form by artisanal action, in a fascinating passage of *Generation of Animals* (730b–740b). Plato did finally address the problem of the being of motion in the Eleatic Visitor's

allegory of the battle between Gods and Giants in the *Sophist*. See Jonathan Beere, *Doing and Being: An Interpretation of Aristotle's* Metaphysics *Theta* (Oxford: Oxford University Press, 2009), pp. 6–17.

7 Gerald Frank Else, 'The Terminology of the Ideas', *Harvard Studies in Classical Philology* (1936) 47: 17–55.

8 No doubt as science progresses, more and more 'disinterested' knowledge emerges; but the modern history and sociology of science have been showing for a long time how complex the imbrication of human interests, technology and action with our knowledge of the real remains. See in this connection the classic work by Ludwig Fleck, *Genesis and Evolution of a Scientific Fact*, ed. Thadeuss J. Trenn and Robert K. Merton, trans. Fred Bradly and Thadeuss J. Trenn, with introduction by T. S. Kuhn (Chicago: University of Chicago Press, 1979). I'm grateful to Edwin Hutchins for calling this essential book to my attention. See also Lukacs, *Ontology of Social Being*, ch. 3, 'Labor.'

9 The main discussion within which this question arises is about how things got their original names, and Socrates, characteristically, analyses name-giving as a techne, a branch of the law-giving techne, and the name as a form of *organon* in its service. How does a lawmaker, an artisan of name-giving, know what form to give to the names he invents, Socrates asks? To answer the question, he reduces the more abstract question of name-giving to the transparency of one of the primary technai, carpentry, and this leads to the discussion of shuttles.

10 Julia Annas, *An Introduction to Plato's Republic* (Oxford: Oxford University Press, 1981), p. 230.

11 Quotation from 'On Ancient Medicine' from Roochnik, pp. 48–9.

12 Cited by Roochnik, p. 49.

13 Stephen Halliwell notes that *ho esti* in the middle books of the *Republic* is used 'as a virtually technical expression for Forms', and concludes from this that in 597a the form in question cannot be 'a simply logical or conceptual idea', while conceding that 'it remains entirely opaque . . . what the transcendent reality associated with "couch" is supposed to be" (pp. 112–13). However, Halliwell's conclusion that a transcendent reality is intended here involves interpreting *physis* as 'a realm of perfection clearly transcending the "natural" world of living things and matter' (p. 114), whereas the *Cratylus* suggests that for Socrates, when it is a matter of techne, the concept of physis is not so easily detachable from the natural world. Stephen Halliwell, *Plato: Republic 10* (Warminster, UK: Arris and Phillips, 1993).

14 Christopher Janaway economically sums up these criticisms in his *Images of Excellence: Plato's Critique of the Arts* (Oxford: Clarendon Press, 1995), p. 112.

15 One might object that the artefact is superior to its Form because the latter lacks functionality, but this is not an objection Plato would countenance.

16 Derrida, *Ltd Inc abc*, in *Glyph 2*, trans. Samuel Weber (Baltimore: Johns Hopkins University Press, 1977), pp. 162–254. Quotation from p. 190.

17 'The equation between knowledge and experience is surprising, since elsewhere Plato *distinguishes* between mere experience and the rationality of true knowledge' (Halliwell, p. 130).

18 For an overview and synthesis of the latest research on this, see Andy Clark, *Surfing Uncertainty: Prediction, Action, and the Embodied Mind* (New York: Oxford University Press, 2016).

19 He also mentions the erga of horses and sense organs in this discussion, but this is clearly a generalization of an analysis that is fully at home only in the realm of techne, and in the final analysis on the model of a tool. He is able to include living things in his list as things whose form is determined in relation to use because in the *Republic* he thinks of animals as a sort of tool; thus at *Rep* 1 352d ff., he treats horses as analogous to such a tool as a pruning knife. Socrates apparently has in mind domesticated animals, like horses and the dogs mentioned earlier in *Rep* 1, and domesticated animals are indeed a form of organon for humans, an organon that has, like any other tool, to be given its ergon by a shaping techne such as the *hippike* 'horse techne', which includes both horsemanship and horse husbandry.

20 Ludwig Wittgenstein, *The Blue and Brown Books* (New York: Harper and Brothers, 1958), p. 3.

21 For a glimpse into how cunningly our bodies have been fitted with cognitive power by evolution, see, e.g. F. J. Valero-Cuevas, J. W. Yi, D. Brown, R. V. McNamara, C. Paul and H. Lipson, 'The Tendon Network of the Fingers Performs Anatomical Computation at a Macroscopic Scale', *IEEE Transactions on Biomedical Engineering* (June 2007) 54.6 (Pt 2): 1161–6.

CHAPTER FIVE

From Aristotle to extended mind

With Aristotle, techne theory comes to maturity. Aristotle takes the Platonic/Socratic concepts discussed in the previous chapter and thinks further along the roads they had opened up, in a way I will try to elucidate. However, as Joseph Dunne has shown in meticulous detail, there is a deep split in Aristotle's texts between what Dunne calls the 'official doctrine' of techne, articulated in *Nicomachaean Ethics* 6.4 and *Metaphysics* 7.7 – the doctrine that is usually recounted in scholarly discussions of Aristotle – and what Aristotle says in many other passages that are unsystematically scattered throughout his treatises, passages that address the practical intricacies of techne. In such passages techne is usually introduced casually as a secondary topic, often as an analogy to illuminate something about biology, and so have been largely ignored, except to the degree that they can be made out to agree with the official doctrine.[1] Yet, considered honestly and in depth, the official doctrine and these passages do not, in fact, agree.

The official doctrine is unquestionably of the type Gilbert Ryle attacked in *The Concept of Mind* as the 'intellectualist legend', the notion that what makes an action intelligent is an 'anterior interior operation of planning', one that mentally posits the form of the completed action before performing it.[2] This notion is not even adequate as an explanation of ordinary intentional action, and aestheticians and literary theorists alike from Collingwood to deconstruction have rightly objected to it as an account of actual art-making. Fortunately, Aristotle was no dogmatist and did not allow his own doctrinal statements about techne to keep him from probing deeply into the reality of artisanal practice.

Those stubborn forms

As is well known, Aristotle rejected the Platonic notion that authentic *ousia*, 'being' or 'substance', belongs only to the separate Forms, in favour of the notion that ousia 'in the primary sense' is a 'this', paradigmatically a living being, in which form and matter have been joined by nature itself (*Metaphysics* 1032).[3] However, precisely because in organisms form and matter are so thoroughly joined, it's easier to illuminate the form–matter distinction in a secondary type of beings, made things, and Aristotle often uses the making process – say the sculpting of a statue – for this purpose. Regardless, whether made directly by nature or by humans through techne, all form ultimately comes from nature. As Stephen Halliwell explains, techne 'has to be comprehended ultimately in terms not of contingent human choices and tradition, but of natural teleology mediated through, or channeled into, acts of human discovery of what was there to be found . . . Not only do human productive activities form an analogue to the generative and purposive patterns of nature, but their individual histories evolve in accordance with intrinsic seeds of natural potential.' Techne, as Dunne says, is something like 'a strategic detour through which nature goes . . . in order to bring about a new class of being (artefacts) which it can neither produce nor reproduce through its normal channels' (p. 338).

Both natural and artefactual forms, then, start out as 'intrinsic seeds of natural potential' in Aristotle. This natural potential is intrinsic to matter itself, which, although it is itself formless – or perhaps because it is formless – feels inexorably drawn towards form, longing for it, as Aristotle says in a stunning image, 'as the female desires the male' (*Physics* 192a23–4).

The marriage of form and matter that Aristotle posits could thus hardly be more profound. And yet, as implied by the analogy of matter to the female and form to the male, they are not equal partners; in the last analysis, the composite of form and matter derives its being from the form. Form, though it is in reality inseparable from matter, nevertheless remains intellectually distinguishable as alone ousia in the primary, the most irreducible sense (*Metaphysics* 1029a, 1032b). Matter, by contrast, while it is intrinsically oriented towards form, is, as such, formless and a principle of formlessness, and is ousia only in a secondary sense.

Thus, despite Aristotle's radical new conception of the unity of form and matter, despite his rejection of Plato's separate Forms, his eide remain, in the final instance, impregnably ideal, metaphysically superior to matter, and the forms that techne conveys to matter seem to be as impervious to modification by their contact with empirical reality as those of Plato. Thus, in the same chapter (*Metaphysics* 7.7) that tells us the form alone is ousia in the primary sense, Aristotle characterizes techne as a disembodied dynamis that resides in the psykhe 'mind' of the artisan (cf. *On Generation and Corruption* 324b). This active power comprises two phases, *noesis*, 'thought', by which the technites figures out the steps towards a desired end, and *poiesis*, the doing that implements these steps. The first, mental or noetic, phase of the process determines the steps the subsequent making will take, and this mentally inscribed prescription for making guides the action of the maker, an action that shapes the materials accordingly, imposing on them the eidos in the maker's mind. This process is described in an important passage from *Generation of Animals*:

> The *morphe* [physical shape; sometimes synonymous with eidos] and the *eidos* [form] are imparted from [the carpenter] to the material by means of the *kinesis* 'motion' that he sets up. It is his hands that move the *organa* 'tools' that move the material; it is his knowledge, and his *psykhe*, in which is the eidos, that move his hands or any other part of him with a kinesis of some definite kind, a kinesis varying with the varying nature of the object made. (*GA* 730b)

On its face, this account is mentalist or intellectualist in Ryle's sense. The passage cited is introduced by Aristotle as an analogy for the process of sexual reproduction: as the artisan's knowledge of the eidos uses hands and tools as vehicles for the shaping motion of the techne, so nature uses semen to carry the shaping kinesis originating in the human eidos to the egg. This analogy implies that the artefactual eidos should migrate intact from techne through artisanal psyche to the artefact, just as, unless some accident happens, natural eide migrate in their pristine form from semen to egg.

But a closer look at *GA* 730 complicates this picture. Socrates leaves unmentioned the physical forces by means of which the artisan looks to the form and transfers it to his material; but Aristotle introduces the notion that form is conveyed into the material by means of a *kinesis*, 'physical motion', that passes from the techne-equipped psyche into the hands of the artisan. This kinesis is 'of some definite kind', a kind appropriate to 'the varying nature of the object made'. We recognize here a refinement of the *Gorgias* account in which Socrates spoke of 'the nature of cutting and being cut' in a specific case of making; Aristotle has abstracted the notion of a formed kinesis from this account. The artisan conveys the form of the object being made through the form of the kinesis that is performed, a kinesis that is conveyed to the tool, which then shapes the material. Aristotle comments that 'in the tools lies in a certain sense the action of the techne', or, as Klaus Bartels puts it, the eidos is, as it were, 'encoded (*chiffriert*)' within the action of the tool; but by the logic of Aristotle's account, in order to be encoded in the action of the tool, the form must first have been encoded in the action of the artisan's hand.[4] Thus, even though the techne itself is a disembodied power, according to Aristotle's own account it must be *serially embodied*, first in hand, then in tool, before finally winding up in the artefact; and it makes the transition from one of these embodiments to the next by means of a physical motive force (kinesis), one that plays out spatially and temporally.

But the materialization of techne in the movements of hand and tool, and the fact that these movements form a temporally articulated series, open a spatial and temporal interval (what Derrida would call a space of *différance*) between the eidos in the soul of the technites, on the one hand, and the thing being made, on the other hand. Each moment of the making process can carry only one bit of the encoded form across the interval; and what can guarantee that it will all be reassembled in perfect correspondence to the original conception?

Presumably the guarantee would be the ideal nature, impervious to empirical deviation, of techne, psykhe and eidos that constitute the origin and destination of the making process. But now consider Aristotle's description of the 'soul' or 'mind' in *Peri Psykhes*. This treatise is traditionally translated as *On the Soul*, but psyche is far from synonymous with soul. On Aristotle's account, the psykhe is the eidos of the body, and the two have a *koinonia*, 'commonality' of nature that makes them inseparable in a way comparable to the inseparability of wax and its shape (412a18–b9). This commonality is, however, much more than that of physical shape and the object of which it is the shape; psykhe is more closely bound to body than the analogy with the shape of wax can suggest. It is the cause and source of the body's livingness, the actuality of the organic body's potential for life (415b). This aspect of the meaning of psyche in Aristotle is a reminiscence of the original meaning of psyche as 'breath of life'. But psyche does more than just animate the body; it enables each of the body's organs to perform its specific function; and it too dies when the body dies (408a). The koinonia between psyche and body, Aristotle argues, is so tight that not just any kind of soul can go into any kind of body, as the Pythagorean doctrine of transmigration of souls implies; it is necessary to give the 'bodily conditions' required for the ability of just *this* kind of soul to inhabit just *this* kind of body. And to underline the absurdity of Pythagorean transmigration Aristotle uses the analogy of techne: to say souls can migrate to different kinds of bodies, Aristotle remarks, 'is as absurd as to say that the art of carpentry could embody itself in flutes; each techne must use its tools, and each soul its body' (407b).

Comparing the relation between soul and body to that between techne and tool projects a different, more dynamic conception of the relation between form and matter than that which is suggested by comparing the soul-body relation to that between form and artifact. The soul is the form of the body not in the way the shape of the statue is the form of the marble, but in the way that techne is the form of the *activity* of form transmission that is encoded in the action of the tool.

The techne–soul analogy brings out in an especially illuminating way Aristotle's most radical revision of the Platonic theory of form: the introduction in his mature system of the concept of *energeia* (or *entelecheia*), traditionally translated as 'actuality', but more precisely, as Aryeh Kosman argues, as 'activity'. Ousia, Aristotle gradually realized, is not simply there, 'present' with the presence of either a sense-object or a transcendent Form; it has to go through a developmental process in which it passes from its beginning in the seed or sperm as dynamis, 'potential' or 'ability', to its condition of maturity as energeia, actuality/activity. The fullness of the being's being, then, is its ability to act put optimally into motion – the kind of dynamis techne makes possible. And since being, ousia, in the primary sense is form, form is, in the final accounting, not that of an 'inert and static' thing, but the specific way in which a being is what it is. The point of translating energeia as activity is to spotlight the 'ontological centrality' of activity in Aristotle's metaphysics. A physical entity is not ousia merely by virtue of its thereness or presence; this presence is only the 'material condensate' of ousia's activity, 'the activity of things being what they are' (Kosman, 176–83).[5]

In the case of artifacts, which are not self-moved, their energeia is in the final instance the actualized ergon 'work activity' of the techne-guided artisan who made them. In some mysterious way 'the act of building is the thing that is being built', 'the ergon is the telos, and the energeia is the ergon', 'therefore even the word "energeia" is derived from "ergon"' (*Meta* 9.8). (Cf. my discussion of Plato's account of the dynamis of tools in Chapter 4.) This beautiful and profound conception is Aristotle's mature notion of form.

In terms of this new non-substantialist metaphysics of energeia, the techne–tool relation is peculiarly apt as an analogue to the soul–body relation, because techne has both shaped the tool into its physical form, giving it the potential or ability to perform a specific ergon, and also animates it in use. As in Plato, the example of the tool-organon is paired by Aristotle with that of the biological organon. If the eye were an animal, *the ability to see* would have been its soul. The eye's ability to see is like the axe's power to cut (guided by techne, presumably), and the energeia/entelecheia of the soul is analogous to both of these. These two analogies together suggest how Aristotle can understand soul as form and form as activity. What sight is to the eye, and what techne is to the tool, the whole faculty of sense, the *aisthetikon*, is to the body as a whole. This suggests that the psykhe, as form or dynamis/energeia of the body, just *is* the aisthetikon, the receptive-active, functional aliveness of the body to its own sensations and to the environing world. It is other things as well; in humans it is also the seat of the intellect, the non-material faculty of the body that is capable of taking the imprint of disembodied forms. But the intellect is seated in the aisthetikon (*Peri Psykhes* 412b).[6]

And since the Aristotelian psykhe, as aisthetikon, is, as Dunne notes, 'present in the whole body and in all its parts', making 'each integral part capable of its specific functioning', it is inescapably the case that psykhe is as much in the artisan's hand as it is in the eye, or anywhere else.

> Without the presence of soul we might have an inert lump of flesh but not a human hand. The very potentiality for dexterity and coordinated action

> which makes a human hand is already due to the presence of soul. And when this raw potentiality is gradually disciplined into actual capacities for specific types of skilled activity, techne is present, we may say, as much in the hand as in the soul; it is what makes the hand of a *technites* different from the hand of an unskilled person. (Dunne, p. 348)

Soul, hand, tool

Although Aristotle officially distinguishes techne from empeiria 'experience', praxis 'practice', and *phronesis* 'practical sense' or 'prudence', he has a great deal of trouble keeping them distinct (Dunne, pp. 253–61). A symptom of this confusion is the ambiguity in Aristotle's treatment of the 'stochastic' technai like medicine, navigation and rhetoric that are least 'mechanical' and which require constant adjustment to the factors arising unpredictably in different contexts. In his canonical analysis of techne into noesis and poiesis in *Metaphysics* 7.7, he uses medicine as his paradigmatic techne; yet in *Nicomachaean Ethics* 2.2 he says that praxis cannot be governed by techne because in praxis the agent must be attentive to the particulars of the occasion or 'moment of decision' (ta pros ton kairon), 'as in the case of medicine and navigation'.

Dunne opines that the technai of the kairos 'occasion, moment of decision' are 'philosophically orphaned' by Aristotle (pp. 257–8). Sometimes Aristotle treats them as technai, other times he 'orphans' them because they do not meet the test of exactness. Aristotle officially defines techne as theoretical, concerned with universals, and distinguishes it sharply from praxis, which is governed by the practical sense (phronesis) that opportunistically adapts itself to circumstances (*Meta* 1.1). Yet *all* technai, however exact, must continually deal with particular cases. Thus, whereas Aristotle treats the more exact technai as paradigmatic of techne, Dunne proposes to elevate the technai of the kairos to that role. In fact, as Dunne correctly stresses, *all technai are technai of the kairos*; it's just that in some this is more obvious than in others (p. 355).

Techne must involve something like phronetic responsiveness, for the carpenter and the mathematician as well as the doctor or navigator. No doubt the area that is left open for deliberation is much larger in medicine than in at least the simpler branches of mathematics; but as anyone who has struggled to learn math knows, there is a great deal of 'programming' of our intuitions that must take place before the operations can become automatic. And for them to become automatic means simply that they become 'intuitive', capable of unreflective adaptation to the particulars of the problem at hand. The more skilled we are in a techne, the quicker and more effectively we can modulate and tweak it to the requirements of the kairos; that's why we tend not to notice that it's still a matter of responsiveness to the particulars of the occasion.

This sort of conception is consistent with many of Aristotle's observations on techne, but he cannot integrate it theoretically because he defines the knowledge involved in techne primarily in mentalist or intellectualist terms, and cannot quite formulate the concept of an embodied knowledge in touch with the particulars of experience. We owe Joseph Dunne a considerable debt for the comprehensiveness with which he has demonstrated how much, nevertheless, Aristotle managed to articulate of such a concept.

So deep is the connection between techne and practical experience in Aristotle's thought that he considers the very existence of the human hand a consequence of our ability to wield tools – a sort of anticipatory back-formation from techne. The hand is *organon pro organon*, the organ/tool for using tools, sprouted from the human body by the form-giving impulse of nature, because humans are the animals 'most capable of acquiring the most varied technai', and therefore needed an organ with the ability to grasp tools (*Parts of Animals* 687a). The hand is the means by which, for Aristotle, nature takes the detour delegating to techne the making of beings nature cannot make on its own. By our lights, he is wrong in ascribing such purposeful agency to nature. But he is profoundly correct in his intuition that the hand is the nexus between tool and 'mind', and that the mind-hand-tool complex is inextricably bound together, as it were, by nature itself.

Neither Plato nor Aristotle is able to conceptualize the soul except in terms of the mind-hand-tool complex. The Platonic-Aristotelian notion of the essence or nature of a thing, of its very *being*, is fundamentally conceived as an ergon, a function or work power that they conceive as ensuing from a functional design like that of a tool or biological organ. And abstract entities like techne and soul yield readily to this analogy. As each organon has its own proper ergon/dynamis, so does the soul. Hence at *Rep* 1, 353, Socrates conceptualizes the soul by analogy with a pruning knife, concluding that its ergon, optimally exercised, is justice; and Aristotle compares the soul directly to the hand as tool of tools. As the hand is able physically to grasp all tools, so the psykhe is the *form of forms*, able intellectually to grasp all eide.

But before techne can animate the tool it must animate the hand of the technites, as a skill learned through teaching and practice. Psykhe, hand, and tool form a tightly knit system along which artefactual forms circulate, driven by techne know-how.

The notion of a form-making impulse in nature that is teleologically oriented toward technology, and which therefore provides human beings with their first tool, the hand, points away from Romanticism, and equally from Heidegger's influential account of Greek techne. It opens a door into an entirely new realm of nature, the realm of the co-evolution of human biology and culture, which essentially involves the development of tool-making and tool use. Aristotelian teleology warps strangely in the transition from nature neat to nature expressing itself as techne, via the hand.[7]

I will examine the nature of this teleology in the next section, but first let us revisit the passage with which this discussion began, in which Aristotle describes the transmission of kinesis from techne to artefact. The way Aristotle articulates the scene of making in this passage, considered against the background of *On the Psykhe*, is rich with possibilities for further development. The notion of a *skilled hand*, one capable of passing a well-formed and form-making kinesis originating in techne, to a tool that then passes this kinesis through to a set of materials, resulting in a finished, well-formed artefact, articulates well with Socrates's account of how tools are *epi touto ergasthenti*, fashioned for a specific task (see pp. 57–8 above). The skilled hand has had the know-how of a techne trained into it, and this know-how has co-evolved with the tool in a way that has gradually optimized the tool's ergon 'potential work-power, functionality' that in turn enables the hand to optimize its practice of its skill.

The Socratic notion of optimal tool-design, of the tool that is 'fashioned for the purpose', is an essential supplement to the account of *Generation of Animals* 730b, because it points towards the history of artisan-empeiria by means of which the design has been honed – a history that Aristotle does not address. Socrates does not explicitly develop the account of the co-evolution of skill and tool towards which the notion of the properly fashioned tool points, but he provides a toehold towards such an account in *Republic* 10 when he describes the empirical trial and error process (described in my previous chapter) by which the design of a tool is improved by being submitted to the test of experience in expert use. A chain of such cases over time would encode in the design of the tool a historical inscription of what has been discovered, in previous acts of making, of what works best – acts that in sharpening this blade here, say, also sharpened the artisan's sense of how to sharpen, and of the best design in the sharpening tool.[8] This encoding in the *form of the tool* is prior to the encoding in the *action of the tool* of the *form of the object-to-be-made*, of which Bartels speaks. Aristotle takes Socrates's analysis of tool design for granted, but it needs to be made explicit, because without it Aristotle's account of making remains crucially incomplete.

The birth of tragedy, according to Aristotle

If Aristotle did not quite tumble to the notion of the tool as historical inscription of techne-episteme, however, he did give an account of a specific techne, that of poetry, as a historically accumulated archive of know-how. Aristotle's *Poietike*, 'The Techne of Poetry-Making', or 'Poetics', is the only treatise in which Aristotle attempts to explain how a techne emerges from nature. If only for this reason, philosophers should take more interest in this treatise than they have done.

According to Aristotle's official doctrine, making by means of techne involves the transmission of a pre-existent eidos, residing in the techne-enabled soul of an artisan, to a receptive material of some sort; and this transmission is supposed to be analogous to the transmission of a biological eidos from sperma to egg. Aristotle appears to think biological eide do not evolve; they have always been there, unchanged and unchanging, co-existent with nature; and eide that are transmitted by techne seem to be similarly resistant to alteration. Nevertheless, as the opening of the *Metaphysics* shows, Aristotle was well aware that technai have been discovered by human beings, one by one, in a specific historical order, the most practical ones first, the theoretical ones last. But *how* have they been discovered? Unlike organic species, which Aristotle treats as co-existent with nature itself, technai cannot be born like new individuals of a species, from pre-existent individuals of that same species. Technai have to actually *emerge* in some way from nature, by human agency of some sort; but the kind of agency by which humans originally give form to a techne itself must be of a different kind from the agency of an artisan trained in an already existing techne. How is this human-mediated formation of form to be explained?

In the fourth chapter of the *Poetics* Aristotle describes poietike as a historical formation that very slowly emerged out of non-form by initially *non-intellectual* human faculties. The earliest, crudest, forms of poietike, Aristotle says, were discovered by a kind of 'improvisation' (*autoskhediastike*) that follows from two natural human aptitudes. The first is our propensity for imitation, 'by means of which we learn our earliest lessons'. The Greek concept of *mimesis* 'imitation' is notoriously shifty, but apparently Aristotle here means the 'monkey see, monkey do' kind of imitation by which infants and small children begin to acquire their basic skills. That this is the kind of imitation he means is implied by the second faculty that he says has enabled the emergence of poietike: the human sense of harmony and rhythm.

It is thus, according to Aristotle, by means of two sub-intellectual faculties that the earliest forms of poietike were discovered. These earliest forms were then improved by a slow historical process that culminated in the discovery and then optimization of the genre of tragedy. In this development, successive practitioners took up the art from the stage at which the previous discoverers had left it, from dithyramb to epic to the various stages by which the specific genre of tragedy developed. The key names in this process are Homer, Aeschylus, Sophocles and Euripides (who is not named at this point, but who later is said to have made the most tragic of tragedies). 'And after going through many changes,' Aristotle summarizes, 'tragedy stopped, having attained its proper physis (1449a).'

This is in fact a very promising sketch of the evolution of Greek tragedy, certainly more historically reputable than Nietzsche's. The final, teleological bit, about poietike ceasing to evolve when it attained its physis as tragedy with Sophocles and Euripides, is problematic but not fatal, because this isn't the naïve kind of teleology that we can automatically disqualify, the kind analogous to human purposiveness, conceived as the aim at a mentally proposed goal (Ryle's 'intellectualist legend'). The fundamental concepts of the teleology involved in Aristotle's account of the evolution of tragedy are not intellectual or psychological but *functional*. The central concept in the understanding of techne is *ergon* in all its senses, as physical work, as the product of artisanal work, and as the function or work potential, *ergon/dynamis*, embodied in the design of tools and methods. Hence the main burden of the *Poetics*, as an inquiry into the *ousia* 'essential being' of the genre of tragedy (1449b), is the analysis of its techne into its component parts, as understood in relation to the techne's function or work-power (*ergon* 1450a–b): to produce the pleasure proper to tragedy, the catharsis of pity and fear. The most important element by far is the plot, which must be constructed in such a way as to maximize this effect; and Aristotle stipulates that it was by chance, *tykhe*, and not by techne (*ouk apo tekhnes all' apo tykhes heuron*), that poets discovered the most effective plot devices (1454b). This implies that first they found, by chance, that certain things *worked* to produce a certain effect; then, because they had been seen to produce this effect, they were integrated into the evolving art. Nor is there is for Aristotle anything regrettable or, one might say, *accidental*, about the intervention of chance in this process; as he says in *Ethics* 6.4, citing Agathon: 'Techne loves tykhe, and tykhe loves techne.'

Aristotle protests against various kinds of tragedy-making that do not adhere to his account of tragedy's proper nature and effect, and I would argue that this is a defensible position, not just an expression of his taste. He analyses tragedy as an optimally functioning system, and argues that the works called tragedies that are differently organized from this system simply don't work to produce the major effect of which tragedy has been shown to be capable, the catharsis of pity and fear, and are therefore functionally inferior. One might object to this as a prescriptive definition and argue that whatever the Greeks called a tragedy is rightly so called, but however we decide the question of naming, Aristotle's arguments about the specific functional system that he analyses are strong.

The function 'ergon' is that which the product is designed to do, the inscribed intelligence or cunning of its form, designed into it by a process of trial and error that has adapted the thing's form to the needs of a specific work, such that it has the dynamis 'capability, work power' to best facilitate this work. What we see evolving in Plato and Aristotle out of their meditation on the tool and their exfoliation of the meaning of ergon from its root form in the organ/tool is the notion of an interacting system of parts, each functioning in such a way as to serve the functioning of the whole system. The roots of this notion go back to Hippocrates, whom Plato cites in a crucial passage of the *Phaedrus* (270c) to the effect that the first step in acquiring 'expert knowledge' of the physis of anything that is made of parts is to determine all the parts and the dynamis of each.

A little earlier in the *Phaedrus* (264c) Plato has introduced the notion that a rhetorical composition should be like a living creature, with each of its parts adapted to its function as part of a whole. Since the parts of an organism are its organs, Plato is implicitly thinking of the parts of such a composition as organa 'organs, tools, instruments', and of the dynamis of these parts as an ergon in the sense of function.Thus the notion of 'organic unity' originates in Plato as a strictly dialectical notion, devised in the service of intellectual analysis and conceived in purely functional terms, with a purport very distant from that of the Romantic notion of organic unity. Socrates is explaining how to 'reverse engineer' physis, to figure out how the ergon of the whole is made up of the interaction of its parts so as to form that specific functional system, whether biological, mechanical, or linguistic. The Greeks tend to reify this functional nature as essence or form in a way that we do not find useful, but this reification is not dictated by the logic of their functional-dialectical analysis, and we can safely abstract from it for present purposes. There is a 'nature' of the whole system, but this nature is not of a metaphysical or spiritual character; it has no essence over and above the interaction of its parts. Its essence just is the functional nature of the whole ensemble.

Socrates's reflections on functional systems in the *Phaedrus* are continuous with his observations on techne and tools in the *Cratylus* and *Republic*, and closely related to Aristotle's analysis in the *Poetics*, which adapts to the analysis of tragedy what Socrates says in the *Phaedrus* about the necessity of the systemic ('organic') interconnectedness of the parts. The techne in question for Socrates in the *Phaedrus* is rhetorike, a language-ordering techne, which Socrates believes does not yet exist; hence there is no question here of taking its forms as pre-existent, already 'perfect', as he had assumed for ordinary craft-objects. Yet the dialectical method will, he thinks, reveal the fundamental ordering principles of rhetoric *as it should be*, according to its as yet undiscovered ideal template. Aristotle, by contrast, treats the techne of tragedy-making as something that evolved 'naturally'. This evolution, of course, is itself ultimately determined by the telos towards which it is theoretically oriented, yet his sketchy remarks on this evolution clearly show that it is not dictated top-down by the form towards which it evolves, but involves a reciprocal relation between the evolving system and its parts. The structure of this reciprocal relation is necessarily open to the contingencies of occasion; that is what it means that new 'organs' of the techne can be discovered by chance. Understood in these terms, the end-state of the evolution of poietike as described by Aristotle may be conceived as the equilibrium-point of a dynamic system that has reached its optimal state of function, a type of system of which Socrates had begun to discern the first rudiments.

The optimal state or 'end' towards which the system's evolution tends is in no way a projection of a mental template; on Aristotle's account, there is no reason to think Homer or Aeschylus felt that the forms they produced were imperfect approximations of some 'proper physis' of tragedy that was their true aim; much less should we think this of the earliest improvisers, or the unnamed discoverers of the earliest genres, the dithyramb and phallic song. To improvise means, precisely, to have little intellectual sense of the form that is going to eventuate, to use opportunistically whatever happens to come up, and to be alert to what works, and subsequently to what works better. Initially one might not even have much sense of just what the working is for; one might discover or invent a purpose along with, or subsequent to, the discovery of the function. Presumably the intellectual component becomes more prominent in later stages of this historical process, but it remains ancillary to the system-dynamic of the historically established and evolving techne-practice. As the system-dynamic of poietike develops, the possibility, and desirability, of adding a second actor, for example, was somehow implied by it, and Aeschylus perceived this implication. Eventually all the 'improvements' that could be made, given the nature and purpose of Attic tragedy, were made, and at that point the development of the specific form of tragedy identified by Aristotle (though not of the historical institution of the tragedy as a whole) stopped.[9]

Now of course we would see a great deal more of chance and historical contingency in this development than Aristotle does; but we should not underestimate the tenacity of the system-dynamics of certain literary forms. There is no doubt that some forms have a tensile strength that enables them to endure across long spans of time. Homer's hexameter is a good example; and the sonnet form, which has now been around for more than 500 years, is another. So too, fundamental elements of the system of Attic tragedy as described by Aristotle have had a continuing life in Western literature, from the neoclassical drama of France to Walpole's *Castle of Otranto*, which in turn founded the durable form of the Gothic narrative. The vagaries of history have much to do with the survival of cultural forms like these; but the fact that the forms keep coming back across different periods of history, in vastly different sociohistorical circumstances, shows that they embody a certain excellence of design that empowers the art of poem-making. They are kept alive because they *work*, and they keep working across historical periods because they can be adapted to serve new purposes. The 'proper nature' of a functional system, to the degree that the phrase can mean anything to us, is whatever works optimally for whatever purpose it serves, and there is no better example of a system functioning optimally than an art form at its peak – as Greek tragedy evidently was with Sophocles and Euripides. Aristotle knew that the Attic drama had many forms that did not correspond to the template he laid out, and of course it kept evolving after Euripides; but that there was something very special about the form it attained with the three great tragedians can scarcely be doubted.

Techne in an archaeological light

The origin of poietike at which Aristotle is guessing lies immensely farther back in time than he suspected. We now know that even Homer's art was preceded by hundreds or thousands of years of Indo-European poetics, a development Homeric poetry shares with the Indian Vedas.[10] And this Indo-European tradition itself must have been preceded by a process of cultural evolution stretching back tens of thousands of years. But Aristotle shrewdly depicts the evolution of poietike out of just such a process of what Gary Tomlinson calls 'technosociality' as must have been involved in the earliest beginnings of human culture. Basing himself on the most recent archaeological findings and theories, Tomlinson argues that the earliest tools were likely made by hominins whose brains were not yet sufficiently evolved to be capable of language or complex mental representation. They must, however, have already possessed primitive versions of the two natural instincts that Aristotle posits at the origin of poietike, the knack for imitation, and at least a primitive form of the sense of rhythm. On Tomlinson's synthesis of the available evidence, these two capacities are at the origin, not of poietike specifically as poetry, but of poiesis in its original sense, as skilful making in general.[11]

Archaeologists have accumulated detailed evidence for this conclusion from intensive study of the earliest tools and their evolution into more sophisticated forms, tools shaped by flint 'knapping' or flaking techniques, in a period long before language or music could have emerged. Skilfully driving flakes off a large piece of flint involves a kind of rhythmic movement of striking the stone with a cutting tool, and in the absence of language the knowledge of how to make these early tools was evidently 'externally stored' as a mimetic tradition, and in the shape of the resulting tools. This know-how could then be transmitted from generation to generation in the form of what the anthropologist André Leroi-Gourhan called a *chaine operatoire* 'operational sequence' that could be wordlessly demonstrated and imitated.

> Young hominins, inhabitants of an elaborated taskscape, watched their elders fashioning tools, came to be familiar with the patterns involved, and set about duplicating them, thus growing up in a 'community of practices' involving ancestors and descendants. Their own expertise resulted from both repeated observation of gestural repertories and a capacity for mimicry and practice. The skills they honed required no direct, and certainly no verbalized, pedagogy. (Tomlinson, p. 71)

This account gives new and unexpected meaning to Aristotle's notions that humans are 'the most mimetic of animals' and that we 'learn our earliest lessons by mimesis'. And it coheres very well with the view of the nature of mind promulgated by the new cognitive science.

The slow development and 'archiving' as socially preserved practices, learned by pure imitation and practice over hundreds of thousands of years, of techniques like flint knapping, would have contributed to a co-evolutionary process that has to a certain extent shaped the brain and the hand into their modern forms. As Tomlinson explains, 'tools functioned as material extensions of the body that altered the selective landscape and its pressures'. This would mean that toolmakers would be 'advantageously selected' over long periods of time, and with them the kinds of aptitudes suited to toolmaking, 'self-initiated motor sequences, mimesis of others, rehearsal loops' (p. 82).[12]

Although Tomlinson's historical subject matter is very far from Aristotle's, it shows with great clarity how *physical* sequences function as *cognitive* operations that human beings, and even proto-humans, can literally 'think with' by encoding in them a practical logic worked out by generations of trial and error – a logic or know-how that develops towards optimality by the retrospective recognition of what has in the past turned out to work. In this way the erga of tools and technai are slowly improved, and with them the cognitive powers and neurological complexity of the tool-users. Tomlinson describes how, by about 500,000 years ago, more and more complex tool-making techniques began, very slowly, to develop – complex tools, made up of parts; transport of tool-making materials across long distances; hierarchically 'nested' knapping methods – all of which embody increasingly complex cognitive processes that imply an increasingly complex sociality and the slow development of the symbolisms that culminate in full-blown language. Socrates's pruning knife and the skilled motions of Aristotle's artisan are both forms of encoding or 'archiving' of techne of this kind.

By Aristotle's time, of course, it was no longer necessary to pass on a techne purely by imitation – as it is not necessary for us. However, the very fact that we now have so many ways of passing on know-how obscures the persistent and fundamental role that mimetic repetition of chaines operatoire has always had, and continues to have, in the transmission of technai. The intellectualist legend has had such a persistent influence that only very slowly has 'tacit knowledge' (as Michael Polanyi called it) been developed into a field of serious scientific study. Aristotle's official account of techne is an important source of this legend; yet there is a partly underground current in Aristotle that, as Dunne has shown, acknowledges the 'rough ground' of practice in sometimes penetrating detail. I have introduced Tomlinson's account here to raise the visibility of this partly underground line of thought in Aristotle, along which he acknowledges the role in techne of embodied-extended-distributed cognition, while not knowing beyond a certain very limited point what to do with it.[13]

Flexible forms

Aristotle invites us to think that the forms of artifacts are encoded in techne itself, in its tools and in the motions of the skilled hand. This is the central insight that I am trying to conserve. In order to be useful to us, however, this notion must be disentangled from the 'mechanical' interpretation that Aristotle's official doctrine encourages. This doctrine treats the soul as a kind of platform for a techne-program that determines the pattern of its productive activity. As Bartels notes, Aristotle was aware of a primitive sort of programmed machine, the 'miraculous' puppets (*automata*) mentioned at *Generation of Animals* 734b that are endowed with an 'innate motion' (*enousa kinesis*) capable of unfolding as a sequence of new motions, once given an initial push by an external agency. Aristotle mentions these automata in order to compare their automaticity to that of semen, which also carries a delegated power of organization – the same semen he compares at *GA* 730b to the techne-guided tool that shapes an artisan's product. This account would support the notion that techne is a kind of spiritual mechanism, a machine principle within the soul of the skilled craftsman – an extreme form of the sort of account that since the Romantic period has thrown techne into disrepute.

A techne, however, in order to be viable, must archive not only its operational sequences, but the know-how necessary to *flex* these sequences in response to the particulars of the kairos, the occasion or crucial moment of choice. Or say that a techne as such, in the most concrete sense, is *what a master practitioner knows in her bones*, including all the tacit knowledge that is acquired by practice and experience. No one can become master of a techne who cannot flexibly respond to particulars of occasion, and this responsiveness must, therefore, be conveyed to learners as an essential part of the transmission of the practice. As every teacher knows, the pupil who learns best how to perform a practice in the way we demonstrate is the one who learns how to carry it on in her *own* way.

What Dunne has shown is that Aristotle himself provides the foundations of this more adequate conception of techne. On the account for which I am arguing, the revised, flexible, extended-mind version of techne theory represents the convergence, after more than two thousand years, of lines of thought that Aristotle was on the track of, but which he was unequipped to think all the way through. With an assist from Dunne, Aristotle helps us think techne as the total archive of encoded, socially accumulated, practical cunning of a specific kind, the cunning of flexible responsiveness to the particulars of the problem at hand – to the moment of choice that the Greeks called the kairos, and which Socrates already emphasized in the *Republic* (370b).

The forms of techne-sequences have been determined by socially accumulated experience that has designed them with a view to how the affordances of specific task situations can be exploited. They thus have an ergon, a function or work-power, that is analogous to the ergon contained in the design of a tool; but the 'form' of a techne is of a fundamentally different type from that of a tool, because technai are 'wired' by teaching and practice, operational sequence by operational sequence, directly into the psyche-soma of the artisan, and pre-eminently into the hand. And because such sequences are learned by repetition, and each repetition presents the learner with at least a minimally varying set of factors, their 'forms' do not have a rigid boundary of definition, the way physical objects like tools do, but vary with the particulars of each repetition-situation. That is why 'the man who has been trained by practical experience is capable of doing what he has not learnt to do'.[14] The form of a techne can best be conceived by analogy with the forms of phenomena like whirlpools in flowing water, which have a vague, constantly varying outline, and yet can be graphed in such a way as to show that there is, indeed, a form here (described formally in terms of the pattern's statistical relation to an 'attractor'). The ordered variability of a techne itself is what makes possible the flexible responsiveness of the artisan.

A techne is not a unitary form, impermeable to contingency, and it does not produce unitary forms. It is an assemblage of techniques and devices which can be variously combined on different occasions. The working of such an assemblage might be helpfully conceived in terms of the Poincaré-Hadamard-Valéry model I discussed in Chapter 1, which provides a way of conceiving a *techne itself* in a way that does not conflict with the notion of individual 'creativity'. Artisanal work can be formally modelled as the product of very elaborate combinatories something like the one imagined by Poincaré, combinatories that the exigencies of practice keep in constant flux and which can therefore be allowed to come together in perpetually new combinations, from which can be selected the appropriate ones for a given purpose and occasion. Unlike 'forms' in either the Platonic or Aristotelian sense, their structural complexity and variability enables them to be intrinsically 'leaky' to the particulars of occasion, leaky by design, as an essential part of the system's ergon. The role of the inventor is to internalize in the most complete way possible the elements and dynamics of a given combinatory or potentially interacting set of combinatories, and learn how to allow its complex and variable dynamics to generate the kinds of forms that each combinatory has been technosocially evolved to generate.

Aristotle tries to preserve the eidos of the techne against such fragmentation, but he began to fragment it himself, and we can now complete the deconstruction. Yet the notion of a techne *as such* does not entirely dissolve in our hands. It is an idealization, but the idealization is tethered to the reality of the social aggregation of practitioners that is organized around any techne's possession of a specific kind of know-how, and to the aggregation's professional associations, schools, workshops, manuals and textbooks, and so forth. This techne community as a whole is the keeper of the archive of its techne. Because the infinite particularities of occasion, material, and agent guarantee that each new practitioner will pick up a partly idiosyncratic version of her techne, a techne-community will always be irreducibly multiple, as a linguistic community is; it will be more or less widely dispersed or institutionally organized; more or less various in its members' apprehensions of the techne and of its standards of value;

more or less fractious or harmonious (for all we know, Aeschylus did not find Sophocles's introduction of a third actor such a great idea). But it is this dispersed, diverse, and possibly divided community, as a whole, that is the ultimate repository of the techne as an evolving historical phenomenon.

NOTES

1 Joseph Dunne, *Back to the Rough Ground: Practical Judgment and the Lure of Technique* (Notre Dame, IN: University of Notre Dame Press, 1997).

2 Dunne argues that Ryle has Aristotle specifically in his sights in these comments, *Rough Ground*, p. 466, n. 115.

3 Ousia is the present participle of the Greek verb 'to be', thus literally translated as 'being'; but it was rendered into Latin in the Middle Ages as *substantia* and is commonly translated into English as 'substance' – a translation I have always found obscure. For reasons why 'being' is preferable, see Aryeh Kosman, *The Activity of Being* (Cambridge, MA: Harvard University Press, 2013); also Jonathan Beere, *Doing and Being: An Interpretation of Aristotle's Metaphysics Theta* (Oxford: Oxford University Press, 2009). Another possible translation of ousia, which also seems to me preferable over 'substance', and which reaches deep into the logic of the Greek concept of ousia, is Heidegger's 'presence' (which was picked up by Derrida in his critique of 'the metaphysics of presence').

4 Klaus Bartels, 'Der Begriff Techne bei Aristoteles', in *Synusia*, ed. Hellmut Flashar and Konrad Gaiser (Pfullingen: Verlag Gunther Neske, 1965), pp. 275–87.

5 Aristotle conceives this metaphysical activity, energeia, by analogy with ordinary physical activity; but physical activity can be latent (as dynamis) or actualized (as energeia), whereas a being's being is always active, whether the being sleeps or wakes. In the psykhe, thus, which is the eidos of the living body, 'ability and exercise of that ability are always and necessarily together'. When I am asleep I possess merely the ability to be awake; yet waking and sleeping are both the activity of my being (Kosman, 176–83, 239–40). That is why Aristotle is able, confusingly, to say at *DA* 412b that the soul's energeia (or entelecheia, as it is here called) corresponds to the *dynamis* of the tool or eye, their ability to cut or to see.

6 For Bartels, the notion that the soul must 'use' its body as a techne uses its tools implies a dividing line between psykhe and body that keeps their unity from being complete. On this conception, despite its koinonia with the body, psykhe would remain an executive agency like the soul or the Cartesian mind, wielding the body as a craftsman wields a tool. Bartels, glossing the double meaning of organon 'tool or organ', notes that organon is etymologically related to ergon, 'work', and *tool was its original meaning*, applied only later, in medical parlance, to biological organs (p. 6). This semantic background, he argues, eases the way to Aristotle's notion that there is no difference between tools and body parts, except for the fact that organs are permanently attached, whereas tools can be picked up and laid down (*Motions of Animals* 702b).

Thus, according to Bartels, the line we draw between craftsman and tool is instead drawn within the artisan by Aristotle, as the boundary between psykhe and hand. But Bartels ignores the larger context of Aristotle's thought that Dunne meticulously documents.

7 See the lucid new account of the nature of co-evolution in Gary Tomlinson's brand-new *Culture and the Course of Human Evolution* (Chicago: University of Chicago Press, 2018).

8 Considering that flint-knapping, the making of blades and points by early hominins and humans, is a central focus of modern accounts of the origins of techne, it is striking that both Plato and Aristotle resort to the analogy of cutting instruments, a pruning knife or an ax, at axial moments of their meditations on techne and the soul.

9 A full account of the nature of the tragedy 'system' would include its function as a great public ritual of the Athenian polis, a ritual that played an important role in the self-conception of the Athenians; but such an account is beyond my purpose here.

10 See Gregory Nagy, *Comparative Studies in Greek and Indic Meter* (Harvard University Press, 1974).

11 Gary Tomlinson, *A Million Years of Music: The Emergence of Modern Humanity* (New York: Zone Books, 2015).

12 The rhythmic imitation by learners of the knapping motions being demonstrated would have happened through an 'entrainment' of the observer's nervous and muscular response, of a type that involves parts of the brain that evolved early. Tomlinson references recent work on the brain that has revealed cortical networks that 'oscillate in regular cycles linked at multiple frequencies – hierarchies of oscillators, in other words – and suggest that these cycles are fundamental to cognitive processes such as attention and expectancy'. He concludes that 'there are strong reasons to think that the oscillators of dynamic attending theory are very real brain functions, that they engage with cyclic phenomena in the environment, and that these linkages are responsible for entrainment' (p. 80).

13 The idea that humans are the most mimetic of animals and learn their earliest lessons by imitation, combined with the idea that the other root of poietike is rhythm, suggests that poem-making originated in physical imitation of some sort, of a kind that would call for minimal noetic activity. But Aristotle makes his reference to imitation in chapter 4 of *Poetics* ambiguous by immediately introducing intellect into the account, noting that, in addition to its being natural for humans to imitate, it is also natural for us to enjoy merely *seeing* imitations. This pleasure in looking (*theorizein*) consists in recognizing the identity of the object or person, represented in a picture, which involves a reasoning process, syllogisesthai, literally 'to put logoi together'. So in very swift strokes, and apparently unaware of the confusion, Aristotle conveys us from primitive, rhythmic-mimetic nature, which would seem to involve the nerves and muscles at least as much as the eyes, to the more purely eidetic-noetic (visual-intellectual) realm in which his official doctrine of techne is at home. In the present context the crucial aspect of the transition from the performance of physical imitation to the perception of pictorial imitation is

that it involves the transition from a temporally extended to a synchronic phenomenon. Aristotle is trying to understand a termporally extended action on the model of "presence, i.e., as a unified whole with the unity and wholeness and accessibility to the representational intellect, of the form of a visually perceived object.

14 Jacques Perriault, 'The Transfer of Knowledge within the Craft Industries and Trade Guilds', in *The Use of Tools by Human and Non-human Primates*, ed. Arlette Berthelet and Jean Chavaillon (Oxford: Clarendon Press, 1993), p. 343. See also the comprehensive account of techne-cunning in Richard Sennett, *The Craftsman* (New Haven, CT: Yale University Press, 2008).

PART THREE

Where Do Poems Come From?

CHAPTER SIX

A Romantic view: Seamus Heaney

Making poems does not obviously involve physical manipulation of tools and materials – things like mixing paint, handling stone, or wielding brush or chisel. Even music, which is, like poetry, in an ethereal medium, relies on physical instruments. Poetry, by contrast, has historically been viewed as, in Hannah Arendt's words, the 'least worldly of the arts, the one in which the end product remains closest to the thought that inspired it'. A poem, Arendt continues, is 'less a thing than any other work of art'.[1] Arendt here implies that poetry is something higher than a mere *thing* can be, as though there is something about materiality that is inherently degrading to the human essence. Poetry, on this very Romantic view, is the immediate resonance of a human being's inwardness.

Poetry, unique among the arts, seems to provide a direct pipeline to the soul, flowing free of mundane materiality, or at least dominating it with a superior power. Words, of course, are a worldly medium; yet word is Logos, Verbum, breath of spirit. This gives language a special power – but a power underlain by a treacherous duplicity. On the one hand, it is the vehicle of the motions of mind itself, of that which is most intimate, most 'proper' to the self; on the other hand, it is a material substance that has to be shaped by the artisan like any other material substance.

The much admired Irish poet Seamus Heaney has given us an exemplary modern statement of the Romantic view of poetry, in a powerful essay called 'Feeling into Words'.[2] Based on examples from his own experience of making poems, Heaney has provided rare, vivid insights into the earliest beginnings of the creative process in a poet's mind, insights that tantalizingly evoke the feeling that we are getting an intimate look directly into the creative process. But Heaney is committed to interpreting this process in terms of some quasi-magical intuitive power possessed by the poet, a power akin to 'water divining', and this commitment, as we will see, drives his discussion into obscurities and contradictions. I know no better way to show the limitations of the Romantic view of creation than by tracking the contortions of Heaney's argument in this essay.

When Heaney recounts his own experiences of poem-making, it is always specific words or phrases that are the locus of inspiration, what got the poem started; yet he insists that words are secondary, a mere vehicle or instrument for the essential thing.

One of his poems, for example, makes an analogy between spade and pen, an analogy that Heaney says he drew from the 'proverbial common sense' of the country people of his schoolboy days, with their repeated reminder to study hard because 'the pen's lighter than the spade'. The poem, he says, does no more than allow the 'bud of wisdom' contained in those words to 'exfoliate' (p. 42). And when he first began to write poems, what enticed him was 'words as bearers of history and mystery'; 'lists of affixes and suffixes, with their Latin roots'; the exotic names of foreign cities on the wireless dial; the 'enforced poetry' of his household, phrases like Ark of the Covenant, Gate of Heaven, and Refuge of Sinners; certain poets and poems (p. 45).

Yet Heaney insists that these consistently word-inspired beginnings are not where we find the source of real poetry; in this early period, he says, 'nothing happened inside' him, it was 'all craft' and 'no epiphany'. Heaney thus, in typical Romantic-humanist fashion, is quick to jump ship on techne (pp. 46–7). Craft isn't enough for the poet, because the poet has to find his 'voice', and this is a matter not of art but of *nature* at work:

> Finding a voice means that you can get *your own* feeling into *your own* words and that your words have the feel of you about them; and I believe that it may not even be a metaphor, for a poetic voice is probably very intimately connected with the poet's natural voice, the voice that he hears as the ideal speaker he is making up.
>
> . . . this is the absolute register to which *your proper* music has to be tuned. (pp. 43–4; italics added)

On this account, there is a self that is already fully constituted by nature independently of the art of poetry, and what you must learn as apprentice poet is to subdue the devices of poetry to 'your natural voice', 'your proper music', the music belonging to what Heidegger, in the most profound expression of this way of thinking, called the 'ownmost ownness' of the self in its proper, authentic being.

Heaney acknowledges that one initially finds this 'absolute register' of one's own most proper voice in the voices of *others*:

> In practice you hear it coming from somebody else, you hear something in another writer's sounds that flows in through your ear and enters the

> echo-chamber of your head . . . This other writer, in fact, has spoken something essential to you, something you recognize instinctively as a true sounding of aspects of yourself and your experience. And your first steps as a writer will be to imitate, consciously or unconsciously, those sounds that flowed in, that in-fluence. (p. 44)

Yet these alien voices do not conduce directly to the finding of one's own natural voice; the imitation of other voices belongs to the preliminary 'craft' stage of a poet's apprenticeship that stops short of epiphany.

> Craft is what you can learn from other verse. Craft is the skill of making. It wins competitions . . . It knows how to keep up a capable verbal athletic display; it can be content to be . . . all voice and nothing else – but not voice as in 'finding a voice.' Learning the craft is learning to turn the windlass at the well of poetry. Usually you begin by dropping the bucket halfway down the shaft and winding up a taking of air. You are miming the real thing until one day the chain draws unexpectedly tight and you have dipped into the water that will continue to entice you back. You'll have broken the skin on the pool of yourself. (p. 47)

The authentic poem, the 'real thing' that is only 'mimed' by craft, is one that makes contact with the 'self or the feelings' of the poet, that dips into 'the pool of yourself', from which, presumably, the natural voice issues; and this, Heaney says, cannot be attained by craft. Something more is required, a faculty that, in an unorthodox and potentially confusing usage, he calls *technique*, giving as a paradigm case of technique 'the craft of dowsing or divining' by which certain exceptional individuals are able to intuit the hidden presence of water underground. This supposed 'craft' can't be learned, Heaney says; it's a 'a gift for being in touch with what is there, hidden and real' (p. 47); and to allow 'the first stirring of the mind round a word or an image or a memory to grow towards articulation', a poet must exercise a similar unlearnable intuitive power.

A poem, of course, is not 'there', 'hidden and real' in the same sense that underground water is. Rather, it pre-exists itself in the form of a '*potential* for harmonious self-reproduction' within the medium of feeling. The poet's prime imperative is to remain faithful to this potential, and not in the first or even second instance by finding the *right words*. 'Felicity in the choice of words to flesh the theme,' Heaney writes, 'is a problem, but it is not so critical.'

> A poem can survive stylistic blemishes but it cannot survive a still-birth. *The crucial action is pre-verbal*, to be able to allow the first alertness or come-hither, sensed in a blurred or incomplete way, to dilate and approach as a thought or a theme or a phrase. Robert Frost put it this way: 'a poem begins as a lump in the throat, a homesickness. It finds the thought and

> the thought finds the words.' As far as I am concerned, technique is more vitally and sensitively connected with that first activity where the 'lump in the throat' finds 'the thought' than with the 'thought' finding 'the words'. That first emergence involves the divining, vatic, oracular function; the second, the making function. (pp. 48–9; italics added)

Poetic technique, on this account, is unrelated to techne or technical skill, or even language; the 'gift' of divination alone can account for the 'first emergence', the inconceivable first dawning of the poem's being. And what the poet's divining stick discovers is in some mysterious way already there, 'hidden and real', in the feeling, or in the seminal excitement aroused by the feeling.

The unresolved puzzle

In this way Heaney hides the rabbit of the poem in the hat of emotion. The puzzle is how we get from inarticulate emotion to the articulated, articulate poem, and Heaney's solution to the puzzle is divination, which finds the poem *already there*, hidden in the emotion. This pushes the mystery of divination back one step, to the mystery of the poem's 'already there'. Exactly how can a poem, which is irreducibly a structure of words, be hidden in a resolutely wordless feeling, a 'lump in the throat'? Heaney doesn't pause over this question; for him the answer is obvious. It is there in the feeling's 'own potential' for 'self-reproduction' as a poem. This potential is what divinatory technique divines. All technique can do, or needs to do, is allow this potential to fulfil itself, which it does by an action that is 'pre-verbal', a kind of Heideggerean 'letting be' that allows the poem to grow out of the feeling, initially in the form of a 'thought', which is itself apparently wordless, but which, unlike the feeling, is capable of finding words. Only in this final phase does craft come in.

It's surprising, even shocking, to hear a poet depreciate the role of language in poetry this way, as the fleshing out of a pre-existing theme, but careful reading of the whole essay shows that Heaney doesn't really mean it. The bulk of Heaney's essay does not show him thinking about language this way, not at all; but here it seems he has gotten carried away with his commitment to subjective immediacy, and the force of this commitment obliges us to take a deeper look into the roots of the Romantic theory of language as analysed long ago by V. N. Volosinov in *Marxism and the Philosophy of Language*.

As Volosinov noted, Romantic theory depends on a metaphysical dualism that distinguishes an interior, superior substance – psyche, mind, spirit, self – from the substance of the exterior, inferior, physical and social world. The interior substance, the 'I' substance, which Volosinov labels 'the expressible', is what linguistic 'expression' must express. But on the dualist Romantic view, expression into the exterior substance called language must inevitably degrade the interior substance (the nonverbal self), whose essential nature is compromised when it is translated into the forms of the inferior, exterior substance of language.[3] This type of analysis was carried further by Jacques Derrida in his reading of Rousseau in *Of Grammatology*, where Derrida showed exactly why, on a Romantic conception, the expressible is inevitably betrayed by the passage into expression. Romantics conceive the interior substance to be by nature pure 'self-presence', capable of pure 'self-affection', absolute, immediate relation of the self to itself. Derrida in this book and many other places exercises all his rhetorical ingenuity to describe the nature of this self-affection or 'sentiment of self', as Rousseau called it: the self is absolutely proximate and 'proper' to itself; it 'remains close by itself'; it 'touches itself' without mediation.[4] There is a close relation between this Romantic self-affection and the Cartesian 'I' that thinks of itself thinking, in isolation from all exteriority; but the Romantic 'I' is typically characterized in terms of intensity and immediacy of feeling rather than of pure consciousness. What remains constant is that both are rooted in metaphysical dualism, the positing of two ontologically distinct substances with natures of fundamentally different kinds, spirit and nature, mind and matter. Language belongs irrevocably to the realm of the exterior, material – and inevitably *social* – substance, and so is fundamentally alien to the self-affecting self-substance, the substance of *me* that I feel with absolute immediacy in my thought and sensibility but which begins to become alienated from itself by the intrusion of worldliness of every sort. Language is in a sense the deepest wedge that worldliness drives into the self-substance, because it is an exteriority that goes very deep into the interior, becoming the medium of our very flow of consciousness. Thinking from the level of the pre-verbal as Heaney prescribes would be a way of making touch with the pristine interior substance beneath the alienating element of worldly language.

Derrida invented the concept of *differánce* to name that element of intrusion of the outside into the inside that Romanticism abhors, the necessity of articulation of the signifying flow into discrete units which must then be 'spaced' from each other in a syntactically ordered chain. The Romantic soul feels this articulation as a kind of *sparagmos* of the self. It craves proximity to the origin, the unity and purity of the originating whole, and abhors the necessity of drawing boundaries around subunits, separating, dividing them from each other, then constraining them into an ordered relation to each other. Language, as articulation of the expressible substance, is the ruination of the self-immediacy of the self. Thus the Romantic poet is in a difficult predicament with respect to language, because it is the medium of the poetic craft, of the poet's most authentic self-expression, yet comes from the outside and degrades the immediacy of the self-presence that it articulates, of the authentic self and the natural, proper voice.

Heaney, thus, tries to maintain the thesis of unmediated self-affection (the 'lump in the throat'), but is evidently aware that at this late date he cannot,

Wordsworth-like, derive the language of poetry *directly* from authentic emotion.[5] Thus he interposes a mediating agency, divinatory 'technique', which finds, hidden in the emotion, a 'thought' that is, evidently, on one side in *immediate* contact with the poet's emotion, thus capable of maintaining the inarticulate essence of that experience in its pristine inarticulateness, yet on the other side opens onto language. Divination can thus somehow be 'crafty', yet not craft; essentially pre-verbal, yet somehow capable of finding words. We begin to see why Heaney wants to call this faculty 'technique' as well as 'vaticination': so it can be mediation and immediacy at once, a pristine inside that nevertheless opens onto the outside.

Inseminating the poem-egg

Heaney's observation that a person, in order to be eligible to receive a state of this kind, must have prepared for it by long turning of the poetry-windlass, would seem to imply that the divinatory power has *something* to do with the linguistic skills the apprentice has learned, that 'technique' (in the odd sense of 'divination') is connected to craft; yet, on his account, craft skills are to play *no part* in the originating creative upsurge. The apprentice's crank-turning at the well of poetry seems to be no more than a ladder that one kicks away once the desired height has been reached – like the discipline of a Buddhist monk who sweeps the master's house for years to arrive at the correct interior state of receptivity.

Just how technique/divination works, of course, is by definition a mystery, but Heaney consistently describes it by the analogy of organic life. Divination endows 'the first stirring of mind round a word or an image or a memory' with the power to '*grow* towards articulation . . . in terms of its own potential for harmonious *self-reproduction*'. This '*seminal* excitement' is what 'selves', reproduces itself. Without this, instead of a living poem we get a '*still-birth*'. Technique is '*vitally*' connected with that moment when the lump in the throat germinates into the thought; and once technique has done its work, the poem can '*survive*' vicissitudes like infelicity of language (pp. 48–9).

The pre-verbal feeling aroused by word or image or memory, once inseminated by divination is, on this account, the poem in ovo – the vital inner essence that predetermines the final shape of the developing form. This is the full meaning of the seemingly innocent notion of 'potential' to which Heaney resorts. The poem is hidden in the feeling as the chick is hidden in the egg. This is all vaguely reminiscent of Aristotle's biology, in which the egg is inseminated with a potential, yet mysteriously fully preformed, 'form'; and all the questions about the origin of the form, and its mode of inhabiting the embryo, that have arisen in the medical tradition since Aristotle arise here concerning the form of the poem. If it is preformed in the inspired thought, how is this preformation to be conceived? Is it already there as a tiny or implicit whole at the beginning, a little poem-homunculus? Or is the form somehow 'coded' into the thought, in a mystical or sacred code analogous to DNA, capable of lighting the way to the poem's self-construction? And how can all this happen independently of language and of the poetic techne?

Consider: if knowledge of verbal craft weren't part of the poem-containing feeling, this poem-egg would be the same in the best-trained poet and someone who knows absolutely nothing of poetry. Wordsworth came close to drawing this conclusion when he argued that the expressive impulses and powers of the least literate were the ones most pregnant with authentic poetry, so that the poet's best ploy would be to cultivate a hallucinatory identification with such people. Heaney seems to pull against such a conclusion by requiring that the poem-egg be *inseminated* ('seminal excitement') by the additional faculty of technique/divination, which has nothing to do with craft, but if the seminal power remains strictly a movement of self-affection in the inarticulate inner substance, divination can add nothing to the essence of the poem-seed that strong emotion does not already contain *in itself*, qua emotion. All it can do is allow this pre-existing pre-verbal poem to grow its linguistic wings. Everything essential to the life of the poem, to its growth to maturity would already be predetermined in the emotion itself – and every strong emotion in every human being would be a potential poem. Everything essential – apart from the words, of course, which can come later. This hidden implication is no doubt an important part of the seductiveness for the poetry public of the Romantic theory of creation. Yes, the poet-genius is different from us, but he is a creature of feeling, essentially inarticulate, as I am. The poems come to him from out of the mystery.

But if every strong feeling is not a potential poem, if only the feelings of those who have been through some kind of poetic apprenticeship can become 'real' poems, then, logically, technique must be in some way a function of techne. The initiating inspiration might be 'inarticulate' in the sense that the specific details of the intuited poem will be only vaguely felt, but within the limits of this initial indeterminacy there will necessarily be a great deal of determination, along several dimensions of linguisticity.

This would have to be true even in the person who knows least of poetry in the formal sense, because from earliest childhood, in most, perhaps all, cultures, the pleasurable patterned energies of metered language wear grooves in a human being's aesthetikon, any human being, whether destined to become a poet or not.

Hickory Dickory Dock
The mouse ran up the clock

Pin marín de don Pigüé
Cúcara mácara pípiri güé

No such person can think a *radically inarticulate* thought that is impregnated with the germ of a poem, because, if it is actually the germ of a *poem*, it will already in its earliest beginnings be inhabited by forces of linguistic form-making that have been absorbed from the tradition of poem-making that the poem-maker inhabits.

The vague concept of potential deployed by Heaney enables both him and his readers to glide over the most difficult part of the puzzle of where poems come from, because when we speak of potentials in modern usage we don't mean anything very precise, and this lack of precision might even be the point. We speak of 'discovering our potential', for example, by means of which we mean open horizons, no telling what we'll find. But within techne theory, where the concept originated, as we saw in Chapters 4 and 5, a potential or dynamis is fundamentally the work-power or functional possibilities that follow from the way an element or instrument (*organon*) of a techne is designed. This kind of potential has a range of possible actualization determined by the nature of the productive system of elements involved. By contrast, when potential is used to refer to a completely indeterminate possibility, one not grounded in a productive techne, it is used so vaguely as to be meaningless. In the case of someone completely unacquainted with the techne of poetry, even as a reader or hearer, there is no chance at all that a feeling will become a good poem, or even a bad one, no chance that a poem could be 'potential' in such a person's emotion.

Heaney's account of poem-making, for all its sophistication, is a version of the notion of a 'Romantic artist' who creates out of a 'free act of origination'. Because Heaney confusingly combines the notion of magical divination with that of apprenticeship in the poetic craft, he never has to confront the question of whether someone's feelings could contain a poem, if that someone had never encountered a poem before. He clearly does not think that is possible, because he presupposes long apprenticeship, but he obfuscates the relation between this necessary apprenticeship and the poems that eventually result from it.

This is not to say, however – and this is an absolutely crucial point – that the inceptive stage of poem generation of which Heaney speaks must, after all, be 'verbal' rather than completely inarticulate or 'pre-verbal'. In the first place, if it's *completely* inarticulate it's better to call this stage *non-* rather than *pre-*verbal, because the 'pre' suggests the incipient presence of language, its 'potential' existence already in the feeling. Yet, probed more deeply, the distinction between the verbal and the nonverbal, like that between consciousness and the unconscious, turns out to be another of those great muddles of thought that make it impossible to arrive at a clear understanding of what, otherwise, might seem fairly obvious to us. To arrive at such an understanding requires a post-Cartesian rethinking of the entire relation between language and thought – or rather of the structure of concepts in terms of which we picture this relation. This rethinking, which has been underway for at least a century, will be the subject of the next chapter. But first let's follow the further development of Heaney's argument, which now takes a surprising turn.

The example of Wordsworth

Heaney assumes an abyss between the prelinguistic inner substance and the language in which it expresses itself, and posits a mystic power, divination, as the agent by which the abyss can be bridged. Poems, he says, begin in nonverbal form as strong feelings; the poet then uses divination to transform the feeling into a thought, which is capable of using craft to 'flesh' the formerly wordless 'theme' that was hidden in the original emotion. This is how far we have traced the argument of 'Feeling into Words'. Now, to show how the process of divination works, Heaney turns to Wordsworth, who left an account of his creative process in the writing of his lyric 'The Thorn'. As Heaney develops this account, however, the strains in his ambiguous definition of technique begin to tell, as its relation to techne becomes dominant and Heaney's references to divination become marginal.

The pivot away from divination is prepared by a peculiar switch in his description of the divinatory mediation. Technique/divination, he had said, 'mediates between the origins of feeling in memory and experience and the formal ploys that express these in a work of art'. Now, however, he tells us that the mediation in question uses language not to *express* but to *disguise* emotion:

> Traditionally an oracle speaks in riddles, yielding its truths in disguise, offering its insights cunningly. And in the practice of poetry there is a corresponding occasion of disguise, a protean, chameleon moment when the lump in the throat takes protective colouring in the new element of thought. (p. 49)

This formulation is problematic in several ways. To begin with, the ancient oracles did not speak in riddles to 'protect' their vatic truth, but to manifest the awful depth of the god's knowledge, and to humble the human intellect by their potential to mislead. Second, and more to the point, it's a mystery why Heaney would suggest that emotion needs *camouflage* in the 'new element of thought'. If the poet's aim is to express the truth of his pool of self, why would he want to disguise it? As we read further in these paragraphs, it becomes apparent that the rather inapt notion of disguise functions for one purpose and one purpose only: to hide the pivot that is taking place from technique as divination to technique as craft, by a rhetorical segue from the notion of disguise to that of the 'formal ploy' by means of which Wordsworth clothed his theme. For Wordsworth turned his epiphanic experience of the thorn bush into a poem by adopting a traditional poetic 'mask' with which to speak, the mask of the ballad form with a fictional speaker, a garrulous, superstitious sea captain. By means of this transformation, Heaney argues, the wind-tossed thorn in the poet's memory became 'a field of force' into which 'ideas from different parts of his conscious and unconscious mind' – ideas all drawn from the ballad tradition – 'were attracted by almost magnetic power'.

> Into this field were drawn memories of what the ballads call 'the cruel mother' who murders her own baby . . .
>
> there have always been variations on this pattern of the woman who kills her baby and buries it. And the ballads are full of briars and roses and thorns growing out of graves in symbolic token of the life and death of the buried one. So in Wordsworth's imagination the thorn grew into a symbol of tragic, feverish death, and to voice this the ballad mode came naturally; he donned the traditional mask of the tale-teller, legitimately credulous and enacting a convention. The poem itself is a rapid and strange foray where Wordsworth discovered a way of turning the 'lump in the throat' into a 'thought', discovered a set of images, cadences, and sounds that amplified his original visionary excitement. (p. 51)

At this point Heaney has apparently forgotten that Wordsworth's recourse to the ballad form was supposed to be a form of oracular 'disguise', 'protective colouring', merely a 'formal ploy' by which to 'express' the lump in the throat. Now he describes it not as disguise or ploy but as an *amplification* of Wordsworth's 'original visionary excitement'. This shows that the notion of oracular disguise had no other function in his argument than to smooth the transition to the notion of the poetic 'mask' as a set of traditional formal devices that are necessary even on a Romantic 'expression' account of poetry.

But what has happened to the notion that technique is divination, a gift that cannot be learned as a craft is? The choice to write in a traditional genre, Heaney writes, was Wordsworth's 'technical triumph' in the genesis of this poem, and if learning to write in traditional genres and modes isn't what it means to learn the craft or techne of poetry, it's hard to know what would be. If what my poet's dowsing-stick discovers is *which genre* I should flesh my vision in, do we really need such a grand conception of the choice-making faculty as Heaney has proposed?

In fact, near the beginning of 'Feeling into Words', when Heaney first introduced his notion of technique as mediator between feeling and the formal ploys of art, he described it much more modestly as 'dynamic alertness'. I cannot improve on this phrase as a description of the mental state that training in a techne cultivates; it is responsiveness to the critical or favourable moment in the techne process, the moment the Greeks called the *kairos*. And indeed everything Heaney says about how Wordsworth composed his poem corresponds to how, with the help of Hadamard, I described the functioning of techne in Chapter 2. Heaney describes it as a semiautomatic process that took place in the (relatively) unmysterious locale of Wordsworth's memory, which contained the system of motifs of the ballad tradition – a system that Wordsworth, as a master of his craft, had thoroughly internalized; and this process was powered not by any supernatural agency on the part of Wordsworth but by the functional work-power, *dynamis* or *ergon*, proper to the thorn as an element in this system of motifs, and to the erga of all the other elements in the system with which the thorn-motif interacted, a system that Heaney very accurately describes as a *field of force*. In the transition from lump in the throat to poem, everything – thorn, mother, baby, storyteller – became impersonal, everything was infused with the energies that centuries of folk experience and generations of storytellers and singers had woven into the genre that so naturally took over the trained poet Wordsworth's imagination. Wordsworth's own 'pool of self', a dubious asset in any case, rather than crying 'me!' (as in Heaney's quotation from Hopkins, p. 48) here disappeared into the tradition of which he made use, or which made use of him. Within this functional system the thorn was able to exert the power which, in terms reminiscent of Poincaré and Hadamard, Heaney describes as 'almost magnetic power'.

As much as Heaney is attracted to the idea of the 'natural voice', the authentic psychological self, and the lump in the throat, he knows too much about the techne of poetry not to recognize and acknowledge the evident facts of the making of 'The Thorn': that it was made not by divination but by techne that relied on the combinatorial dynamics of the English poetry-system.

His final comment on this lyric reveals his own latent discomfort with the direction his argument has taken: 'The Thorn' is a nicely documented example of getting feeling into words,' he begins, but then he adds, 'although I must say that it is hard to discriminate between feeling getting into words and words turning into feeling.' This is a remarkable admission. The essay itself is called 'Feeling into Words', but having worked his way deeper and deeper into his topic, he finds himself reversing the formula: words into feeling. But if the relation between words and feelings is reversible, this means that the boundary between language and non-language, a boundary essential to the notion of divination, has crumbled. And in fact, the bulk of Heaney's essay demonstrates more words turning into feeling than it does the converse process. Words, that is, conceived not in the impoverished 'abstract objectivist' sense (see Chapter 7), but as the handiest elements, for a poet, of the language flow in which human life is carried along – a flow within which words and feelings are fungible elements.

So, when he speaks in generalities about how poems are born, Heaney speaks a Romantic language; but after his discussion of Wordsworth he returns to the register of his opening pages, where he had described the powers of language that first drew him into the composition of poetry. Now he speaks of 'the almost unnameable energies' that for him 'hovered over certain bits of language and landscape' (p. 12). 'The poem "Undine," for example. It was the dark pool of the sound of the word that first took me: if our auditory imaginations were sufficiently attuned to plumb and sound a vowel, "undine" would probably suffice as a poem in itself'; and later he speaks of 'the lump in throat, or rather the thump in the ear' that this word is for him (pp. 51–3). *Or rather*: this means that *thump in the ear* is more precise a statement of the poem's origin than is *lump in the throat*. This restatement follows in the track of the earlier reversal of the feeling–word relation, but adds something important: that a word is not just what we see on the page but a physiological sensation that is imbued with power, power that is at once meaning- and feeling-full. Heaney also associates this kind of power with the *image* of a thing or landscape, but the central focus is always on the word or words that attract the 'almost unnameable energies' out of which poetry grows:

> the best moments are those when your mind seems to implode and words and images rush of their own accord into the vortex. Which happened to me once when the line 'We have no prairies' drifted into my head at bedtime, and loosened a fall of images that constitute the poem 'Bogland'. (p. 54)

What distinguishes Heaney as a poet from non-poets is, thus, not any magical power but the exquisitely trained susceptibility to the 'force fields' of words, to their magnetic power to attract images, feelings, and other words. 'We have no prairies' aroused in him the response 'but we have bogs', and this was the feather touch that crystallized a set of memories about bogland that he had been vaguely wishing to turn into a poem. The simple power of association is the motor of the entire techne-process. For someone with Heaney's experience, the thought of bogs attracts the memories of bog butter and of an elk skeleton that had been recovered from a bog, and of the warning the older people had given him when he was a child that there was no bottom to the bog-holes.

Such an associative vortex by itself, in the aesthetikon of someone who has not undergone a poetic apprenticeship, would not contain the glimmerings of poetic form; it is a psychological process without any intrinsic centre other than that which anyone's personal experience could give it. The set of associations that Heaney detects in the process by which Wordsworth made 'The Thorn', by contrast, was drawn from the field of ballad conventions, and therefore carried, for the trained poet, an intrinsic reference to ballad forms and the methods of ballad construction. But Heaney was a trained poet who had already been, if only vaguely, thinking towards a bog-poem; hence the associative state into which he fell was not merely psychological, it also involved his techne know-how, and thus was capable of eventuating in a poem.

Earthworm knowledge

A comparison of the notion of divination with that of artisanal feel brings out the nature of the latter with new clarity. The fundamental question of techne theory is, 'How does an artisan know the correct move at each stage of the making process?', and Heaney's answer is that the poet knows it as a predetermined consequence of an initial inspiration, the authenticity of which insures the growing poem's survival as a vital form. On this account, the guidance offered by the poem-embryo's form-determining power is not of the extremely picky sort requiring every word, every formal choice, to be the right one; the important thing is for the force of the inseminating inspiration to be preserved. For techne theory, by contrast, the artisan knows the right next move by a feel learned from apprenticeship in a craft, a feel that leads only contingently, not by necessary predetermination, to an end that, depending on circumstances, might deviate in an indeterminate number of ways from what was originally envisioned. There is some overlap between these two answers: on the one hand, to the degree that craft is essential to making, Heaney allows for something like techne-based artisanal feel; and on the other hand, there is something at least mildly divinatory in the notion of artisanal feel. But Heaney places an impermeable barrier between major divination and techne. For Heaney, the artisanal feel gained from craft produces only a 'capable verbal display', not 'the real thing'. On the techne account, by contrast, techne is at work at every moment of artisanal action, as much in the thoughts, and even in the feelings that give rise to the thoughts, as in the words. Artisanal feel is a function of the resources of know-how that have been designed into the elements of whatever techne the artisan employs, and is, like Aristotle's phronesis or Kant's taste, woven into each moment of the difficult, often frustrating, always fallible work process by which the details of a work are gotten right, the rough edges smoothed, and so forth, until the form shines with 'life', as we call that special quality of a particularly well made form, in what ought to be taken as a catachrestic usage rather than an organic analogy.

Whereas divination is a form of holistic perception-at-a-distance, analogous to vision, artisanal feel is, as the word implies, more like a 'haptic' faculty, a sort of blind touch. This too, like immediate self-affection, is an experience we all have; everyone who has ever learned a skill of any kind (that is, everyone) knows in some measure what artisanal feel feels like; but what we know this way doesn't seem adequate to explain Art, which our Romantic ideology has taught us to venerate as something grander than the kind of earthworm-knowledge bestowed by apprenticeship in a techne – a kind of knowledge that knows only whatever it's immediately in touch with at each moment.

Yet, even though artisanal touch is local, a shrewd orientation towards a goal has been woven into each techne by its evolution, which like that of living beings, has shaped it, and every element of it, to perform a certain function (to 'supply a lack', Plato says), and has survived long enough to evolve only because it has from the beginning, in whatever originally crude a way, actually conduced to an at least marginally more effective way of performing this function than is available without it. The system as a whole, thus, is capable, in a trained artisan, of providing a kind of peripheral guidance to the local movements felt out by touch. Sensitive responsiveness to this guidance is what constitutes *mastery* of a techne. When technai reach an advanced level of complexity this teleological or *problem-solving* design both requires and makes possible a faculty in the artisan that goes beyond touch, the faculty that following Hadamard I have called 'physiognomic' perception. Such perception is required to tie together structures larger than those artisanal feel by itself can attain, and has presumably co-evolved with the increase in complexity of our technai. Physiognomic perception is, obviously, also – like divination – analogous to physical vision, but whereas divination is a mysterious inner power that precedes all articulation, physiognomic perception ensues on an advanced exploration of the combinatorial and articulatory possibilities of a techne-system in which an artisan has been thoroughly trained.

Form is a product of the combinatorial possibilities of the well-designed organa of a well-designed techne-system; and such form is what physiognomic perception of any kind, including aesthetic perception, perceives.

A poem, thus, does not become 'the real thing' when the poet dips the bucket of craft all the way into the pool of self; it becomes a real poem when it manifests a certain degree of mastery of poem-making. And we the readers learn the feel for such mastery the same way the poet does, from experience of the exemplars that have set the standard for us. What we judge is not some absolute quality in the poem, something simply present or absent that would make it 'the real thing'. There is no litmus test for the success of a poem. There is a threshold of quality a poem must cross before we will take it seriously as a poem, of course; there is indeed such a thing as what Heaney calls 'capable athletic display' that a poet can achieve, while still writing what is essentially an empty poem. But crossing this threshold is the minimum qualification, not the ultimate achievement. Once a poet is writing poetry worth taking seriously, there are still many ways in which we might deem it to fall short, because there are many vectors of value, not just one, that our critical judgment might pursue. One of the things one might criticize is, indeed, the quality of the feeling; but not on the basis of whether what is represented in the poem is the poet's true feeling or not. Once a poem manifests sufficient mastery to be taken seriously by the community of poets and readers, the judgment of value becomes a matter for debate, and no basis of judgment is more imponderable than that of the poem's correspondence to the truth of the poet's feeling.

Heaney's essay offers invaluable insight into the workings of a poet's constructive imagination, but even when he leaves behind the claims of supernatural power he can think of poem-origins only in terms of what Valéry called the 'poetic state' – the state the poet's aesthetikon is in when it is roiled with the kind of energy that truly contains the 'potential' of a poem. Valéry's account, which will be the subject of Chapter 8, recognizes the limitations of this state and locates the origin of the poem on the other side of this state, in the poet's labour. But first I will briefly lay out the new conception of language that I referred to earlier, the view that overthrows the old dualist conception to which Heaney still subscribes.

NOTES

1 Hannah Arendt, *The Human Condition*, 2nd edn (Chicago: University of Chicago Press, 1958), p. 169.

2 Seamus Heaney, 'Feeling into Words', in *Preoccupations: Selected Prose, 1968–78* (London: Faber and Faber, 1980).

3 V. N. Volosinov, *Marxism and the Philosophy of Language*, trans. Ladislav Matejka and I. R. Titunik (Cambridge: Harvard University Press, 1986), part 2, ch. 3, pp. 83–98.

4 Jacques Derrida, *Of Grammatology*, trans. Gayatri Spivak (Baltimore: Johns Hopkins University Press, 1976), pp. 141–3, 165–6.

5 Wordsworth, however, in contrast with Heaney, did not depreciate the importance of 'finding the words'; on the contrary, his probing inquiry in the preface to the *Lyrical Ballads* into the nature of 'real' emotions worth expressing was motivated precisely by the need to find the authentic language of poetry.

CHAPTER SEVEN

Excursus on language

As is common in intellectual controversies, the question about the role of language in thought has been muddled from both of the opposing extremes – the side that promotes the supremacy of the verbal and the side that denies it. The notion that 'all thinking happens in words' is based on the same narrow view of language as the Romantic side, a view derived from the mirage of words as a sequence of 'lexical items' of the sort the dictionary imposes on our imaginations.

Volosinov called the kind of linguistics that takes words in this way, 'abstract objectivism'. The problem with this view, he says, is that it atomizes language into its constitutive units and then fixes these units as freestanding forms that have a unitary self-identity at any given moment in history, and which evolve in such a way that the history of the development of a given word can be abstracted from the multiplicity of contexts in which the word is actually used when it belongs to a living language. In reality, however, at any moment in the evolution of a language, its words are being used in a multiplicity of contexts – often *conflicting* contexts – with a continually varying sense that cannot be fixed. The living reality of language, Volosinov argued, is flux, and the proper unit of analysis is the entire utterance-situation within which language use occurs.[1] Wittgenstein conduces to the same conclusion: meaning is best understood by attending to the way specific words are *used* in specific contexts, and what we find when we look at meaning this way is that flux of which Volosinov speaks, the sense of the words continually slipping and diverging, expanding and contracting. The entries in the dictionary represent only one facet of the shimmering, always changing flow of the full worldly phenomenon that language is, a phenomenon that, as Andy Clark has richly documented, is densely interwoven with our movement through the world as physical, socialized, entechned psyche-somas.

Understood in this way, *language itself* might be said to be in large part, not preverbal or transverbal, but supraverbal, meaning that it isn't just strings of lexical items of the sort you are looking at on this page (the 'verba'), or the Saussurean system of differences behind them, but, in addition, the entire ensemble of forces that gives sense and coherence to such strings. Learning language is isomorphic with learning to be a human being, a *person*, and to negotiate the world as a human being; and language necessarily involves all the elements and aspects of this experience. We conceive of 'thought' as something distinct from language in part because it seems to be so much richer than language; but this impression is created by our having first impoverished the concept of language.

Even the artificially isolated units we call words are rich bundles of sound, reference and emotional resonance: Heaney's 'thump in the ear' that can be unfolded into a poem. And the flow of language in use is in addition a flow of syntax, intonation, tone, gesture, facial expression, dynamics (loudness and softness), interactions with context and of larger organizations of utterance such as those Volosinov called 'speech genres'. A child can understand the complex *force* of a word in an utterance, in a broad, 'inarticulate' way, from the way the word is intoned by a specific person in a specific situation, in the context of other intoned sounds that might be words or not and might be understood or not. I vividly remember asking my two-year-old son Marco in a scolding tone whether he had moved a toy I had ordered him to move, to which he replied, 'I *totally* moved it!' and then, after a pause, looked quizzically at me and asked, 'Dad, what does "totally" mean?' He had heard this word used in certain situations, with a certain intonation, and had perfectly picked up this particular colloquial usage, which he now replicated. This illustrates how language is heard first, understood first, as a feeling-intoned flow of a signifying substance made of heterogeneous elements, including gestures, expressive sounds like 'oh!', facial expressions and objects that are being manipulated or pointed to – as well as of what is implied in the given speech context, everything comprised in what Volosinov calls 'ideological structuration' (in a very broad sense of 'ideological') as well as everything that comes in at the psychoanalytic level, as the 'I' that is beginning to form introjects the imagos of the mother and father that represent the nuclei of the self. All these aspects of language are supraverbal, which is to say that they function at the level of the entire communicative flow, of our entire experience as human beings whose world has been given form by our socialization – at the cost of that elusive self-immediacy for which the Romantic in us yearns. Our experience of ourselves as conscious beings is our sensation of the more or less coherent flow, articulated in *differánce*, of all these together; and our ability to use words is a function of this coherence. The mirage of a separate substance called 'mind' or 'thought' is the counterpart of the impoverished 'abstract objectivist' conception of language.

How could we not have the sensation that thought, the flow of consciousness, is so much more than words, when even word-language itself is so much more than words, and when there are so many more kinds of signifying substance in the human world than just language? Thought is like a flooded river swollen not only with water and fish but with chicken coops, old tires, dead cows, children's toys and everything else it has washed away. The flow of this river is the temporal, articulated flow of personhood, and its elements are all the elements of a human world. That's why, as Wittgenstein said in *The Blue Book*, the difference between the inner and the outer doesn't matter. Strings of lexical items are only one dimension of language, and even verbal language is a stream swollen with heterogeneous elements.

The supraverbal level at which we experience and then are able to produce language, and which creates the mirage of a separate thought-substance, involves the way we cognize whole blocks of language at a higher level of integration than that of words or sentences. We see this operating already in the mere ability to begin a sentence without having consciously in mind how we're going to shape the rest of it. If we picture this process in terms of the mythology of mind, we might imagine that one's thoughts flash ahead across the whole subsequent set of words and unconsciously preselect them. But this picture seems explanatory only if one is committed to the mythology of mind, according to which thought is a super-substance capable of doing inexplicable things, like going so fast that our conscious thoughts can't keep up with it.[2]

According to the alternate, non-dualistic model, thought is not the inexplicable action of a non-natural super-substance but the structured flow of signifying elements in a psyche-soma or aesthetikon that is involved in constant interactions with the world, some conscious, most not, some 'in the head', most involving exterior instruments or tokens, all of them informed in some way by techne.

To understand the dictum that 'meaning is use', think of the way a musician's fingers know just which keys to push or strings to pluck, and just how hard and for how long. Words are like the keys of an instrument, and our use of language is like a skilled musician's use of an instrument. If we ask, how does a pianist know which key she wants, we all know the answer: she has learned the techne of piano playing through endless hours of practice. And that's how we learn to speak, too – by practice – though of course the practice of language happens not at a conservatory but in the ordinary course of our lives.[3] To touch a key or to use a word is not an isolated event corresponding to an idea in the mind, it is a function of our feel for the dynamics of the entire system that we are 'playing'.

Think of thought as related to words in the way that expression is related to the notes the pianist plays. The pianist controls the actions of her fingers not at the level of the individual notes, which are sounded automatically by her hands, but at the level of expression. This higher, more comprehensive level of relation to the articulations of which the piece is made is the level at which the pianist's aesthetikon experiences the piece – having learned from much experience of model performances how to experience it this way – and is able to shape it as her own skilled performance. Thinking or having ideas is related to words in something like this way. If we think of the notes of a musical piece as analogous to words, we can see that it makes no sense to ask whether the pianist's experience of shaping the piece at the level of expression is 'verbal' or not. The individual notes (the 'verba' of music) don't enter her consciousness. At a certain elemental level the notes are constitutive of what she does, but, at the 'control level', what she has learned to play is not notes but *songs*.[4]

Like all analogies, this one has its limitations, but I am trying to evoke dimensions of our experience as conscious agents that do not fit into the classical dualist account of mind that yields the hard distinctions between verbal and nonverbal, conscious and nonconscious. This is the Cartesian 'mental theater' conception that treats consciousness on the model of visual perception. On this model, verbal consciousness parades lexical items across the stage of the mental theatre, open to the eye of the mind. But our use of language is not like that. Our experience of language is very varied, and little of it involves anything like clear and distinct perception on the Cartesian model.

Consider the experience of having a word 'on the tip of my tongue'. This is the tantalizing feeling that you know exactly what word you want, the word that would express precisely the meaning you intend, yet you're not able to bring it explicitly into consciousness. This experience, which is familiar to everyone, is like a controlled laboratory experiment in which we can observe precisely the phenomenon under study. Here the difference seems crystal clear between thought or meaning on one side and the word on the other. I know *precisely* what I want to say, yet I am drawing a blank as to the corresponding word. Doesn't this prove that there is thought – and indeed, very precisely formed conceptual thought – without words?

On the contrary: if I'm certain that there is a word that is precisely right for this wordless concept, and the certainty is well founded – as is proven by the fact that almost always, in a moment or an hour I remember the word I wanted – this implies that before it came to me I already had an *inarticulate* consciousness of the articulated word. This only sounds paradoxical if we're locked into the Cartesian model and insist on the 'abstract objectivist' distinction between the verbal and nonverbal. But our experience of meaning can't be neatly divided into these categories. I earlier moved away from Heaney's term 'preverbal' because of its ambiguity, which creates part of the obscurity of Heaney's account by vaguely suggesting that somehow, even though the poem-generating emotion is languageless, language is somehow incipient in it. By contrast, the tip of the tongue experience is genuinely preverbal, a threshold experience that can occur only in a language-equipped consciousness.

From the techne standpoint, that a word is on the tip of my tongue means that I have first constructed a preceding word-sequence that, given the functional dynamics of the whole sequence, already implied that word, and which thus created a 'slot' for it that I experience as a strong feeling that the non-present word is pulling at my tongue. The word-sequence is oriented towards the missing word as a sequence of chords might, in the pianist's aesthetikon, from the outset be oriented towards the concluding chord. My feeling that I know the word I need, even though I can't think of it, is a product of knowledge that is 'distributed' throughout the system-dynamics that are producing the sentence. To know how to speak a language is to have mastered the entire technique of building language structures, to know how to do it the way a pianist knows how to shape a melody, or a master builder knows how to shape an arch in such a way that it 'implies' the keystone. The evolution of the verbal articulation by which we were being carried along was, at each step of its unfolding, building towards that specific meaning-block that, when we get there, needs to be fitted into that slot. The feeling that we know the word we want, even when we can't think of it, is the articulated sense of the architecture of the entire utterance. This is that relation of 'feel' for larger language-based, articulated 'physiognomies' of meaning that I've been trying to define.

We should take literally the figure of having a word on the tip of the tongue. We sometimes actually open our mouths and activate our tongues with the expectation that this word, which feels so proximate, will come (as a pianist or guitarist who has forgotten part of a song might play it up to that point to see if the fingers will automatically produce the forgotten part); and sometimes it actually will. This reminds us that speech is something we produce not just with our brains but with the entire vocal apparatus. Terrence Deacon has explained in extensive detail how, according to current research, our brains and bodies co-evolved with language, showing how deeply *embodied* a phenomenon natural language is.[5] Who knows how much of our bodies is involved in the production of any given sequence of words, or any kind of signifying configuration by means of which we think? Recall Albert Einstein's revelation to Hadamard that he sometimes kept track of the physiognomy of his mathematical insights by means of muscular movements.

There are as many aspects, modes, and levels, of consciousness as there are of the aesthetikon as a whole, and what is 'conscious', even at the blindest, most generalized levels of consciousness (of the sort we call preverbal or subconscious, subliminal, and the like) is continuous with and in constant interaction with, constantly changing places with, processes that our brains and bodies as a whole carry on entirely beyond our awareness. In human beings, the aesthetikon is trained into an entire tapestry of techne-organized patterns of behavior that henceforth structure our activity and our experience, including our most solitary interior self-experience. To be able to think is to have this entire tapestry of competencies at work inside us, structuring the flow of our interior experience. Hence when conversation is going well and we speak, the words just appear on our tongues, the right words at the right moment. It would never occur to us, from this kind of experience, that there is a separate process called thought that accompanies our speaking. Thoughts, reveries, feelings, images, old or new music or poems or mathematical formulas, surge up in our consciousness, or perhaps flow out of our tongues or fingertips, unanticipated by us, because this flow in its entirety *is us*, the spontaneity of our life-surge as techne-formed human persons.

The part of this process that happens 'in the head' cannot be adequately described in terms of the visual, mental theatre model; but there is a revised version of this model according to which mental perception is neither instantaneous nor 'clear and distinct' in the way visual perception appears to be, and which remains useful for thinking about techne. In the mental theater model, consciousness is what Husserl called a 'darting ray', like the lantern on a miner's hat, that illuminates only what is immediately before it in the present moment. In later work, however, Husserl opened the way to the more complex and adequate analysis of experience of mature phenomenology when he analysed the 'now' of consciousness into a complex that has, packed into it, a lingering awareness of the sequence of conscious nows that have led up to the present now, each successive now embedded in the following now (as in a Russian doll structure), as well as a structured anticipation of what is likely to come in the sequence of future nows. On this model, consciousness is full of 'implication', the in-folding in the present *now* of internal time-consciousness of the more or less indistinct traces of a world left in our consciousness by previous nows, implying a series of future nows. Husserl's conception of a present awareness that has a temporal structure, which probably influenced Heidegger's *Being and Time*, enables us to conceptualize a penumbral or peripheral awareness of what is not presently in full view on the mental stage.[6]

Such penumbral awareness might have a great deal of conceptual articulation folded into it, in ways that depending on circumstances will be more or less accessible to explicit awareness. Think of the memory a paragraph we have just read in a philosophical treatise leaves in our minds. No matter how carefully we've read it, and how well we've understood it, our memory of it (unless we have the fabled 'eidetic memory', which has its own problems) will be relatively indistinct. In the best case, I can, by directing close attention to this memory, reconstruct the idea in the original paragraph in its essential detail; but even in this case, as soon as I am no longer focusing my attention on it, it will recede into a ghostly presence that I can feel in the immediate vicinity of my thought-train, and perhaps recall to centre stage at will, but which for the time being is no more than a mental blob, comparable to the blobs Hadamard tells us he drew on paper to remind himself of the physiognomy of his mathematical ideas.

Call the memory of the paragraph a *conceptual ghost*, an indistinctly articulated conceptual complex that remains somewhere in the mental mansion, and whose presence I feel from time to time, for example when I read in some other book something that reminds me of it. 'I think I read something related to this before, let's see, what was it, oh yes.' The key point is that the entire conceptual complex articulated in that paragraph has become a single loosely defined entity for me, one whose densely layered structure I perceive blurrily on the periphery of my conscious awareness, but can to some degree or other bring back into explicit consciousness.

Now turn this around. Hadamard says there is 'no essential difference' between understanding a new mathematical argument already developed by someone else, and building a new one of one's own; in both cases what is involved is the perception of a physiognomy. This, I think, is right. Say I come up with what seems to me a new idea. It will necessarily be a recombination of articulations that I have picked up from my previous study and experience, and I can initially perceive the new combination that is 'dawning' in my consciousness in the same generalized way that I peripherally remember a paragraph-ghost, as a semantic block of considerable complexity, but without a distinct perception of all the details and links of the argument.

These semantic blocks or blobs, which integrate complexes of word concepts, are the basic supraverbal units with which our thought process works. They are a kind of 'lingpack', 'a set of mental items . . . that hang together and are packaged via a public symbol as a manipulable item for use in propositional thought', except that, where lingpacks are individual lexemes available in a language, our blobs are assemblages of lexemes.[7] These higher-level blocks, that package together more or less complex sets of combinatorial elements, and which appear as single entities, can be handled much more efficiently than the elements treated separately. Think of carrying a dozen disparate grocery items in one's arms, as opposed to carrying them in a bag. The bag that carries a dozen thought-elements seems, by comparison with thinking each element serially, a 'lightning thought', something carried on in a medium with inexplicable powers; but the price of speed is, necessarily, vagueness. It can only be rendered lucidly articulate by being slowed down and stretched out into a chain of signifying elements.

These semantic complexes comprise signifying elements of all kinds, according to the 'swollen river' principle mentioned earlier, elements that would involve memory images from every sensory modality. At the level of vagueness and complexity of the semantic blocks involved, images for example of smell or taste can function as elements that add combinatorial possibilities. Poetry of course is the linguistic techne that humans have developed for maximal mining of language at the level of such possibilities, above all in the making of metaphors. The complexity of these blocks and their ability to incorporate signifying elements of all kinds (their ability, in fact, to turn any percept into a signifying element) provides them with many more semantic 'hooks' with which they can combine with other semantic blocks, than mere strings of lexical items have. We can think more quickly with these thought-bags than we can with individual words, and, because of the wealth of connections afforded by the multiplicity of hooks, they are also much more generative, much more likely to produce something new; on the other hand, precisely because of the speed and vagueness of the operation, there's a much greater chance that the finished result will not turn out as our supraverbal intuition or guess appeared to promise. Hence all those wonderful moments of illumination when we're writing that we feverishly try to capture in spoken or written words, but wind up discarding. One important reason for this will-o'-the-wisp character of such insights is that these blocks come together more out of an automatic tendency towards coalescence that is built into their elements by the engineering to which they have been subjected by use over the history of the race, than they do out of any intentional activity on the part of the thinker. The Romantics were intensely aware of this, and tried to maximize the action of spontaneous coalescence by techniques of lowering of conscious control; Freud famously cited Schiller as an inspiration for his technique of free association. But freeing up of the blind combinatory powers of such complexes, precisely because these powers are indeed blind, can only be a preliminary phase in the production of actual poetry, as Paul Valéry explains in the essay that we will consider next.

NOTES

1 V. N. Volosinov, *Marxism and the Philosophy of Language*, trans. Ladislav Matejka and I. R. Titunik (Cambridge, MA: Harvard University Press, 1973), part 2, ch. 2.

2 In which case, there would have to be *two* thought processes going on at once, one that goes at a pace our consciousness can keep up with, and another that runs on ahead, blazing the trail for the conscious process.

3 Noam Chomsky has very influentially argued that syntax would be impossible to learn if humans didn't have a pre-adapted syntax learning module in the brain. But Chomsky has had little interest in explaining how such a faculty could have evolved, and, in the absence of a convincing evolutionary account the syntax faculty remains what Daniel Dennett calls a 'skyhook', an explanation that hovers in the air and does its explanatory lifting without any terrestrial support. In the past three decades, however, Terrence Deacon and others have developed a much more comprehensive account of language than Chomsky's, involving the 'co-evolution' of the brain and language. On this account, language itself has evolved in a way adapted to the learning capacities of young humans. My own account harmonizes with this approach. See Terrence Deacon, *The Symbolic Species: The Co-evolution of Language and the Brain* (New York: W. W. Norton, 1998).

4 What I'm describing is the structure elegantly descried as 'attending from'/'attending to' by Michael Polanyi in *The Tacit Dimension*

(London: Routledge, 1966). The pianist 'attends from' the level of the individual notes in order to 'attend to' the level of expression.

5 Deacon, *The Symbolic Species*.

6 Edmund Husserl, *The Phenomenology of Internal Time-Consciousness*, ed. Martin Heidegger, trans. James S. Churchill (Bloomington: Indiana University Press).

7 Quoted from Andy Clark, 'Minds, Brains, and Tools', in *Philosophy of Mental Representation*, ed. Hugh Clapin (Oxford: Clarendon Press, 2002), p. 75. Clark borrows the term 'lingpack' from S. Henser, 'Natural Language Use in Habitual Propositional-Type Thoughts: Support from Japanese-English and English-Japanese Bilingual Codeswitching Data', PhD Thesis, University of London, 2000.

CHAPTER EIGHT

An anti-Romantic view: Paul Valéry

Paul Valéry's 1939 essay 'Poetry and Abstract Thought' took important early steps towards the modern theory of techne. Valéry did not, in this essay, quite attain a clear grasp of the nature of techne, and this creates problems for his account; yet, when interrogated, even the ways in which he misses the techne standpoint yield significant new insights into it.

His description of what he calls the 'poetic state' in which poems originate tallies with Heaney's description of the vortex of word, feeling and image in which his own poems initially came to him; for Valéry, however, this state is only a preliminary to the real making of the poem.[1] For Heaney, the poet's wizardry acts essentially to maintain the authenticity of the poem's origin in inarticulate affect. Poetic 'divination' somehow effects a direct transmigration of feeling into thought, which then mediates the work with language that will result in the finished poem; but this work is, literally, an after-thought to the inarticulate labour of creation that has already taken place. For Valéry, by contrast, those poems that most convey the sense of miraculous genesis are in reality masterpieces of *labour*. There is no value in the initial creative excitement; it produces only materials for the essential form-giving work, the 'modification' or 'transformation' of these materials by the poet-artisan.

When his mind is in the poetic state, Valéry writes, 'all possible objects of the ordinary world, external or internal, beings, events, feelings, and actions, while keeping their usual appearance, are suddenly placed in an indefinable but wonderfully fitting relationship with the modes of our general sensibility'. In this state, 'well-known things and beings – or rather the ideas representing them' become '*musicalized*, resonant, and as it were, harmonically related', so that they 'attract one another, are connected in ways quite different from the ordinary' (p. 59). Here is, once again, the idea advanced by Poincaré and then by Heaney, of an associative automatism by which ideas in the mind are drawn to each other by some attractive force intrinsic to them. Valéry theorizes that this automatism is unleashed when the poet's aesthetikon slips out of its ordinary division into the 'specialized senses' and functions as an undifferentiated whole (a 'general sensibility'), such that connections spontaneously arise across sense modalities and across the boundaries usually drawn by the rational consciousness (just as in Heaney's vortex).

There are, Valéry remarks, 'extensive analogies' between this musicalized 'poetic universe' and the dream state, in which the 'meanings, relationships, modes of variation and of substitution' of things function like symbols and allegories. But Valéry does not use the analogies between the dream state and the poetic state to argue that the dreamer is a kind of poet; he uses it to bring out the fact that the poetic state is as incapable as the dream state of making art. The poetic state, like the dream state, is 'completely irregular, involuntary, and fragile, and . . . we lose it, as we find it, *by accident*'. 'This state is not enough to make a poet, any more than it is enough to see a treasure in a dream to find it, on waking, sparkling at the foot of one's bed' (pp. 59–60).

This is the crucial insight that opens the way to techne theory. Whatever it is that happens in the pre-craft state of inspiration is pure accident, no more an art-producing state than dream is. 'A poet's function . . . is not to experience the poetic state: that is a private affair. His function is to create it in others' – not to feel inspired himself but to make the *reader* feel 'inspired'. The notion that poets are inspired, according to Valéry, is a back-formation from the reader's feelings. Readers think the state of exaltation that the poem arouses in them must be the state out of which the poem was created, but

> poetic feeling and artificial synthesis of this state in some work are two quite distinct things, as different as sensation and action. A sustained action is much more complex than any spontaneous production, particularly when it has to be carried out in a sphere as conventional as that of language. (p. 60)

Musicalized states and dreamsongs

In order to illustrate further the difference between the inspired state and the 'artificial synthesis' of this state that is necessary for a poem to emerge, Valéry describes at length a visionary experience of music that he once had, but which, because he utterly lacked the musical knowledge, could result in nothing. He was out walking when he was gripped by two rhythms that were playing off against each other, and then by a song that he felt produced *through* him rather than being produced *by* him; and the song grew more and more complicated, far beyond anything he was normally capable of producing. Then, after about twenty minutes, the musical inspiration vanished as mysteriously and suddenly as it had arisen. How could such a thing happen? He theorizes that the rhythm of his walk somehow set going the musical rhythms that took possession of him and became autonomous, and that this entire phenomenon was in the end a discharge of energy in his brain that was set off by 'mental activity while walking'. Whatever the cause, it is evident that this kind of state, like dreaming and poetic inspiration, is completely irregular, involuntary, accidental. But, whereas Valéry's mastery of the techne of poetry enabled him to turn some, at least, of his accidental poetic states into poems, he could do nothing with his musical vision, which disappeared without a trace (pp. 61–3).

He recounts this experience, he says, to bring out 'the profound difference existing between spontaneous production by the mind – or rather by our *sensibility as a whole* – and the fabrication of works'. He was freely given 'the substance of a musical composition', but 'the organization that would have seized, fixed, and reshaped it was lacking'. Here Valéry reiterates the nineteenth-century French notion of art-making as labour of fabrication that we hear also from Flaubert, Rodin and others. In another essay, he writes that the poems 'whose intricate perfection and felicitous development give their wonder-struck readers more strongly the notion of a miracle, a stroke of fortune, a superhuman accomplishment' are in fact 'masterpieces of labor and are, too, monuments of intelligence and sustained work, products of the will and of an analysis that exacts qualities too multifarious to be reduced to those of a machine for recording enthusiasms and ecstasies' (p. 213).

Juxtaposing the three 'musicalized' states – poetic, dream and properly musical – opens a rich avenue of investigation of the nature of techne. But the concept of techne cuts obliquely against Valéry's distinction between labour and these three states, which, despite being accidental and undependable, with no direct pipeline to the productive process of art, are yet not entirely uninformed by techne. The productive or form-giving work of techne begins, and must begin, long before any particular artisanal labour can be accomplished. Techne must organize, give functional articulation to, the subject's aesthetikon ('general sensibility', in Valéry's terminology) before it can, through the agency of the artist, give form to a work of art. Labour is an activity, but techne is a settled possession or 'disposition' (*hexis* for Aristotle) that does not disappear when it is not being used, and traces of which can be activated when we are not actively engaged in the corresponding work.

Technai are no respecters of the boundaries drawn by the 'specialized senses'; they organize the entire aesthetikon along whatever mixed-mode lines (think of eye–hand coordination) required for the interaction with the world defined by the specific purpose of that techne. And this is particularly true of poietike, which both facilitates the linguistic-perceptual-kinaesthetic-synaesthetic vortex and then uses its products as the material for the colder and more restricted forms of poetry (which are nevertheless rooted in this vortex and draw their sustenance from it). Because Valéry's general sensibility is already organized by poietike when he enters one of his poetic states, his associational vortex cannot but exhibit a tendency to fall into the grooves of poetic form. Techne is not only the logos of the artisan's worldly labour but also of the preliminary stages of form-giving or form-facilitation that are carried on in the mind-body before the conscious intentionality of the artisan takes over. Most of the time, this preliminary stage will be only the roughest pre-shaping of the material, roughly analogous, say, to the quarrying of a section of rock that is destined for a sculpture of a certain size and shape. But there is no in-principle limit to how much of the mental work of giving form can be done in a state of inspiration, as we know from examples like 'Kubla Khan', and from such homelier examples as the common phenomenon of 'dream songs' that one hears, fully formed, in one's sleep, and which one can record on awaking, as Paul McCartney is known to have done with the melody of 'Yesterday'. As we have seen, Hadamard discusses the phenomenon of such 'unconscious' coalescence of forms with great precision in relation to mathematical invention.

Scholars have mostly scoffed at Coleridge's claim that 'Kubla Khan' came to him full formed in an opium dream; but this disbelief is not based on any factual evidence that I know of, and I see no reason why it couldn't be true. However, it's easy to misunderstand the story as lending support to the Romantic notion of creation. The fallacy of the spontaneous poem is not the belief in its spontaneity, but the accompanying notion that in order to be formed spontaneously it has to take shape in a transcendent mental substance that possesses an intrinsic form-creating power. Heaney argues something like that in 'Feeling into Words'; but Heaney doesn't suggest that the poem can be fully formed in this way – word choices, meters, the whole thing – as Coleridge seems to claim for 'Kubla Khan'. Obviously, if the poem was formed in a dream, it was, in a sense that needs updating, in the purported 'mental substance' that it was formed; but the crucial question concerns the *formative power* that made it, not the site ('mind' or paper) on which the poem was first inscribed. In order for the actual poem, as we have it (which Coleridge testified to have been only a portion of the original dream, the part he could remember) to have been fully formed in the dream, it would have had to be in words belonging to the English language, arranged in intelligible English syntax and ordered in measures of iambic tetrameter. And if, in Coleridge's dreaming mind, it was already in English and iambic tetrameter, and if all its formal characteristics were indistinguishable from those the poem would have had if it had been written slowly on paper, then it wasn't a creative power ontologically prior to that of the techne of English poetry that made it, it was this very same techne, the same that would have made it if it had been made slowly on paper. If, alternatively, these characteristics had to be added in the transition onto paper, then the mental poem was not yet a poem at all, and we are thrown back to the conundrum in which Heaney left us.

Intrasomatic inspiration

The primary conceptual boundary, then, lies not between the inspired state and the labour process, but between the strictly psychological aspect of the state and the techne know-how to which the psychological dynamics can have a highly variable relation, from the most random and disorganized to the most disciplined and thorough. But the range of this variability is not, as Valéry suggests, restricted to the binary of artisan/non-artisan, because one picks up techne not just from formal apprenticeship but from all kinds of informal, often apparently passive, experience of it. As I noted in Chapter 7, everyone as a child hears the rhythms and chiming sounds of verse, and so in a rudimentary way internalizes some very basic elements of the poetic techne. This experience is not entirely passive, because children repeat rhymes with pleasure, moving their bodies in rhythm, and so incorporate the techne in an active way.[2] All of this is also true, and to an even greater extent, about music, with which our own culture is saturated. It is not surprising that someone like Valéry should have experienced the spontaneous emergence of a complex new musical composition, given that he is known to have had an intense interest in, and non-musician's knowledge of, music. No other human-made symbolic forms are as spontaneously self-reproductive as those of music, and rhythmic forms above all. The most mimetic of animals picks up rhythms very readily, and musical rhythms coursing through and out of the body quickly become autonomous and then spontaneously mutate and become more intricate. When Valéry says that he couldn't turn his musical ecstasy into a musical work because he didn't 'know music', he means that he didn't have the professional musician's ability to perform the form-completing and form-fixing labour necessary for that; but he had to 'know' music in another sense in order to have the musical experience that he had. Even if he didn't know how to write musical notation, there doesn't seem to be any reason in principle why he couldn't have captured at least the essentials of his musical vision in some other way, and then perhaps gotten a musician to write it down, as Don Van Vliet (Captain Beefheart), who had no formal musical training, did with the music for *Trout Mask Replica*.

Thus Valéry's musical vision has a very different nature from the dream state, one much closer to the poetic state in a trained poet like him, because, while he was not a musician, he had internalized important aspects of the musical techne. The dream state can at least theoretically be techne-independent, but his musical vision could not be and manifestly was not; Valéry's sophisticated non-musician's knowledge of music enabled him to experience a complex organization of rhythm and song, even if one that was only 'roughed in' in terms of details and formal aspects of which a professional musician would be aware, and without which the composition could not be realized as a work.

However, even the dream state, though it presumably *can* be techne-free, is not necessarily so, when we move from the digital scale proposed by Valéry – according to which one is either poet or non-poet, musician or non-musician, and the creative process is either merely psychological experience or artisanal realization – to our new, analog scale of more or less techne, at work already in the intrasomatic process of inspiration.

Before we consider dreams, it is necessary to distinguish two primary, interacting, dimensions of variability in this analog scale. The first concerns the amount and kind of know-how that is available to the subject of the associative process: the difference between someone who has only the most casual acquaintance with poetry and someone like Valéry or Heaney. This is the dimension explored in the above remarks. The second dimension concerns the degree to which, whether one has much or little knowledge of a techne, that knowledge will be activated in a dream. In a dream even a master poet can have a confused vortex of associations that provide no useful clue to how they are to be given the form of a poem, and which either will not issue in a poem or will require a lot of follow-up labour; and a person with very limited knowledge of a techne might find that little bit coming to life in an inspired moment in which it suffices to give at least modest form to something.

In the dream state, thus, the differences between artisan and non-artisan are considerably levelled out, because of the latter factor. The artist is almost as helpless to make well-formed work in his dreams as anyone else, and non-artists can occasionally create works that in their waking lives they are powerless to produce, such as the dreamsongs to which I referred earlier. I myself have been the recipient of half a dozen such songs, despite my only rudimentary training many years ago on piano and guitar, and my almost complete lack of musical talent. All these songs but one (an elaborate symphonic piece, an experience similar to the one recounted by Valéry, and which I was similarly incapable of reproducing on waking) were thoroughly conventional, in the standard idioms of American popular music (ranging from bluegrass to country to rock 'n' roll); but they were actual, original songs, with music and lyrics, well-formed, and I could remember enough on waking to reproduce substantial chunks of them. I cannot claim any great merit for these songs; they were generic product. But the important point is not how good they were, it is the fact that in my waking life I am utterly incapable of creating a new song, not even generic product of this type, and have never done so. The spontaneous appearance in my dreaming consciousness of such songs vividly manifests the fact that *new forms are created by the effervescence of old forms*, forms at work in our mind-bodies in ways that intersect consciousness only partly.

The conscious intentionality of the individual agent is never completely in charge. The dynamis that pulls forms together comes out of the socio-historically 'programmed' intentionality of the techne-system to which they belong. Even when one is 'fully' conscious of what one is doing, our neurons are doing most of the work, hidden far out of our sight; and when we are dreaming we exercise even less control. But neurons by themselves cannot give coherence to forms any more than our conscious intentions can. The neurons fire in the service of the 'magnetism' that pulls formal elements into new configurations, and that magnetism arises at an entirely different level of functioning than that of the neurons: the level of the techne.[3] The songs that have popped into my dreaming mind have been produced by the spontaneous recombination of forms of American popular music, by a process that must in principle (though not in detail) be the same as that by which a skilled musician comes up with a new song. We are of course not talking here about the most radically inceptive kind of art, either in my case or that of the popular musician; but once we have broached the boundary between pure repetition and repetition-with-a-difference – no matter how small the difference – the creative process can be thought in terms of evolutionary logic, and there is no conceptual limit to the degree of newness that can be explained in its terms. In evolutionary logic, even the tiniest differences can add up to make radically emergent new forms.

The forms of song or verse are by nature 'formal' in a way that contrast sharply with the randomness of dreams, but there is another kind of form that dreams quite easily take on, that of narrative. That is, no doubt, because there is a kind of incipient narrativity in the connected sequences of action of our ordinary lives. We know that some animals dream, and perhaps some of their dreams have this incipiently narrative form. Anyone who has ever seen a sleeping dog's legs twitch, while he half-barks, will find it easy to think that the dog is dreaming of chasing some prey or other – a necessarily sequential activity. However it might be with dogs, human dreams are highly susceptible to taking on the form of narrative. Today, of course, the question has been further complicated by the fact that there are many dreams to which we can attribute a narrative form only because since Freud, Kafka and the Surrealists we have learned to accept as artful narrative forms that are themselves modelled on the chaotic nature of dreams. Independently of that, however, many dreams do constitute fairly coherent narrative sequences of a more conventional kind that are doubtless at least partly informed by our constant experience of narrative through books, movies and television, as well as through the anecdotes frequently recounted in conversation. Thus even dreams cannot be construed as entirely techne-independent.

Slow and quick creation

So all of these qualifications must be made regarding the empirical boundary between dream and techne, which is not nearly as clean as the conceptual boundary between inspiration and actualization. Nevertheless, it remains the case that dream experience is typically chaotic or nearly so, an associational vortex uninformed by techne or influenced by it in such a scattered way that no graspable form emerges from it. Hence the boundary stressed by Valéry between the inspired state and artisanal labour remains as decisive for techne theory as it was for him. Being a musician in my dreams doesn't make me a musician, even if on awaking I remember a song that I can sit down and skeletally tap out on the piano. Dream songs, opium poems and inspired states in general are *marginal phenomena*, gee-whiz occurrences that tell us nothing significant about art, the reality of which is the teachable and learnable practices of communities of artisans. The dream song is a product of the musical techne, but it is a savant production, one that doesn't involve my agency as artisan but only uses me as a 'platform', and which doesn't involve the methodical know-how that can be consistently put to work by the expert artisan and taught to an aspiring artisan. It remains true, as Valéry says, that 'poetic feeling and artificial synthesis of this state in some work are two quite distinct things', and there are only negligible exceptions to the rule that such synthesis is a product of artisanal labour.

But Valéry's further observation that 'a sustained action is much more complex than any spontaneous production' can now be seen not to draw as absolute a boundary as he wants to draw, and to very subtly confuse the matter, because the value of *complexity* is not one that necessarily adheres to either side of the sustained-spontaneous binary. The real complexity of an artwork is that of the skill and knowledge that are involved in its making, not that of the action by which it is made, and while it is true that the actualization of sophisticated techne typically requires sustained effort, it doesn't always. 'Kubla Khan' is the same poem, with the same complexity, whether Coleridge laboured long over it or dreamed it in an opium stupor.

There is a sort of accordion flexibility, expanding or contracting in accord with the particular case, in the relation between the complexity of the know-how involved and how long the action of making will be sustained, or how complex the action in itself will be. Indeed, one of the best results of increased skill is the simplification and shortening of the action by which we achieve our desired result. There is no more intrinsic art-merit in achieving a result laboriously than there is in achieving it quickly or spontaneously, *as long as the latter reflects the same level of artisanal cunning*. One admires long, dedicated labour on its own merits, but that is a different matter.

Valéry of course knows this, and when he describes how poems are actually made, he silently drops the notion that spontaneity is alien to fabrication. The crucial thing, he now says, is the 'modification' or 'transformation' in the initial materials that is effected by artisanal labour, and it doesn't matter whether this transformation is 'sudden or not, spontaneous or not, laborious or not'. Whereas Heaney suggests that it is the inspired poetic 'thought' that 'finds the words', Valéry locates the transformative work of the poet very precisely as intervening *between* 'the thought that produces ideas' and the discourse called verse that is 'so curiously ordered' (p. 63).

This – the *curious ordering* of language that makes it into verse – is what needs explaining, and cannot be explained by Romantic theory. For Heaney, this ordering is merely verbal athletics, empty as such, needing to be filled with the poet's emotional truth. For Valéry, *the ordering process itself* is the only instrument the poet has for turning a poem into the real thing; there is no extra something that must – or indeed *can* – be added to the resulting order of words to make it feel inhabited by the full conviction or passion of the poet. A poem is ultimately and irreducibly words and nothing but words, and there is no other way to make a poem feel authentic, in Heaney's sense of authenticity, than to select the right words and order them in the right way. What Heaney interprets as dropping the bucket of craft into the pool of self is just a mystified way of describing the poet's coming into full mastery of the craft of making poems, such that he acquires the ability to hear or feel the rightness or wrongness of each choice, until the whole poem is right, and can be heard to be right by its audience.[4] 'A poem is really a kind of *machine* for producing the poetic state [in the reader] by means of words', and the poet's art is measured by just how cunningly he constructs his little verbal machines to accomplish this end. If we're put off by the 'mechanical comparison', Valéry says, 'please notice that while the composition of even a very short poem may absorb years, the action of the poem on the reader will take only a few minutes. In a few minutes the reader will receive his shock from discoveries, connections, glimmers of expression that have been accumulated during months of research, waiting, patience and impatience' (p. 79).

Interior universes

Despite the fact that Valéry conceives the art of poetry as a kind of engineering, however, he is even more expansive than Heaney about the notion that the origin of a poem is a kind of miracle or prodigy. The miraculous bit is the poetic state, that 'special phase in the domain of [the poet's] psychic existence' in which sound and meaning become indissoluble and 'all the properties of our language are indistinctly but harmoniously summoned' (p. 75). This element plays a fundamentally different role here that it does in Heaney's essay, because Valéry has no use for the pre-verbal; his magic is all word-magic. He finds it necessary to posit the inspired state, the state in which the poet's mind opens to Heaney's word-vortex, because he sees no other way that what he considers the *chaos* of ordinary language could possibly be given the extreme order of poetry; but there is never any question of dissociating the state of inspiration from language. Thus Valéry's 'poetic state', magical as it might be, lies this side of the Romantic abyss that separates the wordless inner substance from the social outside.

Since the function of Heaney's divination was precisely to preserve the primacy of the wordless inner substance, it isn't entirely clear why Valéry, who has not one romantic bone in his body, feels the need to invoke magic at all. He attempts to derive it by drawing a contrast between the materials out of which music and poetry are made, respectively tones and language; but the logic of his argument is questionable.

In the case of music, he says, out of the universe of *noise* that the human ear is immersed in, we have isolated the system of musical tones and invented musical instruments that 'are, in reality, *measuring instruments*', measuring out their sounds in accord with the laws of harmony and melody. 'The musician is thus in possession of a perfect system of well-defined means which exactly match sensations with acts.' And the listeners who have been apprenticed into the musical system are able, as soon as they hear a recognizable tone, to 'unconsciously *organize*' themselves to hear music, because inside them is a 'musical universe', ordered by the 'associations and proportions' imbibed from previous experience of music. These associations and proportions are comparable to the ordering principles of crystals, exemplified in a saturated salt solution that needs only a slight mechanical shock to the container for the dissolved salt to suddenly solidify into a crystalline form (pp. 66–7). Valéry thus describes the dynamics of the functioning of music in the human mind-body in a way that sounds very much like the way techne works. The metaphor of crystallization, used by the Romantics to evoke what they took to be the self-organizing impulse of spirit-inhabited nature, here evokes instead the interior dynamics of the functional system of the musical techne. And, interestingly, it is with respect to the *listener*, and not to the musician, that he describes it.

According to Valéry, thus, the musical universe is a scientifically ordered system, but poetry is a different matter. The poet lacks what the musician so abundantly possesses, 'a body of resources expressly made for his art'. The poet

> has to borrow *language* – the voice of the public, that collection of traditional and irrational terms and rules, oddly created and transformed, oddly codified, and very variedly understood and pronounced. Here there is no physicist who has determined the relations between these elements; no tuning forks, no metronomes, no inventors of scales or theoreticians of harmony. Rather, on the contrary, the phonetic and semantic fluctuations of vocabulary. Nothing pure; but a mixture of completely incoherent auditive and psychic stimuli. Each word is an instantaneous coupling of a sound and a sense that have no connection with each other. Each sentence is an act so complex that I doubt whether anyone has yet been able to provide a tolerable definition of it. (pp. 67–8)

And so forth in this vein. Valéry sees ordinary language as a vast wilderness that the poor poet must tame without tools or instruments or system of any kind, and he concludes that the task of making poems would be unmanageable if the poet 'had *consciously* to solve all these problems'. It follows that they can only be solved by the marvellous alchemy of the poetic state; and yet when Valéry describes how this alchemy is made possible, it becomes unclear just what is magical about it:

> In my eyes a poet is a man who, as a result of a certain incident, undergoes a hidden transformation . . . I see taking shape in him an agent, a living system for producing verses. As among animals one suddenly sees emerging a capable hunter, a nest maker, a bridge builder, . . . so in a man one sees a composite organization declare itself, bending its functions to a specific piece of work. (p. 69)

An *agent* is an instance capable of *doing* something, and this agent takes shape as a productive 'system' comparable to certain animal agents that act by instinct. This sounds very much like Valéry's description of the way the musical universe organizes the interior of the musician or listener; and if Valéry had known more about evolution he would have realized that birds and beavers and so forth have had their instinctual 'systems' organized by evolution in a way that is, properly considered, formally parallel, at the species level, to apprenticeship in a techne (see Chapter 12). Yet he has explicitly denied that there is any such techne-system available to the poet. The system of music is something known, scientifically measured, technologized; but the system that takes shape in the poet is something that doesn't seem to be a system at all. Valéry describes it, surprisingly, as 'marvellous', 'in the sense we give that word when we think of the prodigies and miracles of ancient magic' (p. 74).

It's very strange for Valéry to say that the poet has no 'body of resources expressly made for his art' considering that within a few paragraphs he will show himself acutely aware of the resources that the techne of French poetry has provided for his own work. It's equally strange that he thinks the *musician*, by contrast, has complete scientific control of his medium. His argument implies that musical making, being scientific, is completely conscious, as though anything at all that human beings do could be completely or even mostly conscious – much less a complex and mysterious activity like music creation. It's only by contrast with such an idealization that poem-making could be conceived as emerging from mere chaos.

And yet Valéry acknowledges that poetry acts on us like a kind of music. He cites a couple of lines from poems that he admires, and exclaims that the unity of sound and sense in them makes them 'act on us like a chord of music'. 'The impression produced depends largely on resonance, rhythm, and the number of syllables; but it is also the result of the simple bringing together of meanings' (pp. 74–5). But it doesn't occur to him that from hearing this kind of poetry-music the aspiring poet *learns* about the system of poetry, about its elements and their interaction, and about how a successfully constructed line of poetry comes to sound like a chord of music – just as a musician learns about the system of music from hearing it, something that most musicians in most of the world through most of history have learned without an inkling of any more 'science' than what is embodied in the system of tones and in the construction of the instruments (which is, admittedly, a lot, but implicit in the system and not something typically known by the musician).

The reality is that we learn to enjoy poetry as we learn to enjoy music, by hearing it (or reading it, but poetry has traditionally been made to be heard), and once we have become practiced in hearing poetry, hearing it organizes a 'poetic universe' within us just as surely as hearing musical chords organizes a 'musical universe' in us. This process begins the same way in both the person who will become a poetry-maker and the one who won't, it just goes much farther in the poet. Poets learn their trade from the work of the poets who precede them; how strange that Valéry should fail to take this fact, of which he is eminently aware, into account at this point in his argument. Language may be so complex and variable as to merit the hyperbole of 'chaos' with which Valéry describes it, but the level of complexity is vastly reduced by the ordering strategies that are embodied in any poetic tradition – most famously, in the European tradition, the 'formulas' of Homeric composition. Valéry himself says that one of his most famous poems (*La Cimetére*) began 'as a rhythm, that of a French line . . . of ten syllables, divided into four and six', with no idea how to fill out this form; but gradually words 'settled into' the line, and after that it was all labour. This example shows in the simplest way how the 'grooves' of the techne can lay down the patterns along which the creative labour can then find its way. Another poem, *La Pithie*, came to him as a complete eight-syllable line, 'which implied a sentence, of which it was a part', and this sentence, which he now had to complete, 'implied many other sentences'. 'A problem of this kind,' he continues, 'has an infinite number of solutions. *But with poetry the musical and metrical conditions greatly restrict the indefiniteness.*' I have added italics to the last sentence because with this remark Valéry essentially takes back what he had said about the disorder that the poet, as opposed to the musician, must deal with. And it isn't just the musical and metrical conditions that restrict the indefiniteness – it's all the kinds of good moves in poetic design space that the poet learns from all the poets she reads during her apprenticeship, as well as the specific kinds of moves each poet develops for herself. Here is how Valéry describes the further evolution of *La Pithie*:

> my fragment acted like a living fragment, since, plunged in the (no doubt nourishing) surroundings of my desire and waiting thought, it proliferated, and engendered all that was lacking: several lines before and a great many lines after. (p. 80)

Here is that characteristic testimony of the modern writer concerning the independent life of the work that seems in some inexplicable way to call forth its further development. We are once again back to an organic analogy, but one with a radically different import from the one proposed by Heaney. The poem-egg figured here is not something that belongs to the self-immediacy of the subjective substance but to the dynamis of the specific configuration of design elements of Valéry's poetic techne that had begun to come together in the eight-syllable line of French poetry that originally popped into his head.

No doubt the generative system of poetry is far less formalizable than that of music, but Valéry sets too high a bar for system of the techne type when he demands fully conscious control and a high degree of scientific regularization. This is a version of the problem that arose historically when Aristotle demanded such precision from techne as to make it unresponsive to the vagaries of empirical particularity.

Valéry needlessly retains one last element of Romanticism in his conception of the poetic state. For a brief moment he is almost as rhapsodic about the magic of creation as Heaney is. This shows just how hard it is to get entirely free of the magical view of creation. Still, the miraculous nature of the poetic state plays an essentially different role for Valéry than it does for Heaney. Lest we attribute too much virtue to the power of inspiration, Valéry proceeds immediately to demote it to a very humble place indeed. This miracle 'is not enough to produce that complete object, that compound of beauties, that collection of happy chances for the mind which a noble poem offers us'. From the poetic state

> we obtain only fragments. All the precious things that are found in the earth, gold, diamonds, uncut stones, are there scattered, strewn, grudgingly hidden in a quantity of rock or sand, where chance may sometimes uncover them. These riches would be nothing without the human labor that draws them from the massive night where they were sleeping, assembles them, alters and organizes them into ornaments. These fragments of metal embedded in formless matter, these oddly shaped crystals, must owe all their luster to intelligent labor. It is a labor of this kind that the true poet accomplishes. (pp. 75–6)

The magic of inspiration, so warmly described by Valéry on the preceding page, is here remarkably deflated, in a way reminiscent of how Kant deflates the balloon of genius when he says that by itself it creates only nonsense. Valéry now describes the products of inspiration as 'fragments of metal embedded in formless matter' and as 'oddly shaped crystals' that owe all their lustre – *all* – to the poet's intelligent labour. Valéry seems unable to quite free himself from the notion of natural creation or to quite believe in it either. He solves the problem by separating the two into separate-but-far-from-equal compartments, at the cost of a certain obscurity in his account.

We see in the case of Valéry just how close literary theorizing has come to an adequate conception of art as techne, and how even the theorizing that comes close flails in the dark in its absence.

NOTES

1 Paul Valéry, 'Poetry and Abstract Thought', in *The Art of Poetry*, trans. Denise Folliot (Princeton: Princeton University Press, 1958), pp. 52–81.

2 An essential reference here is E. A. Havelock's study of the psychophysiology of the ancient Greek pedagogy that was based on the rhythms of the Homeric poems: *Preface to Plato* (Cambridge, MA: Belknap Press of Harvard University Press, 1963). This aspect of Havelock's great book has unfortunately been cast into shadow by his controversial thesis, in this same book, on the origins of Greek philosophy.

3 Cf. A. Roepsdorff, J. Niewöhner and S. Beck, 'Enculturing Brains Through Patterned Practices', *Neural Networks* (2010) 23: 1051–9. This study strongly supports the notion that the functioning of our brains when we perform social practices cannot be understood without reference to the logic of the social practices themselves.

4 I can't resist citing Wallace Stevens's 'Of Modern Poetry' here. Stevens says modern poetry must 'like an insatiable actor',

> . . . slowly and
> With meditation, speak words that in the ear,
> In the delicatest ear of the mind, repeat,
> Exactly, that which it wants to hear, at the sound
> Of which, an invisible audience listens,
> Not to the play, but to itself, expressed
> In an emotion as of two people, as of two
> Emotions becoming one. The actor is
> A metaphysician in the dark, twanging
> An instrument, twanging a wiry string that gives
> Sounds passing through sudden rightnesses, wholly
> Containing the mind, below which it cannot descend,
> Beyond which it has no will to rise.

PART FOUR

Studies in Modernist Techne

CHAPTER NINE

T. J. Clark's Picasso

Artworks are skilfully contrived assemblages of constitutive elements, elements that have been honed by long traditions of techne before they come into the hands of present-day makers. The most gifted artisans coax newness out of their assemblages, but new forms are not born out of the makers' souls: new forms are brought forth out of old forms. Techne is the knowledge of how to bring about such births, and the intentions of artist-artisans are guided by this kind of knowledge.

A person with very minimal drumming skills can have a first-hand experience of how this works by simply participating in a drum circle. Such a circle will settle into a given rhythm for an indeterminate number of repetitions, but eventually that rhythm will wear out and a new one will emerge in its place. The way this happens is that, after the group has played one rhythm for a while, someone in the circle feels a variation of it emerge from within the dynamic of the prevailing rhythm; this new rhythm, if it is played with conviction by its 'originator', and if it is a viable revision of the existing rhythm, will gain adherents in the group, a few at first and then very quickly the whole group. Then the cycle will be played out once more, as the satisfying new rhythm is repeated a number of times until it starts to 'wear out', and a new one surges up to replace it, and so forth. The basic pattern of this cycle can be modelled by a single person. One can simply beat on a single drum, or even a table or other resonant surface, playing a simple rhythmic figure over and over, and at a certain point a variation will almost inevitably emerge from it. The variation is motivated in part by the need to liven up the rhythm as the original one becomes boring; but there is something very nearly – at times completely – automatic about the emergence of variation. One can't 'think up' a new rhythm as an idea in one's mind as one drums; rather, it's as though the going rhythm builds up a pressure in one's hands and arms until one's hands, in response to that pressure, spontaneously break into the new rhythm. In a slightly more advanced version of such a process, anyone who knows how to strum a few chords on the guitar, and has a feeling for rock 'n' roll, can strum a simple rhythmic guitar 'hook' from a rock song over and over until it generates variations of itself.

Only hands that have had at least a very minimal measure of apprenticeship in drumming or guitar playing are capable of this kind of 'spontaneity'. One part of that apprenticeship is simply to have listened to a lot of rhythms of this type; another part is to have practiced enough to have the flexibility and motor pathways necessary. These forms of competence constitute the elementary techne involved here, and provide a rudimentary model, as transparent as possible, of the way in which old forms give birth to new ones, through the agency of a human being who is skilled enough to make it, or allow it, to happen. With this simple model we are a long way from understanding the creativity of an ordinarily skilled musician or other artifex, much less the Beatles or Picasso, but more complex kinds of making are evolved out of metamorphoses of forms that work in analogous ways.

It is remarkable, considering how often writers, painters and other artisans have described the complex intentionality/non-intentionality of the creative process, how crude the concepts of intention have remained in debates on the topic. It's commonly assumed by both sides that the concept of intention denotes something *geistig* (involving Geist, 'consciousness' or 'mind' as super-substance), and, this being so, one must either defend intention as something preciously human or dismantle it as a mystified idea. It seems extraordinarily difficult to accept the obvious, that artist's intentions are essential to the making of art, and that nevertheless intention is not mainly 'in the head' but is dispersed across time and across the social-historical dynamics of embodied techne and of 'the art world'.

The artwork is indeed a public product, as W. K. Wimsatt and Mondroe Beardsley said in 'The Intentional Fallacy', their epochal manifesto of anti-intentionalism, and it follows from this that its value and meaning do not depend on the private mental activity of the maker.[1] But Wimsatt and Beardsley became tangled in the confusion I have just described when they claimed that 'the design or intention of the author is neither available nor desirable as a standard for judging the success of a work of literary art' (p. 3). The key word in these remarks is 'design'. Wimsatt and Beardsley see the design as something strictly intrapsychic, 'in the author's mind', 'the intuition or private part of art' (p. 6). But the artist's design, which for Wimsatt and Beardsley can play no role in the interpretation or evaluation of art, is for techne theory the central fact of art-making, because to intend a *design* cannot be private any more than a skilled chess player's intention to start with the Sicilian defence can. Whether one actually intends to use this defence on a specific occasion is of course 'private', in the sense that only the person involved knows that this is what she is intending, and might have all sorts of psychological motives for doing what she does at this moment. But the *this* that is intended is not at all private; it is a complex social fact.

In order to intend the Sicilian defence I must know how to play chess, with everything in apprenticeship and practice that involves, including the entire background of the institution of chess, with its rules and conventions. That knowledge, we could say, provides the 'structure' of the intention. Similarly, the intention to write an experimental novel or a Shakespearean sonnet, or to make a Cubist painting depicting the suffering of the victims at Guernica, is, *precisely to the degree that the work intended is a work of art*, not structurally private.

Because this is so, there can exist extensive bodies of evidence for the nature of the intention involved in the making of a given work of art, evidence that helps us to reconstruct the process of making, the way this process is woven into the unfolding of the artisan's career as a whole, and the way this career is woven into the evolution of the techne with which she works – all of this without trenching on anything that is essentially private. From the standpoint of techne theory, any kind of information that provides insight into how the work was made is admissible – 'how' not in the sense of the empirical series of events simply as such, and 'why' not in the sense of psychological motives, but in the sense of the *logos* or techne-logic that structured the series.

The road to Guernica

T. J. Clark, in his recent *Picasso and Truth*, has superbly demonstrated how this kind of reconstruction can be carried out in his recent *Picasso and Truth*, a misleadingly titled book that shows a profound understanding of the way techne, mediated by the artisan, makes new work happen.[2] Clark's comprehensive account of Picasso's career from Cubism to *Guernica* shows how to talk about Picasso's artisanal project in a way that does not run afoul of the intentionalism/anti-intentionalism dichotomy. The key piece of 'biographical' evidence that Clark uses is the dating of the works, which Picasso was exceptionally careful to document. Knowing when the works were made enables Clark to line them up seriatim in ways that are strikingly illuminating, not about what Picasso was experiencing or thinking as a value in themselves, but as a perspicuous representation of the techne-design at which he was aiming or (another way of saying the same thing) which was evolving out of his repeated attempts. Clark shows how this aim or design can be discerned in the unfolding series of works, and, in the end, how three decades of its unfolding culminate in *Guernica*.

Clark's reading of Picasso circulates around what since Clement Greenberg has generally been recognized as the central question of the techne of modernist painting, the flattening of the picture plane. Clark suggests that, in the case of Picasso, the movement away from deep, perspectival space towards, the literal surface of the painting was motivated by the change in the historical character of lived space that had occurred in the nineteenth century. Clark infers this from the striking obsession of Picasso's Cubist work with the intimate 'room-space' of bourgeois life with its personal possessions.

> Truth was proximity. An object in a painting . . . was true if it was tangible – meaning touchable, usable, possessable, playable. And the guarantee of this tangibility was a kind of space, a kind of containment or intimacy, Room-space, to use my shorthand. The room for the Cubist was what the river surface had been for Monet or the village street for Pissarro: the real-world condition under which appearances became substances. (p. 150)

This sense of 'proximity', 'tangibility', 'coziness' (p. 81) is literalized in Cubism by being placed in a way that appears to be close to the surface, or on the surface, of the painting – not securely on the other side of the perfectly transparent, imaginary window into three-dimensional space that is called the 'picture plane'. This movement towards the surface culminates in the 1927 *Painter and Model*, but it is there from the beginning in Cubism, notably in the collage technique. Clark argues that collage represents 'the *triumph* of room-space':

> Not for nothing was its key material wallpaper. The space [collage] conjured was now literally put together from the little bourgeois's belongings: his newspaper, his 'sheet music, his matchbox, his daughter's scrapbook, his friend's or dealer's calling cards . . .' Never was painting more in love with nearness, touch, familiarity, the world on a table. (p. 82)

The tendency towards this kind of proximity always kept reasserting itself in Picasso's Cubist work throughout its various phases and motivated 'three great re-imaginings' of Cubism as Picasso became dissatisfied with what he was doing and pushed Cubism in new directions.

Clark analyses the tensions in Picasso's work in terms of two overarching dichotomies, between 'structure and substance', and between 'room-space' and its outside. He sees the dichotomy between structure and substance instantiated in two paintings from 1920, a small untitled watercolour – a Cubist work that Clark refers to as *Composition* – and an oil representation, mainly of a hand, called *Fingers and Face*, done in Picasso's 'antique' or classicizing style. *Composition* represents one extreme of the Cubist style, in which objects are not only reduced to geometrical forms but their colours washed out, made translucent. This is the pole of 'structure', of 'a feeling less for the specific identities of things than for the conditions of their being-together in our field of vision. A feeling for interlock and juxtaposition. A sense that objects are most fully themselves for us at their edges' (p. 32). On the other side, the chiaroscuro rendering of the hand, with its 'heavy opacity', represents the pole of 'substance'. Clark then reproduces five drawings from

1919 to 1920 in each of which Picasso, strikingly, put together these two opposed representational tendencies on the same support. These drawings are all variations on the same themes, with substance represented in each case by a hand, and structure in each case centred on a Cubist rendering of a guitar. But the objects depicted in the opposed styles never form a single composition; even though in each case they're paired up on the same sheet of paper, they always 'remain in separate compartments'. However, in one of them, from autumn 1919 (fig. 1.21, p. 46), it looks as though the hand, even though it occupies a different pictorial space from the guitar, is reaching towards it, as though the two styles are being pulled towards each other, implying that each one by itself is somehow insufficient. (From the standpoint of the present discussion, it's striking that this fascinating drawing represents a hand reaching towards the organon of a techne.)

By putting these related pictures in sequence, Clark reveals how Picasso massages his forms, over and over, as a skilled drummer massages his rhythms, feeling for the contours of potential new forms in them, with the stylistic tendencies of the work evolving across time through these successive attempts.

The second major dichotomy, between room space and its outside, Clark reads off from the way windows become central to Picasso's Cubist room spaces in the late 1910s. In 1919 the painter experiments with pushing his objects away from the front of the picture space that they inhabit in Cubism's classic phase, back to the threshold of the window, on the borderline between the room's interior and its outside. The opening up of the window and the migration of the room's objects towards its threshold show Picasso beginning to break out of the restricted confines of room space, 'an outside overtaking and informing the enclosed space of a room' (p. 91), and thus signals the end of the first great phase of Cubism.

But the experiment with putting objects at the threshold between interior and outside does not initially work. The test of a painting idea for Picasso is whether he can make a big painting out of it (p. 98), but the big 1919 *Open Window*, where the still life is located on the threshold between the room and the balcony, is a failure: 'The objects on the table have been reduced to flat tokens, with light leaking in and across their perfunctory contours' (p. 101). Not until 1924, in *Guitar and Mandolin on a Table*, does Picasso work through the dilemma of this phase. Here the table is pulled back away from the window, putting Picasso's objects back 'firmly into the room'.

What interests Clark most about these paintings is the way the edges of objects are related to the light that comes through the window, the question of whether they are given definition by the light or instead 'blurred or evaporated' by it (p. 102). In *Guitar and Mandolin*, with the object safely back in room space, Picasso attains the 'weight and opacity' that were missing in the 1919 painting; the light coming through the window surrounds and defines the objects rather than dissolving them. Yet at the same time the objects in the painting 'lack substance', in the sense of lacking depth, modelling; unusually for Picasso's still lifes of the 1920s, the paint is 'paper thin, almost unmarked by the brush', and the detail is 'laid on with minimal, cynical efficiency'. Clark interprets this technique as a new way of overcoming the intimate availability of objects in bourgeois room space, not by moving objects to the threshold of the outside, but by making them insubstantial, lacking in the tactility of his earlier objects, and thus distanced from the viewer's grasp. The shapes are enveloped by the outside that floods in through the window, and are themselves reduced to outsides; they are mere facades of objects. This, Clark argues, is the first of Picasso's 'three great re-imaginings' of Cubism (p. 152).

Clark's reading is not 'formalist' in the commonly accepted sense of the term. His great overarching thesis is that Picasso's paintings express his response to the horrors of the century, mainly in terms of taking refuge from those horrors in bourgeois room space. Now obviously there is a great deal of interpretation in all this, and so, much room for disagreement with Clark. One need not be convinced by his overarching thesis, or by the notions that 'The world for the bourgeois is a room' (p. 79), and its objects usable and possessable, and in this different from the objects in *Guitar and Mandolin*; or that the thin paint of this painting is intended to overcome this inwardness and is successful in so doing. Analysing a work in terms of techne cannot be limited to pure description. But it should be obvious from my summary of Clark's arguments how very different his mode of argumentation is from the way most art criticism, certainly most Picasso criticism, is done. Each of his judgments is (1) anchored in the closest attention to the details of the materials, techniques and form of each painting; and (2) these detailed observations are contextualized in terms of the evolution of Picasso's techne across decades of his career. This sets a new, and very high, standard for disagreement. If one wants to counter Clark's interpretations, one must do so with a similar depth of knowledge and observation, with a comparable grasp of the nature of the relevant line of development of the painting techne. Clark always sees the relation of painting to world from the perspective of the painter as technites, as the problem of finding the right techniques by which to translate the world into the terms of formal constraints of the painting's physical being: its rectangular shape and size, its flat surface, the nature of the paint or other materials that are deployed on the surface of the canvas. This is the only true formalism, the one the medium in its worldly entanglement imposes on the artisan, and only because of this, on the viewer; the authentically formalist reading of art is one that follows the track of this imposition. Because the evolution of Picasso's techne is the process of working out new ways of transforming content into form, the distinction between the formal level of explanation and explanation at the level of content or context is not a simple, fixed distinction; what Clark calls the 'semantics' and the 'syntax' of painting are always running together in new ways as the work evolves.

Formalism can speak of the relation between work and world, but it must do so differently, not by trying to find coded 'reference' to this or that aspect of world, but by showing how in making the artwork the artifex has struggled to *transform* world into the material of which the work is made, at the same time – in the most ambitious art – struggling to transform the already existing transformative capabilities of that techne itself. All of this together can then be read, not as a reference to, but as an *index of* the historical situation within which it happens, and of the artisan's relation to that situation; but reading the indexicality of an artwork is an additional, more speculative level of interpretation, and one that should be both rigorously grounded in, and methodologically distinguished from, the elementary analysis at the level of techne. Thus, for example, in a highly distorted representation like the 1927 *Painter and Model*, the persons and objects in the painting, and the features of the room itself such as wainscoting and window, are barely recognizable, indicated by minimal visual signs, lines and rectangles. In a sense they have become mere geometry, forms without real world content. Of course, even though they retain only a shred of reference to the reality of room space, they are still recognizable as such, and the title of the painting invites this recognition; yet there's very little interest in merely recognizing the reference. What Clark is interested in is how Picasso's paintings rely on such referential marks to come together at the level of form, and what it is about the way Picasso transforms them that makes certain works succeed better than others. In the best work, Clark argues, the objects indicated, however minimally, are opaque, definite, substantial – and of course indoors, in the illusory room space where Picasso feels most at home as a painter. But the objects in the painting do not have the solidity and palpability of classical representation, of perspective and chiaroscuro, rather, they are a solidity and palpability that maximally exploit the immediacy of the painting surface itself.

Integration of the outside

In the narrative structure of Clark's book, the great dramatic interest of the trajectory he traces through Picasso's art comes from the way it leads up to the climactic *Guernica*. The problems of spatiality and light and form that Picasso works through during these decades provide him with the resources to make the most famous painting of its century. On Clark's telling, this trajectory is fundamentally a matter of Picasso's working his way out of the enclosing familiarity of bourgeois room space into the monstrous, tragic space of contemporary history. Picasso takes a crucial step in this direction with *The Three Dancers* of 1925, the second of his great reimaginings of Cubism, which builds directly on the advances made in *Guitar and Mandolin*. This is another 'window' painting, but one in which the outside enters the room in an entirely new way and invades not inanimate objects but human beings. Clark focuses on 'the pressure of the blue' in the painting, the way the blues that come through the window, which seem to come 'straight from the world of crude chromolithography', become 'part of the world up front', surrounding the bodies of the dancers, actually penetrating the body of the demonic dancer on the left (p. 128). The figures are paper cutouts doing a dance of death; Picasso is painting his way 'out of entrapment in style' (p. 123) and allowing something truly new and strange and other to enter his pictures. *The Three Dancers* 'is a turning point . . . in leaving collage behind' (p. 136); the painter is learning how to thread the 'wild outside to existence through the life we have' (p. 146).

The third great reimagining comes in the previously mentioned *Painter and Model*. This picture features one of Picasso's monstrous, distorted female nudes, with a stick-figure artist painting her. The room is a dull grey, but there are two large areas of light, on the left one shaped like the blade of a sickle, on the right a shape like a fat boomerang with the curved side down. It's a mystery just how these shapes function pictorially; they can be read as spotlit areas lightening up the gloomy room, or 'as holes punched through the picture surface – holes that dramatize and materialize the strange fiction of European painting since the Renaissance called the "picture plane"' (p. 156). To learn how they should best be understood, Clark observes their genesis in the 'psychic material' of Picasso's sketchbooks, where these shapes slowly emerge. Nietzsche says in *The Birth of Tragedy* that all human beings are artists when they dream, but there is a dazzling demonstration of the difference between dream and art in Clark's reading of these notebooks. The notebooks document how Picasso initially captures the monsters that emerge from his imagination in the disorderly dream-form in which they emerge. Some are little more than doodles, in which Picasso keeps reworking the same vaguely obscene forms, vaginas and genital hair, heads and penises, or heads that become penises, and are beheaded or castrated; then little by little, in drawing after drawing, Picasso trims and prods this 'loony material' into formally satisfying shape, working out the 'brilliant, contrived reworking of Cubist space' (p. 164) that we see in *Artist and Model*. The blade shape is of particular interest; it starts out as a literal blade with which one monster is in the act of beheading/castrating another (p. 165; fig. 4.12); but eventually these and all the other shapes become 'fully and only facts of painting' as Picasso works them into a new form of 'Cubist spatiality' (pp. 189, 164). They are neither representations of blades, nor holes through which we look into the space of the room, nor light that falls on it; Picasso makes them 'consubstantial with the gray surrounding them' by his treatment of the painting surface: 'a hard, encrusted, tamped down opacity, like high-grade plasterwork or stucco stiffened with sand'. They are 'here on the screen, the surface' (p. 187). 'The picture plane was opened and materialized. The room was nowhere but in it, on it' (p. 189).

In the years after *Painter and Model* Picasso searched for ways not just 'to bring the outside into the room', as he had tried to do in his 'window' paintings, but 'ways *into* the outside'. He puts his monsters on the beach, out in the open air. 'He wanted to see if the openness of the outdoors could be made into a picture; that is, made present and coherent within the four sides of the [picture] rectangle' (p. 194). But as wild as Picasso's designs at times become, and as much as he tries to locate his monsters and monuments in outdoor scenes, they keep gravitating back within the rectangles of room space, which sometimes become indistinguishable from formalist rectangles that merely echo the shape of the painting. 'Always the few square feet of Cubism lie ready to recapture the imagination' (p. 220). Clark demonstrates this thesis by means of a truly eye-opening series of drawings from 1929 to 1930 that show one of Picasso's monsters migrating gradually from its initial place on empty ground under the sky, where it is apparently of monumental size, to a role in a still life on a table with tablecloth, with wall and wainscot behind and a picture frame drawn around it, as though the monster he had initially pictured had to be enclosed, domesticated (p. 221).

Thus the best of Picasso's later work does not try to break out of room space entirely, but through the three great reimaginings, his art learns how to allow the interior to be 'penetrated – energized – by space of a different character' (p. 152).

The culminating challenge

Picasso needed everything he had learned from his decades of technical exploration to paint *Guernica*. It was a tremendous exertion for him. He did not choose either the format or the subject matter – a very large, public work, a mural, on the subject of the aerial destruction of the Basque city of Guernica, symbolic centre of Basque freedom, by Franco's Nazi allies. At first he told the representatives of the Spanish Republic that he didn't know if he could do it. Profoundly a painter of intimate interiors, and of paintings of moderate size, he was being asked to paint an outsized outdoor scene (25 ½ by 11 ½) depicting a monstrous public event, one that announced a new kind of modern horror. But Picasso's paintings need a 'sense of containment', of space as 'fully *there* in the painted rectangle', if they are to provide a set of 'felt equivalents for the things – the bodies, the agonies – the space contains' (p. 246). They 'lose hold' of everything 'if the top boundary of the picture is not every bit as present and determinant a fact of viewing as the line along the picture's floor' (p. 246). How can this be accomplished in a painting this large, when the top edge of the painting is so far above the viewer's head that it cannot be made present in this way? And how can Picasso open out the spatiality of the painting to the magnitude of the monstrous event that he has been called on to commemorate?

By immense good fortune, an extensive documentation – most crucially the photographs taken by Dora Maar – exists of the stages that Picasso's thinking about this picture went through during its five-week evolution.

Drawings from May 1 and May 2, done in the 'old master' medium of pencil on gesso, show him conceiving the scene of the bombing as entirely outdoors. These first attempts are reminiscent of the kind of outside that had become ordinary in Picasso's unimpressive work of the mid-1930s, where the outside is conceived in a surrealistic or fantasized way, with mythic monsters and classically idealized figures. This is the kind of 'dreamscape' outdoors with which Picasso apparently felt comfortable; but now it must be 'put back into the world – given weight, made ordinary and substantial' if it is to do justice to the horror and tragedy of Guernica (p. 256). On May 9, Picasso makes a small drawing that already contains many of the elements of the final painting, but still as an outdoor scene, with the suggestion of a deep ground plane. Then, when the full size canvas is stretched and Picasso begins work on May 11 (stage one), he lays out the full design of the painting as a line drawing that collapses the middle space, moving everything closer to the picture surface. But line 'cannot make space materialize, as the palpable, close thing Picasso felt it to be' (p. 260). How to provide this substantiality?

In stage one the women's bodies are eroticized in the familiar Picasso fashion, but Picasso will gradually de-eroticize them, by such devices as working the roundness out of their breasts and giving them nipples that look like spikes or bolts. This development occurs in tandem with the bringing forward of the picture plane. It seems only to be expected, given the story Clark has told about Picasso's career, that gradually as it proceeds through its various stages, *Guernica* also becomes more and more an interior. A ceiling light is added, and then ceiling lines, though part of the original city roofscape remains, making the space ambiguously indoor/outdoor; and in stages six and eight, patterned paper stick-ons are added ('a last effort to preserve room-space'; p. 275). This late return to collage is not, however, motivated by nostalgia; it addresses the need to keep the 'light-dark geometry' of *Guernica* from 'opening the illusion backward, into a space that was simply vague' (p. 276). But Picasso finds a better way to achieve this end; he permanently removes the collage pieces after stage eight and instead secures the picture to its surface by covering most of the horse's body with lines of stippling (p. 274). And finally, when the painting is almost finished, he secures the picture's spatiality to its bottom edge by adding a grid of tiling on the floor, a grid that gives the giant figures in the foreground centre, the horse and the falling woman, ground to stand on, but also makes them seem even closer to the picture plane. This is 'flatness finding its feet'. When the tile is painted in, the spatiality of the picture 'seems to harden and clarify' (pp. 277–9).

In the end, what matters most is not whether the scene is inside or outside, but that it is '*here*, lower down, closer to us, in the weighted, bottom heavy world of the giants' (p. 272); the top of the painting is secondary. Light does not enter this space as it enters a room, through the window, but as 'inruption' (p. 257), as the light of an exploding bomb. 'Everywhere in *Guernica* the shards of the painting's light-dark architecture (its blast effect) slash across women's bodies' (p. 270). This effect of inruption is registered in the suffering of the organic bodies, shared by human and animal; and this suffering, which is 'the agony of a polis' (p. 240), is brought up close to the viewer, and set down on the ground, made 'earthbound' (p. 246), in giant size.

The movement towards form

This, then, is how, according to Clark, Picasso worked out the kind of spatiality appropriate to the event he had to depict. Clark makes vividly evident how new this was, and how different from the kind of space that was habitual and congenial to Picasso this was, how much of a torsion he had to put his art through in order to arrive at it, and why it had to be precisely this way.

From the techne perspective, the centre of interpretation is not, as in ordinary formalism, the individual work as a finished object, but as a specific intersection of techne-energies, the *dynamei* of the specific techne-system, or combination of techne-systems, involved. I am thinking here of Hadamard's mathematician walking around (mentally) in the edifice of mathematics, perceiving how the equations that constitute a particular wing of the mathematical architecture contain the possibility of a new expansion of the edifice. The trick for the viewer is to see what the artisan sees when looking at a conjuncture of techne-forces – to see, for example, what Picasso saw when he looked at the techniques of his early Cubist work and worked out from them to the techniques of his later work. The already existing work is a set of structures that represent actualized potentialities of the techne, and which contain, for the eye or ear or hand of the skilled artisan, potentialities, *dynameis*, for new structures.

One of the central impulses of modernism, what distinguishes it as the specific kind of artistic and intellectual movement that it was, is its direct, intentional exploration of the various forms of art as such conjunctures of techne-elements and potential energies. Greenberg points generally in this direction when he says, in a much-quoted remark about the modernist 'discipline', as he calls it, that its 'essence' lay 'in the use of characteristic methods of a discipline to criticize the discipline itself, not in order to subvert it but in order to entrench it more firmly in its area of competence'.[3] But Greenberg excessively narrows his definition when he describes this self-analytical turn only as the techne or 'discipline's' self-criticism. Clark shows how Picasso's experiments with style over the decades constitute a slow-motion analysis of the generative system of the techne of painting as it stood in the aftermath of the Cubist revolution, experiments the purpose of which was not merely to criticize the techne but to grab hold, at the deepest possible level, of its *generativity*, its ability to generate new forms.

Clark's reading of *Guernica* demonstrates in comprehensive detail how a painting can be read on the basis of this way of understanding what art-making is. He focuses at each moment on the question of *why* this or that change was made in the developing work – where the answer to *why* that is called for is always a techne-reason, the solution to a problem of how to make the picture's design fulfil the artistic goal, a goal that is only darkly envisioned and must be discovered in the process of painting, perhaps through much trial and error. These techne-reasons of course always come out of the messy imbrication of techne with history and the artisan's own psychological world – and the richest account of art takes account of as much of this as possible. But if this is to be an understanding of the *art* in works of art, all of this information must be funnelled into the analysis through the techne-reasons.

Now imagine that a 'genius' could somehow avoid all the trouble Picasso actually went to in making this painting. Imagine that the final finished image of *Guernica* popped into Picasso's head one day, and he then in one titanic, convulsive session slavishly rendered this mentally preconceived image onto canvas. It would still remain the case that, in order to manifest the formal mastery visible in the painting, the instantaneous mental image itself would have had to incorporate all the painting knowledge that slowly and painstakingly went into *Guernica* as it in fact evolved. What the existence of the actual process, and of the record of that process – especially Dora Maar's photographs – provide is rich clues to the precise nature of that techne-knowledge and the way Picasso put it together, clues that would be missing otherwise. This lack would considerably impoverish the kind of analysis that could then be done. But we know a priori that techne would have had to be at work in the making, no matter how mental or instantaneous the process. And to the degree that we are familiar with the techne-tradition or mixture of traditions within which the artisan was working, and the specific artist's own body of work, this techne could be deciphered, to a greater or lesser extent, from the finished work, regardless of how much or little we know about its empirical genesis.

Whereas formalism stops short with the work as already complete, from the techne standpoint we read the work as a system of clues to the constructive process that made it, and more fundamentally to the power/knowledge of the techne that guided this process. That is to say that the aim of techne theory is to read the power that we feel in the finished form as a clue to the *nascent movement towards form* that circulated across the stages of the work's emergence or making, and that initially did so – to the degree that the work is truly new – in the absence of the form towards which this movement moved, and which only emerged in the process of making. This is what Clark does so well in his reading of Picasso, and most fully of *Guernica*. From this standpoint, our enjoyment of the exquisite refinement of a detail doesn't end in the immediate sensation; it involves attention to how the detail functions in a whole economy of forces that were involved in the making of the work as a whole, to how this economy constitutes a moment in the unfolding economy of the painter's larger project, to the way this larger project itself is involved in a complex dialectical struggle with the *techne*, and how the techne, the individual project and the individual work are a product of and a response to the historical process within which they are contained. All of this is accomplished by Clark in his reading of Picasso.

Each work of art is a functional system, with each element performing an *ergon* that is interdependent with the *erga* of all the other elements. This work never stops taking place *in* the work, for the eye that knows how to trace its functioning. A painting, no matter how much it is a depiction of something, even to the point of the most precise realism, is also at the same time a movement of that painter's work, a push forward or backward, a further development of lines of force already established or a revision or undermining or deconstruction of such lines; and at the same time as it does this within the individual painter's work, it does it also at the level of the techne as a collective, historical unfolding. This is the activity or *energeia* of the work, its character not as mere thing but as work in its root sense, as the activity of the work's functional organization, where this organization is itself the encoded, techne-guided, work-activity of its maker, and, through that maker, of the accumulated work-cunning of an entire techne-community.

NOTES

1 I cite the version of this essay published by Wimsatt in his widely influential book *The Verbal Icon: Studies in the Meaning of Poetry* (Lexington: University of Kentucky Press, 1954).

2 T. J. Clark, *Picasso and Truth* (Princeton, NJ: Princeton University Press, 2013).

3 Clement Greenberg, *The Collected Essays and Criticism, Vol. 4, Modernism with a Vengeance* (Chicago: University of Chicago Press, 1993), p. 85.

CHAPTER TEN

What's radical about radical painting?

The work of Joseph Marioni – 'radical painting', as he and a few colleagues have most often called it – and his reflections on it, have a singular place in the history of techne theory. No other artisan of his stature has so resolutely opposed the conception of art as Art, to the point of rejecting even the name of 'artist' for himself, in favour of the techne-specific title of 'painter'. In the 1986 manifesto he co-authored with his former collaborator, the German painter Günter Umberg, he and Umberg went so far towards the craft-idea of art as to describe paintings as functional objects comparable to chairs – objects made for a specific use that defines their essence as objects.[1]

This comparison, however, has a double, complexly tangled, bearing. On the one hand, by placing the objects produced by painting on the same plane as those produced by carpentry, it also places the art of painting and carpentry on the same plane, at least at the ontological level. On the other hand, Marioni and Umberg introduce this modest comparison in the service of what is often considered the most elitist stance towards art, the modernist stance that defines the arts in purist terms, seeking the *essence* of each. Just as chairs are defined by their function of being made to sit on, so paintings must have a function that defines them as paintings and therefore the painter's goal as painter.

There can, however, be an enormous difference between one search for the essence and another. In the case of painting, a myopic definition of essence as the *single* aspect of an art that it shares with no other led Clement Greenberg to define this essence as flatness and its delimitation, and this alone. By definition it couldn't be image or colour or paint or anything that painting shared with any other art, and certainly not the relations among this whole ensemble, so, Greenberg reasoned, it must be the simple fact of a flat, delimited surface. Hence, he famously concluded, a mere blank canvas pinned to a wall would qualify as a painting, 'though not necessarily as a successful one'.[2] The rather artificial debate over flatness as an essence has largely obscured the historical reality in which Greenberg was interested, that since the late nineteenth century avant-garde painters had indeed been progressively flattening the picture plane – a movement that, as we saw in the preceding chapter, T. J. Clark tracks in the development of Picasso.

There is no more perspicuous way to understand the development of Modernism in painting than in terms of this 'flattening' movement, of which Manet and Cézanne are central figures, which was further developed by Cubism, then by such figures as Malevich, Matisse, Pollock and Newman, and entered a new phase with the early work of Frank Stella, followed by two figures of special relevance to Marioni, Brice Marden and Robert Ryman. Ryman and Marden, with whom Marioni almost immediately connected when he arrived in New York City in 1972, were working in the direction of radical, concrete, or as Marioni has recently called it (and this, I think, with its Aristotelian overtones, is the best name for it yet), *actualized* painting. Marden's work subsequently turned in other directions, but Ryman's work has continued to be a central point of reference for Marioni's reflections on art.

So, even though flatness is not the *essence* of painting, taking it as an interpretive focus has yielded a great deal of insight into the history of modern painting *practice*. It's unfortunate that the single, rather isolated remark about the unpainted canvas has distracted attention from the fact that this practice in all its aspects was Greenberg's persistent concern. As Michael Fried explained in *Three American Painters*, in response to readers who thought Greenberg was positing an immutable objective teleology in the history of painting, the only 'inner artistic logic' that Greenberg saw in the development of modernism was a '"logic" that has come about as the result of decisions made by individual artists to engage with formal problems thrown up by the art of the recent past'.[3] It is, in other words, not a matter of metaphysical essence or objective teleology but of *techne*, of looking at each canvas in terms of the specific practical *logos* that guided its making.

Modernism of course ceased to occupy centre stage in the art world many years ago, overwhelmed by pop culture, social movements and the dominance of financial over aesthetic values. But Marioni's work and that of several other painters – notably the late Karen Baumeister, who tragically died in mid-career – shows that the modernist style of investigation of the techne of painting, including the inquiry into flatness, is far from exhausted.

Marioni's fundamental concern for many years now has been how to think the dynamis of the elemental material ensemble of the art of painting: paint, canvas, stretcher, means of application, means of attachment to the wall. This concern is what lies behind the analogy he and Umberg made between a painting and a chair. The search for the specific essence of an art, properly understood, is really just the artisan's quest to refine her intuitions, as an artisan, about the nature of her practice, to reach more deeply into the art's capacity to generate new forms out of old forms, in the way that Picasso, in Clark's reading, did with his own painting practice.

Greenberg's reduction of painting to flatness 'and the delimitation of flatness' is incomplete for Marioni, not because of the talk of essence, but because it doesn't question the *function* of flatness in painting. A canvas, Marioni observes, is not a natural object, it is a human-made thing, designed and manufactured to serve a specific purpose: for someone to apply paint to it (p. 19). This is its intrinsic function or final cause, that for the sake of which it has been made. Marioni addresses this point directly in a recent essay on Fried's contribution to the debate over modern painting.[4] When Greenberg defined flatness as the essence of art, Marioni argues, he 'had the cart before the horse'. He was ignoring the 'use-function' of flatness, isolating the stretched canvas from the functional system of which it is a part – a system that gives each element its function and what I am calling its work-potential (ergon and dynamis). The elemental material ensemble of the art of painting is an interacting, interlocking set of elements that has evolved across the history of painting, each element of which emerged for reasons both intrinsic and extrinsic to the art, but in the modern era increasingly intrinsic – at least along the line of development to which Marioni belongs. The canvas is the part of this elemental ensemble that exists, and is stretched flat, Marioni argues, not as an end in itself, but in order to have *paint* applied to it. Correspondingly, the painter's fundamental task is to do the applying. Hence, as Ryman has put it, the primary question for the painter is 'what to do with paint'.[5] Painting is indeed, as Greenberg held, a *specific* art, but not because of some single element unique to it; rather, it is specific in its functional ensemble, an ensemble that is, inevitably, organized around paint and the application of paint. Now, of course the fact that the canvas only exists in view of its purpose, to be painted, doesn't tell us *how* it should be painted. Marioni, however, purports to deduce the imperatives of his art from the nature of his materials themselves. Representation, on his account, is external to the 'logic of the material form' of the painting. 'The material itself has perceptual content that is intrinsic to its function' (p. 24).

Deducing the functional essence

The conclusion of this esoteric debate so far would seem laughable to the average museum goer: that a canvas in order to qualify minimally as a painting must have *paint* applied to it. But it is the essential first step in Marioni's deduction of the principles of the techne of painting from its elementary materiality.

This deduction cannot be made simply from the materials themselves – certainly not from paint alone – however much they may have been preformed to serve the ends of an art. A palette of paint, a stretched canvas and a brush can equally produce a Rembrandt portrait or a Mondrian abstract. We need, rather, to understand these materials in the context of the specific historical moment and place in which they will be utilized; and that is precisely how Marioni, who has an encyclopaedic knowledge of the history of art, does it. In order to follow the logic of this deduction, we must understand the way in which the dynamis of paint has been progressively exfoliated across the history of Western painting since the Middle Ages, and in particular since Impressionism.

By the late nineteenth century painters were developing techniques that, instead of inviting the eye to look into the painting as though it were looking through a window, more and more attracted it to the painted surface itself. This is the flattening of the picture space to which Greenberg refers. Cézanne's late style is generally credited with accomplishing the crucial step towards the autonomization of the painted surface; here is representation on the verge of dissolution into the blocks of paint that constitute it, a movement carried further by Cubism. Yet Cubism remains both explicitly and implicitly representational. Not only does it abstractly depict guitars, tables, and room space, but, as Clark notes, 'it seems preternaturally aware not just of the two dimensions of the actual object it is making, but of the object's enclosing outline' (*Picasso and Truth*, p. 70).[6] That is to say that the shapes in the picture often echo the shape of the picture support – a square or rectangle. The preoccupation with this shape from Picasso and Braque through Malevich, Mondrian and others, suggests a radical reduction of the subject matter of painting to the representation of a painting's own shape. So painting grows increasingly abstract; but abstract representation is still representation.

The next step was taken by Frank Stella, in his black paintings of 1958–60, the surface of which is covered with evenly spaced bands of black paint that radiate concentrically from the picture edge, separated by thin lines of unpainted canvas. The ruling principle that Stella set for the making of these paintings was that the geometry of the bands should be mechanically derived from the shape of the support. This was a radical new development, because, while it was still a matter of abstract representation of the shape of the support, the representation was rigidly parallel to the picture edge, as though it were mechanically determined by that edge; and the mechanical nature of this determination was made explicit by the repetition of the same shape over and over, the lines separated by precisely the same distance, as one moved inward from the edge.

In these works the picture plane is no longer being flattened, it has been completely eliminated. Even Mondrian still gives the eye a certain pictorial interest, but with Stella this is much diminished if not eliminated, and one has much more of a sense of the presence of the painting as a unitary physical object, 'a single thing', as Donald Judd put it.[7] Like Judd, Marioni took note of the presence, as objects, of these paintings, which is truly striking; but he noted also that there was little interest for the eye in the painted surface of these works, which Stella intentionally de-emphasized by using housepainter's paint and brush, and by hiding the traces of brushwork in order to eliminate the 'expressive' reference to the painter's subjectivity that visible brushwork carries. The elimination of all painterliness, and the fact that, as Judd commented, these works 'suggest slabs, since they project more than usual', leaves them poised on the edge of sculpturality, which for Judd was a gain, since, in his conception, three-dimensional 'actual space' is 'intrinsically more powerful and specific than painting on a flat surface'.[8] Marioni's interest, by contrast, was in finding a more powerful way, precisely, to paint on a flat, rectangular surface; what the suggestion of sculpturality taught him was a feel for the boundary between what the elementary material ensemble of the painting art can do and what begins to be something other than painting – a direction *not* to go in.

The importance of Ryman

Much more significant than Stella's work for the evolution of radical or actualized painting is that of Ryman, who is truly a watershed figure. The entire development of modernist painting, and Ryman's place in it, can be illuminated in terms of the Russian Formalist notion of 'laying bare the device',[9] as this notion was further developed in the poststructuralist period. A work of art lays bare the device when it is constructed in such a way as to reveal rather than hide the nature of the artifice by means of which it is creating an artistic effect. In representational or 'figurative' painting, even so basic a gesture as making the individual strokes of the brush visible, as opposed to hiding them, or the creation of a thick texture of paint that is visibly a material mass on the surface of the canvas, are forms of laying bare of the device, because they reveal how the paint that creates the representational illusion is being worked. This kind of thing – painterliness, as it is called – is not new; Rembrandt's late work is notable in this respect, as is the late work of Turner. Individual devices like these, however, cannot be evaluated in terms of the logic of 'laying bare the device' in isolation from the nature of the entire work within which they occur, which itself must be understood in relation to the larger art-evolutionary context within which that work belongs. Thus in an abstract painting, where there is no question of realist illusionism, the visibility of the materiality of the paint, or of the gesture of application, can acquire a function the opposite of that which it has in representational painting: rather than revealing its artifice as a device, it can become the device itself, in a new kind of mimeticism. Thus in the 1950s the gesturality of a painter like Pollock was read as a direct expression of something about the psychological reality of the painter – a

Romantic rather than Realist mimeticism. In this context, Stella had to hide rather than reveal the gesture of application of the paint, so that it would not perform any kind of mimetic function at all, neither realistic nor expressionistic. In his black paintings there is a shift to a new dynamic of laying bare. What is being revealed, made visible, is not the artifice by which a representational illusion is created, but the principle that determines the pattern inscribed on the painting's surface.

But once he had accomplished this shift to a new dynamic, Stella stopped working in this direction and turned to other interests, and that's where Ryman comes in. Ryman has spent much of his career exploring every aspect of the art of painting in terms of the logic of 'laying bare'. He has sometimes been labeled a minimalist, but this is a mistake, because there is considerable interest for the eye in his brushwork, though of a 'cool', non-expressionistic sort. The texture of the paint and its articulation by the brush are always foregrounded, but he paints almost exclusively in white, and his brushwork tends to be repetitive and controlled, so there is no temptation to read it as expressive. Ryman's works remain paintings, that, as Marioni would say, reveal their 'objectness' *as paintings*, rather than becoming minimalist painted objects.[10]

Ryman himself has said that the paintings are white because white is less obtrusive than other colours and allows the material of the support to assert itself as an integral part of the painting. 'The gray of the steel comes through; the linen comes through . . . all of those things are considered,' Ryman says. 'The white just happened because it's a paint and it doesn't interfere.'[11] Other painters had unsystematically revealed the texture of the support, but Ryman turned such revelation into a field of exploration that he has tried to explore as exhaustively as possible, systematically probing the immense variety of effects of texture, colour and reflectivity that can be achieved by means of white paint interacting with the variety of surfaces to which it can be applied (linen, paper, plastic, metal). But what most unignorably alerts the viewer to the distinctive logic of what Ryman is up to is his thematization of the ways in which the support can be attached to the wall, a very rich element for Ryman, who has used such things as masking tape, bolts and tacks, exposed to view and made part of the composition of the work. The means of attachment has traditionally been hidden – treated, like the stretcher, as substructural elements that are not part of the aesthetic effect intended. Revealing them, and even making them obtrusively large, like bolts or aggressively unaesthetic, like masking tape or tacks, makes it evident that they are that way on purpose, that the painter is thematizing them as an element of the painting. Ryman has also placed a painting horizontally, with the 'top' edge against the wall and two narrow supporting rods near the 'bottom' edge, so that at first sight it looks like an odd, rather tall table. This last is not, to me, notable for its aesthetic quality, but, like the play with attachments, it reminds us, by negation, of the force of the convention of attaching paintings to walls. In other works, the paint-image is constructed in such a way as to make visible reference to the underlying stretcher, or to the size of the brush and the amount of paint it will hold, and one large, particularly striking, canvas hangs so loosely from the wall that it bellies out like a sail filled with wind – a startling violation of our expectation that the canvas be stretched flat.[12]

One way of interpreting Ryman's work is that it 'dismantles' the 'vestiges' of modernist painting, revealing its 'essential arbitrariness'.[13] This type of interpretation was favoured by writers of a poststructuralist stripe, for whom everything was a matter of social conventions that were said to be, like Saussure's sign, 'arbitrary'. So Thierry de Duve, in his impressive *Kant after Duchamp*, debates Greenberg's ideas about the 'medium' of painting in terms of its conventions, completely ignoring the role that the materiality of the medium plays in the micrology of painterly practice, or, more generally, the way in which social conventions themselves evolve out of a dialectic between human action and the unpredictable materiality of the medium.[14] In sharp contrast, what Marioni learned from Ryman was not the arbitrariness and conventionality of it all but a heightened awareness of the material presence and functionality of every element of painting's material ensemble, *in terms of their potential for aesthetic impact.*

How Marioni does it

In Marioni's own work, it is the aesthetic dimension that is of prime importance, and if one did not know how important Ryman has been to this work, only the most acute observer would be able to guess it. Marioni is above all a colourist who draws the inspiration for his own distinctive project equally from the great Renaissance masters and the Abstract Expressionists. If Ryman has deconstructed the vestiges of modernism – as indeed he has – this, for Marioni, has not been the end of painting but a way to continue the work begun in the Renaissance in a new, and perhaps deeper, understanding of that work, one that has nothing to do with representation. For Marioni, the flattening of the picture plane has at last freed paint to do the work for which it was, from the beginning of the modern painting tradition in the late Middle Ages, destined, even as it traversed the long representational phase of its evolution: to reveal the nature of light. God is light, he has taken to saying. Marioni was raised a Catholic, and nothing could be more Catholic than this notion, which recalls the function of the rose windows in the great medieval cathedrals, and the 'light mysticism' that inspired them, of which the greatest monument is the *Paradiso* of Dante.

What Marioni learned from Ryman was how to take all the elements of the physical painting object into account in calculating the overall aesthetic effect. Over the years he has learned how to harmonize all these elements in his own paintings – how to make the support, as Fried has recently written, a receptacle that is just right for the painted colour that he will apply to it, such that the impression given by the painting will be 'of color fitting itself perfectly to its container'.[15] Fried has described Marioni's painting technique with great precision and sensitivity, and I refer the reader to him for a finer-grained discussion than I can provide here (or anywhere, for that matter). I will only briefly outline the main points. For Marioni every aspect of the physical body of the painting – its size and shape, the precise texture of the linen, how it is hung on the wall – is determined by the texture and colour of the paint that he will apply to it, because what he is making is, as he and Umberg wrote, a thing 'whose objectness is color'.

> Aristotle defines color as 'the limit of the translucent in a determinately bounded body'. This is a superb definition for the painter. It locates color within a material (even though it is, in Aristotle's concept, the outermost part of a thing) and it implies the limitation of its form as material. (p. 24)

All of the physical parts of which a Marioni is made are brought into unity by their subordination to the colour. Like Stella in his black paintings, Marioni avoids expressive marking, but the logic of paint application of the two painters is quite different. Whereas Stella drew in the lines, within which he then applied paint with a housepainter's brush, Marioni avoids drawing altogether because it's alien to the logic of paint. Everything about his technique is directed at allowing paint to do what paint can do, within the limits of a painting project of the modernist type, or that has evolved out of what the modernists did. Marioni applies his paint with a roller because this allows him to give partly unconstrained flow to the liquidity of the paint, which he applies from the top and 'pulls' down with the roller, guiding it perhaps halfway down and giving it as much freedom to flow the rest of the way as is consistent with the painter's intuitively conceived preconception of the final overall form at which he is aiming. One might think of these individual layers of paint, or 'skins', as Marioni calls them, as the basic unit out of which his paintings are made, producing a logic of making very different from that of a painting built up by individual brushstrokes. The final colour-image produced in this way arises out of the interplay of the various layers of paint, an interplay that Marioni has increasingly come to describe in terms of the level at which the painting captures the light. His paintings are, loosely speaking, monochromes, and usually have carried names like 'Green Painting' or 'Yellow Painting', but, as Fried explains:

> each layer of paint in a single painting differs from the others in hue, density, and transparency/translucency/opacity (though on rare instances two or more layers are more or less identical), so the term monochrome is to that extent a misnomer . . . nothing is more decisive for the final result than the choice of the individual layers; it is precisely Marioni's long experience in working with these materials that enables him to envisage in advance the way in which the different applications of paint will interact

> and bond in the course of making the picture, though of course the result is often somewhat surprising to him. (*Four Honest Outlaws*, p. 158)

From 'long experience': this is how Marioni, like any other artisan, has developed his feel for his materials.

When he first spoke to me about his relation to what he does and how he does it, I was perplexed. At that point in my thinking (in the 1980s) I had a much more 'formalistic' sense of techne than which is developed in this book, and when Marioni, in answer to my question, 'How do you know when the painting is right?' replied, 'When I feel that it's right,' I thought he was being naively romantic. It took me decades to realize the simple answer to my perplexity: that I was focusing on the 'feel' part of his answer and ignoring the 'it's right' part. A master artisan *feels* that a work is right when the work *is right*, where rightness is a matter of at least potential agreement in judgments by the relevant techne community (in the complex senses of community, and of agreement, defined at the end of Chapter 5), or a significant subset of such a community.[16]

Plato says in the *Republic* that each person must practice one techne and one techne only, and must do so as a lifelong devotion, if that one thing is to be done in a *kalos*, excellent or optimal, way. This might be an exaggeration, but it points in the right direction – and it characterizes Marioni's career as well as that of many other artisans of the type we call artists perfectly. This kind of devotion is the means by which, usually over a long period of time, the *historical* depth of the techne is absorbed by the individual artisan. Bellini is as much implicated in Marioni's colour-sense as is Rothko.

The body of light

We can now return to the question of how to deduce the 'essence' of painting from its materials, and centrally from paint. In the recent 'Footnote Number 6: Art and Objectness', Marioni has returned yet again to the flatness of the picture support, continuing his quest to define it functionally. We know that paintings are made on a flat support, but *why*, he asks, does the support *need* to be flat? In traditional representational painting it needs to be flat 'because the particulars of the illusion would be distorted on a three-dimensional object. Pictorial space needs a degree of flatness for clarity and full disclosure of the illusion.' But then, does this mean that 'the condition of flatness is merely something left over from the death of easel painting'? And in that case, why would radical/actualized paintings need flat supports?

If painters no longer need to create a perspective illusion of an image in space on a flat surface, what *function* does flatness now serve that makes it still necessary? When Greenberg rejected colour as an 'essential element specific to painting' because painting shared this element with sculpture and theatre, he treated colour as though it were an independent element in itself. In fact, however, colour is always embodied in what Marioni calls 'the paint medium', and in order properly to pursue the question of the nature of painting one must interrogate this material body of paint itself. After one has done this, one can pursue the question of the relation between this medium on the one hand and flatness and the delimitation of flatness on the other.

The 'paint medium' is not simply synonymous with 'paint'. Interrogating the material nature of paint, Marioni notes that it consists of two elements, the liquid 'paint medium' and the pigment. The function of the paint medium is to carry pigment and make it 'adhere to a surface'. But this is a subordinate function. The primary function, the function with which we at last touch on the central element around which all the other elements of actualized painting are organized, is that of the pigment that is carried by the liquid medium. This function is to 'divide light' by holding some wavelengths and reflecting back others, such that the light 'is revealed to us as color'. And now Marioni can explain why, although painting shares colour with sculpture and theatre, it has a function in painting that is specific to that art:

> A three-dimensional object reveals the direction of the light source by the shadow of its form. Its color is seen in relationship to the form and movement of the object, as in sculpture and theater. So the particulars of its color, and their understanding, are altered by the [three-]dimensionality and movement of the object the paint medium is attached to.
>
> Unlike a sculpted three-dimensional object, paintings, as two-dimensional entities in space, have a specific function for color. In relation to the flat plane, the pigmented medium is seen as an open membrane of divided light. The flat plane of painted color allows us to see the inner movement of the light itself. Light is the energy that activates the pigmented paint, and is the radical opticality of the painting.

In these lines, Greenberg's seminal argument, which he himself did not properly pursue, comes to maturity. Paint is shared with sculpture and theatre, but it has a different function, a function that can be reverse engineered from the function of its elements, the paint medium and – the central element in the entire ensemble – the pigment. The irreducible function of pigment is to divide white light into its constitutive colours, and the support is flat in order to allow the pigment to perform this function in the fullest way. 'So the painting is flat for visual clarity and full disclosure of its color', and the 'energy' that 'motivates' the coming-together in a specific form of the material complex constituting the painting, is light. Light is therefore, Marioni writes, 'in Aristotelian terms, the soul of the form'.[17]

> We are all immersed in light, most or all of our lives. Painting's delimitation is to see a particular moment of the light. So that, in the architecture of concrete painting, function follows light.
>
> The irreducible essence of the art of painting is its moment of light.

In his most recent writing, 'The Last Paintings of Karen Baumeister', an elegiac, unpublished meditation on Baumeister's work, Marioni has produced his fullest statement yet regarding actualized painting's relation to light.[18] Baumeister was a younger Philadelphia painter whose career as an exhibiting artist lasted little more than a decade (she started showing in 2004 and died in 2015), but in the last two years of her career she found her own way to make fully actualized paintings.

These late masterpieces are acrylic quasi-monochromes, as Marioni's are, but they present a quite different material aspect. The dry, paste-like paint lies flat against the canvas, and there is an immediate sense of intimacy because of the way the surface is worked with a delicate pattern of brushwork, which produces an overall sense of horizontality. The light is close in the paintings and they invite you to approach them. Marioni's paintings, by contrast, seem to float in front of the wall with a shiny, almost glass-like surface. There is a strong verticality to the surface of a Marioni, due to the downward flow of his fluid paint medium. The paintings seem to be reflecting the light as though it is hovering in front of the surface. There is no mistaking a Baumeister for a Marioni; but both are made for the same end. Both are, as Marioni says in 'The Last Paintings', 'a disciplined exercise of the materials brought to the forefront of our perception for the conscious seeing of their painted color'.

Marioni became aware of Baumeister's work only a few years before her death, but he quickly realized its importance:

> These paintings of Baumeister's fully acknowledge the material integrity of their being. They are not caught in the duality of the materials trying to represent something. Each element is there in an interconnected relationship to the gestalt of the painting as an object . . .
>
> Baumeister's placement of paint, with its soft pattern of brushwork, establishes a subtle visual texture that gives a location of the surface for the eye to focus on. All things being right with the materials and their placement, we are then allowed to look into the very heart of the painting – to see how it lives. If you stand still and focus on its painted surface, you can see the shift in its colors, each layer slightly different.
>
> Color is visible because pigment divides the light waves and reflects back certain waves that we usually identify as a color. That color can be presented in its full strength as a kind of portrait of its personality, with its emotional or psychological impact. *But Baumeister's is not this kind*

> *of peacock presentation standing alone in the world*. Her color is more internal to the medium. It is an intimate experience of a delicate moment of light. (italics added)

The italicized sentence vividly brings out the difference between the experience of one of Marioni's paintings and one of Baumeister's; Marioni refers to his own paintings as 'peacock presentation' of colour, and notes that Baumeister's colour is even more internal to the paint medium than his own.

> The light she reveals is not an impression of the light in her studio, nor the illusion of light seen elsewhere. It is the actual light of the moment of our seeing the painting . . . If you view the painting in the light of your noon day, what you will see is the life of that noon day sun . . . This is the kind of being the painting is. It provides a stage for a dance of light and gives a promise of another day . . .
>
> These last paintings of Karen Baumeister reflect the very essence of being: that we are all living creatures of the sun.

The function of actualized painting, thus, is to capture the actual light that falls on the painting at the moment it is being viewed, and to divide the light in the way that is specific to its particular layering of pigments, on a support that has been devised in such a way that it is experienced in its entirety as the body of the colour, which in turn is felt as this body's soul or form. To experience these paintings as they are made (or 'intended') to be experienced requires a new way of seeing, a way of seeing that only practice in looking at them can provide. In order to experience them in the fullest way, it helps to know what it is you're supposed be able to see, but the eye of anyone who has followed the adventure of modernist painting at least up through the Abstract Expressionists is poised to make the jump, as Fried recounts in *Four Honest Outlaws* that he himself immediately did when he saw Marioni's mid-career survey exhibition at the Rose Museum in Boston in 1998.

Marioni conceives the painter's task in modest, and at the same time exalted, terms – in something like the way the medieval monk's task in making a religious painting was both humble and exalted. And his work, along with that of Karen Baumeister, spectacularly demonstrates the depths of artisanal discovery to which the single-minded pursuit of one's techne – 'staying within the well done', as Rilke says – can lead.

All art is techne, but what makes actualized painting so strikingly rich for techne theory is that its techne is so immediately bound up with its materials, not only in the making process but also in the *thought* process by means of which the very idea of the work is developed. All painters must work out their ideas on canvas, of course, but the radical painter has jettisoned all concerns that are not bound up with the physical thereness of the painting as this thereness can be experienced by the trained and responsive eye. The radical painter does not only not think about representation, she also does not think about meanings or messages or cultural references or anything at all that does not have directly to do with colour and light and shape and form. For that reason, there is no better way to learn about art as techne than from a radical painter.

Intimate relations

We return here to the complex dual bearing of the analogy between a painting and a chair with which this chapter began, and to the underlying premise of this entire book, the fundamentality to social reality of the labour process. Materiality has not fared well in the world of sophisticated art theory or art criticism since poststructuralism/deconstruction, which turned everything, down to the human body itself, into a function of discourse. There was, indeed, much talk about the body, but in the end it always turned out to be a discursively constituted or 'socially inscribed' body, one in which the materiality of the body disappeared behind an impenetrable veil of semiosis.[19] Marioni, by contrast, talks about the body of his paintings as something real, to which the painter's own body (also real) has an *intimate relation*. The importance for Marioni of 'the artist's intimate working of material' ('Footnote 6') gives it an ethicopolitical resonance of great importance, one that takes us beyond the realm of modernist purism – at least as this purism is usually understood.

A high modernist painter working his paint is, from the techne standpoint, fundamentally and irreducibly, nothing more – *or less* – than a highly skilled manual worker, an 'illustrious artisan', in the term proposed by Dubos in 1709. This observation is both important and necessary because the intimacy of the relation between artist and material, already obfuscated by Romanticism, has become less and less important in the last half-century, to the point that the most famous 'artist' in the United States can sell paintings with his name on them for staggering sums, when he himself never lays a finger on them. Like Donald Trump with his buildings, the artist merely has the idea, attaches his name to the product and reaps the profits. But if the 'artist' does not do the work, *somebody* does, and, as it happens (but is this an accident?), the somebodies who make the specific work in question are paid and treated 'like serfs', as one of them recently testified – paid servant's wages to do excruciatingly detailed brushwork that has been reduced to a mechanical, paint-by-numbers task.[20]

The artisan in her workshop, making things, craft objects, and making them by intimate feel for the materials, a feel that has been educated deeply into her psyche-soma by long practice, is perhaps our final hold on some elemental humanity, rooted in the earliest origins of Homo sapiens, that we may be on the verge of evolving beyond – or may not. Either way, Marioni is a reminder of how such making can become a lifelong devotion, one that is capable of resisting the blandishments of the market, and this, to me, is the most important thing about his career, even more important than the greatness of his work itself. Or rather, it is what gives this greatness its full stature. An essential aspect of this is that Marioni, although in some ways his career reads like the standard popular narrative of the marginalized creator who cares for nothing but his art, has always thought of himself as participating in a *collective* enterprise, the unfolding by a subset of the community of painters of a new phase in the art of painting; hence he has always sought dialogue with other, especially younger, painters, and has made extraordinary efforts to foster the careers of some of them whose work he believes contributes to this development. His greatest ambition is not to become immortalized as a painting genius but for this community of painters to flourish, and for the line of investigation to which he has contributed so much to be continued and taken to new depths by future painters. All of this should be taken into account when one considers his search for the essence of painting in its materiality.

NOTES

1 Joseph Marioni and Günter Umberg, *Outside the Cartouche: Zur Frage des Betrachters in der radikalen Malerei* (Munich: Neue Kunst Verlag, 1986), pp. 23–4.

2 Clement Greenberg, 'After Abstract Expressionism', in *The Collected Essays and Criticism*, vol. 4: *Modernism with a Vengeance 1957–1969*, ed. John O'Brien (Chicago: University of Chicago Press, 1993), p. 131.

3 Michael Fried, *Three American Painters: Kenneth Noland, Jules Olitski, Frank Stella* (Cambridge, MA: Fogg Art Museum, 1965), p. 6.

4 Joseph Marioni, 'Footnote Number 6: Art and Objectness', 17 July 2017, unnumbered pages, https://nonsite.org/article/footnote-number-6-art-and-objectness.

5 Quoted by Sauer in Christel Sauer and Urs Rausmüller (eds), *Robert Ryman*, catalog for Ryman exhibition in the Espace d'Art Contemporain (1991), p. 31.

6 T. J. Clark, *Picasso and Truth* (Princeton, NJ: Princeton University Press, 2013), p. 70.

7 Donald Judd, 'Local History', in *Complete Writings 1959–1975* (Halifax: Press of the Nova Scotia College of Art and Design, 1875), p. 181.

8 Donald Judd, 'In the Galleries', in *Complete Writings 1959–1975* (Halifax: Press of the Nova Scotia College of Art and Design, 1875), p. 91.

9 Boris Tomashevsky, "Thematics," in *Russian Formalist Criticism*, trans. Lee T. Lemon and Marion J. Reis (Lincoln, Neb.: Nebraska University Press, 1965), pp. 94–5.

10 It's not quite accurate to say Ryman paints only in white, but close enough. For a more nuanced account, see Suzanne Hudson, 'Robert Ryman's Pragmatism', *October* (Winter 2007) 119: 217–38.

11 Quoted in Sauer and Rausmüller, p. 31.

12 I had seen a lot of Ryman before, but somehow seeing this bellying canvas was an epiphanic moment for me in my understanding of his work. It raised my consciousness of the convention-informed physical presence of paintings – all paintings – to a new level.

13 These are the words Suzanne Hudson uses in Robert 'Ryman's Pragmatism' (p. 128) to describe Yves-Alain Bois's view of Ryman's work .

14 Thierry de Duve, *Kant after Duchamp* (Cambridge, MA: MIT Press, 1996). I discuss this book in detail in an article, 'Clement Greenberg, Radical Painting, and the Logic of Modernism', *Angelaki: Journal of the Theoretical Humanities* (special issue, Aesthetics and the Ends of Art) (April 2002): 73–88.

15 Michael Fried, *Four Honest Outlaws: Sala, Ray, Marioni, Gordon* (New Haven, CT: Yale University Press, 2011), p. 159.

16 A fine new documentary video by Joseph de Francesco shows the stages through which Marioni makes a painting, and explains, with closeups of the paintings, how the paint is layered. See https://vimeo.com/278926126.

17 This is a slightly unorthodox formulation, but not unjustifiable. For Aristotle the soul *is* a form, the form of living things (see Chapter 5). But nonliving things have forms, yet lack life, so one might think of the form of living things as itself 'ensouled'. Marioni clearly means to indicate that he thinks of an actualized painting as alive in this sense, which is not 'organic' in the Romantic sense but, rather, in its original Greek sense.

18 Marioni wrote this unpublished essay for a joint exhibition of his work and Baumeister's held in the year 2018 at Larry Becker Contemporary Art in Philadelphia.

19 Of course the body is always 'socially inscribed'. The very neurons of our brain are socially inscribed. But this does not happen flatly in the socialization process of the individual; we have barely scraped the surface of what 'social inscription' means when we think of it as 'socially constructed', in terms of such concepts as Althusserian interpellation or Foucaultian discipline. Rather, it has happened across tens of thousands of years of the co-evolution of the human body and human society, a co-evolution that is itself inscribed in return by the environing natural 'taskscape' within which, and in dialectical interaction with which, this evolution occurs.

20 www.nytimes.com/2012/08/19/magazine/i-was-jeff-koonss-studio-serf.html (accessed 3 April 2018). See also https://news.artnet.com/art-world/jeff-koons-radically-downsizes-his-studio-laying-off-half-his-painting-staff-998666.

CHAPTER ELEVEN

The techne of Kafka's *Metamorphosis*

This disparity between the underlying structure of impossibility and the wealth of atrociously detailed facts makes for the uncanny disturbance at the center of the story.
– Stanley Corngold

The project: to read the *Metamorphosis* as an artefact, made out of the linguistic materials, and by the literary techniques, available to Kafka at the moment in literary history when he wrote. To read it in such a way as to account for the experience of the reader across the temporal unfolding of the text – beginning, middle and end – as this experience is shaped, moment by moment, by the overall design of the artefact. In order to do this we must resist the critic's almost irresistible urge to interpret, to go straight for the mirage of 'meaning'. Even the best interpretation of 'meaning' articulates only a residuum of the experience of reading and implies that this experience, as shaped by the texture and topology of the experienced text, is fundamentally irrelevant – that what really matters is the big fish that remain in its interpretive net after all the smaller ones have fallen through.

What follows, then, is not an interpretation, in the sense that it doesn't try to reveal the 'meaning' of the text, but, rather, the way the text creates effects – emotional, imaginative and intellectual – by means of a system of interacting devices, in something like the way a Marioni or Baumeister painting creates effects of light by the layering of pigments, or the way a musical piece creates effects by the interweaving of tones and rhythms.

Looking at this narrative in terms of how it's made, the most striking features are these:

- This strangest of all canonical fictions has the plot of a conventional realist narrative, one that would be at home in Balzac: a bourgeois family that has already descended a full rung in the social scale, as a consequence of the father's business failure, now struggles with the threat of actual poverty because its new breadwinner has become incapacitated and can no longer work. The importance of this conventional realist matrix is obscured from the outset by the fantastic nature of Gregor's incapacitation, but this grotesquery is inserted into the plot structure in a way that minimally disturbs the structure's conventional syntax. The primary plot function of Gregor's metamorphosis is no different from that played by illness, accident or an expensive vice in a realist text: to cause economic problems. Underlying this realist matrix is an even more profoundly conventional plot structure, one that goes all the way back to Aristotle's *Poetics*: a steady 'rising action' that comes to a climax, resolves and has a 'happy ending' for the survivors.
- Gregor's metamorphosis is insensibly 'naturalized' by the texture or style of the language in which the plot is developed (Corngold's 'atrociously detailed facts'), which is also predominantly realist. Gregor's own thoughts and perceptions are the vehicle of this naturalization, because he reacts to his bizarre change with calm, turning his thoughts immediately, and in great detail, to the anxieties of his work life – above all, the immediate need to get to the office so that he can avoid the persecution he anticipates from his superiors. His family, too, after absorbing the initial shock, turns its attention entirely to the practicalities of their new plight. Then, in the second and third parts, the narrative presents a quite plausibly realistic account of the psychological fraying of Gregor's nerves and those of his family, especially his sister, under the stress of their new situation. The result is a sort of lunatic realism, in which we track the decay of Gregor's complex human interiority as the crisis wears on – as though Kafka were some deranged naturalist who carries forward Zola's project into realms undreamt of by Zola, *The Metamorphosis* the mutant offspring of *Therese Raquin*. We can imagine this deranged naturalist saying, 'Let us study scientifically what the effects would be, on the mind of a more or less normal human being, of a sudden and unaccountable transformation into a monstrous vermin, one that throws his family into financial crisis.'[1]
- Thus in Chapter 3, when everyone's nerves are beginning to fray, and Gregor becomes resentful that his sister Grete no longer cleans his room adequately, his aged and ailing mother mops it; but the dampness irritates Gregor and in response he lies 'sour and immobile' on the coach; however, 'his mother's punishment was not long in coming', in the form of Grete's angry reproaches to her

mother for usurping the young girl's role of caretaker to Gregor.[2] He is resentful towards his mother for cleaning his room and also towards Grete for *not* cleaning it; and he callously judges that his poor asthmatic mother, who has worked so hard to clean his room, is being justly punished for having inadvertently made him uncomfortable. This is pure psychological realism, skilfully done; the stress is making the considerate Gregor more selfish and immature. But what then? How are we to judge a selfish and immature *bug?*

- The deranged naturalism of this story is conveyed by a narratorial instance that never manifests any awareness of the strangeness of what it is narrating. Yet what is narrated, which is grotesque to begin with, regularly becomes openly parodic or comic. The openly comic note is struck near the beginning by Gregor's mental description of his boss sitting on some inconceivably tall desk around which his employees gather to hear him speak, while he must bend down to hear them because he is hard of hearing, and later (among other instances) by Gregor's gambols on, and falls from, the ceiling; by the three visually indistinguishable bearded boarders who move about the Samsa apartment almost as a single entity; and by the truly inspired depiction of the bony cleaning woman with the feathered hat, who is the most vividly pictured character in the story.
- These openly parodic or comic effects are a form of 'laying bare of the device' at the level of the design of the entire narrative, because they show that the naturalizing power of the straight-faced realism that predominates has to be considered as an element in a more comprehensive design. As naturalized in the text, and especially in light of Gregor's death, his plight generates considerable pathos, enough to suggest that the grotesque elements should be taken seriously, as having some symbolic or allegorical sense; yet the openly comic elements open up a radically opposed way of taking the narrative, one that is difficult to reconcile with the pathos. The force of these elements is typically minimized by interpretations that stress the tragic-existential aspect of the story; tracing the formal design of the story as a whole, however, reveals how tightly the comic moments are woven into the narrative, in a way that makes them *structural* to it in a way that I will try to explain.

The narrative voice

Put crudely, then: on one side, *The Metamorphosis* invites us to suffer with Gregor, and on the other side, it invites us to laugh at him; and the division between these two sides corresponds pretty neatly to that between the *interior* and the *exterior* narration. Seen from the outside, Gregor is repellent, even disgusting, and his interactions with others tend towards a grotesque kind of slapstick; seen from the perspective of Gregor's inner experience, he remains human, feelingful, trapped in a suffering that is only accentuated by the indignity of its outward manifestations. But because the narration, up until Gregor's death, keeps us mostly within the latter perspective, it magnifies his pathos while diminishing the force of the exterior view.

In order to understand the overall design within which this play of inside and outside takes place, we must be minutely aware of two technical devices by which the narratorial voice conveys Gregor's interiority.

First, from the beginning, narratorial description 'focalizes' through Gregor's perception as he feels his hard back and sees his many little legs waving in front of his eyes, then looks around his room, focusing in particular on the remarkable picture of the woman in furs (another comic note, the full force of which doesn't emerge until later), her right hand immersed in a fur muff that, for some indiscernible reason, she 'holds up to the viewer'. Since Gregor is confined to his room, and, for brief spells to the space immediately adjacent, this rule restricts the power of the nominally 'omniscient' narrator in a peculiarly tight way that can, if the reader is aware of it, make the reading experience feel distinctly claustrophobic. We see and hear only what Gregor sees and hears, and what he can deduce from his perceptions.

Second, the narrator at times uses the style commonly known as 'free indirect', but which Dorritt Cohn has more precisely analysed as 'narrated interior monologue' ('narrated monologue' for short), to transmit the flow of thought and feeling within Gregor.[3] This technique can be used innocently, or, as we know since Jane Austen's *Emma*, it can be designed to obscure the utterance source, making it unclear who is speaking at a given moment, the narrator or the fictional person. As we will see, the designer of *The Metamorphosis* skilfully exploits this ambiguity at crucial moments in the story.

The question of the utterance source is of fundamental importance in the realist text because it concerns the authority of the speaker. If it's a fictional character who speaks, then what is said might or might not be true; but if the narrator says something is objectively the case, then, unless something in the design of the text warns us otherwise, it is true by definition. If the narrating voice reports a picture of a woman in furs on the wall, or the words that pass through Gregor's mind, we must – absent indications to the contrary – accept these reports as 'facts' constitutive of the fictional world we are entering.

But the narratorial voice performs a second function in which its authority is not absolute: it depicts the moral framework of its fictional world. This kind of authority can be exercised implicitly or explicitly. In its implicit exercise, it is interwoven with that of the first, report-of-the-facts function, because the reportorial function paints the portrait of the characters for us, and this in itself is the primary determinant of the moral contours of a fictional world. Thus Gregor is depicted as a generous, self-sacrificing, warm-hearted character, somewhat of a fool – a kind of surreal Candide; his father as cold and distant, quickly roused to aggressive exercise of authority over his son. These characterizations, presented as the facts of who these people are, are shaped in ways that guide the reader's sympathies, without any need of explicit judgments from the narrator. By the very nature of human character, such implicit moral shaping is inevitable in fiction. Only in melodrama is it a matter of good and evil; character has a thousand moral shadings, and it is the great triumph of realist fiction that it has so extensively explored them. But these depictions are not always entirely convincing, so even this implicitly exercised moral authority is not absolute.

Explicit moral judgment by the narrative voice is not inevitable, and as the moral consensus of European society decayed in the second half of the nineteenth century, advanced fiction increasingly abjured it. The banishing of the 'intrusive narrator' of older fiction by Flaubert has been generally admired as a technical advance, one that enabled fiction to capture the real complexity and moral ambiguity of human existence. *The Metamorphosis* represents one variation on this theme of 'effacement of the narrator', carried out, in this case, in large part by the combination of tight focalization through Gregor and narrated interior monologue. The narrator does intrusively comment at one point in the story, as we will see, but for the most part the moral colouring of things is seen through Gregor's eyes. However, the use of narrated monologue at times make it hard to tell who is speaking, with crucial consequences for the dynamics of Kafka's prose.

Gregor's voice, or narrator's voice?

The distinguishing marks of narrated monologue are visible in the following passage, a few paragraphs into the story, in which the technique first appears. Gregor, still lying in bed, has just finished his opening reflections on the gruelling nature of his job, and looks over at the alarm clock:

> 'God Almighty', he thought. It was six thirty, the hands were quietly moving forward, it was actually past the half-hour, it was already nearly a quarter to. Could it be that the alarm hadn't gone off? You could see from the bed that it was correctly set for four o'clock; it had gone off, too. Yes, but was it possible to sleep quietly through a ringing that made the furniture shake? Well, he certainly hadn't slept quietly, but probably all the more soundly for that. But what should he do now? (p. 4)

The narrator has from the outset been focalizing through Gregor, but up to the first sentence of this quotation the narrating voice and Gregor's have been clearly distinguished by devices like quotation marks and tags like 'he thought' that indicate the utterance source. In the second sentence, however, these devices disappear, and Gregor's thought is reported in the past tense of narration, not the present in which the character would presumably think ('it *is* six thirty'). Yet the lack of certainty regarding the objective situation, together with the breakup of the sentence into a series of short clauses separated by commas, indicate clearly that we are in Gregor's consciousness, and that the thought is being expressed in something approaching Gregor's own words. What we are hearing here is Gregor's internal deliberation, as it happens, over the alarm clock question – a sort of 'stream of consciousness' of a type different from the one we associate with *Ulysses*.

The sixth and seventh sentences add the crucial shift characterizing narrated monologue, from the first person in which Gregor would think these thoughts to the third person of narratorial discourse. 'He' hadn't slept quietly; what should 'he' do now? The changes in tense and person, together with the elimination of speech tags and quotation marks, blend narratorial and figural voices seamlessly together. Yet that we are still in the flow of Gregor's internal speech is indicated by subtly colloquial indicators like the 'well' with which the sixth sentence begins, as well as by the subsequent 'certainly' that indicates the lack of cognitive privilege of the observation. These sentences come in the flow of the preceding narrated monologue and clearly continue to transmit Gregor's internal deliberation in a way that is almost citational, yet because of the shift to the third person it seems to be the narrator who is reporting that Gregor had not slept quietly and asking what he should do. In the second paragraph of the story the narrator has said authoritatively of Gregor's awakening in a new body that 'It was no dream', and it's hard to shake the feeling that 'he certainly hadn't slept quietly' in some way partakes of the same authority (although it doesn't). This is Gregor's inner speech, yet the narrator is still audibly present. Are we to take what is said as authoritative or not? It doesn't much matter whether Gregor slept soundly or not, so the ambiguity here is not significant in itself, but this passage shows how subtly narrated monologue can weave the flow of a character's thoughts into the voice of the narrating instance, in a way the unwary reader might not notice.

Gregor and his family

The main effect of the funnelling of the narration through Gregor's subjectivity is to heighten the pathos of Gregor's situation, while throwing that of his family into the background; and this effect creates the conditions under which the use of narrated monologue at certain crucial moments becomes important.

Not that it's only the style of the narration that makes Gregor seem pathetic; he is objectively the victim of an oppressive socioeconomic system. The office, the boss, the horrible life of the traveling salesman and, for a more penetrating reading, the entire social system that demands that he support his family at the level of a certain petit bourgeois respectability. He can also, though less justifiably, be seen as a victim of economic exploitation by his family, in particular by his father, who has secretly withheld money from Gregor's salary, thereby increasing the term of his servitude at the office while he pays back the debts incurred by Mr. Samsa when his business failed. Then, there is a dimension of apparently gratuitous violence in the father's treatment of Gregor: at the end of Chapter 1 he drives Gregor back into his room 'hissing like a wild man', with a voice that 'did not sound like that of a single father'. This makes the father seem like a representation of the punishing Father-in-general, the Father-principle, violently aggressive in its essence, pitiless towards the suffering son. Biographically inclined readers magnify the significance of this moment by bringing in Kafka's relation to his own father; but even without this, the fact that Chapter 2 also culminates in a scene of paternal aggression against Gregor, combined with the mock-militarism of the messenger's uniform Mr Samsa is now wearing, formally foregrounds this aggression in a way that cannot be missed. Finally, the sister's climactic speech declaring that the creature in the next room is 'no longer Gregor' and must be gotten rid of, together with the disposal of his remains by the maid without the ceremony of a funeral, all together present a picture of general heartlessness towards him.

Closer reading of the story reveals that this picture of familial heartlessness is somewhat overdrawn, but the narrative is clearly structured in such a way as to heighten Gregor's suffering for the reader by throwing that of the family into soft focus. The most important aspect of this is the way Gregor's horrific physical transformation is presented. Every inhuman detail is described, including the various disgusting effluvia that flow from his body, but these descriptions are presented either through the deadpan report of the narrator or through Gregor's eyes, which view them with placid acceptance. When Gregor notices such things as the brown liquid that flows from his injured jaws as he uses them to turn the key of his door, he doesn't find them disturbing; and subsequently he even begins to take pleasure in his new bug faculties. We see, through his eyes, that the people around him are horrified, but we aren't privy to their felt experience, only to Gregor's suffering at the realization that he repels them; and from his innocent standpoint their reactions seem callous.

A good example of how the narration 'spins' the facts of the situation in this way is the passage in which Grete comes into his room the morning after his change, to check on how he has dealt with the food she left him the day before. Notice how the passage tends to slip into narrated monologue, at the end in a way that ceases even to bear the technical marks identified by Cohn, yet is clearly channelling Gregor's consciousness through the narrator's voice. I have italicized the words that are switched into narrated interior monologue:

> She did not see him right away, but when she caught sight of him under the couch – *God, he had to be somewhere, he couldn't just fly away* – she became so frightened that she lost control of herself and slammed the door shut again. But, as if she felt sorry for her behavior, she immediately opened the door again and came in on tiptoe, as if she had been visiting someone seriously ill or perhaps even a stranger. Gregor had pushed his head forward just to the edge of the couch and was watching her. *Would she notice that he had left the food standing, and not because he hadn't been hungry, and would she bring in something better?*
>
> . . . But he would never have been able to guess what his sister, in the goodness of her heart, actually did. To find out his likes and dislikes, she brought him a wide assortment of things, all spread out on an old newspaper; old, half rotten vegetables . . . *And out of a sense of delicacy, since she knew that Gregor would not eat in front of her, she left hurriedly and even turned the key, just so that Gregor should know that he might make himself as comfortable as he wanted.* (pp. 17–18)

The final sentence doesn't bear the characteristic marks of narrated monologue. It is stylistically indistinguishable from authoritative narratorial report; yet it quickly becomes apparent that there's nothing authoritative about it, and that the meaning of her hurried departure is not what Gregor takes it to be. The sentence in question is revealed to be the expression of a naïve attempt by Gregor to put his sister's motive in the best light when shortly afterword he learns the real meaning of Grete's hurried departure:

> In time, Gregor, too, saw things much more clearly. Even the way she came in was terrible for him. Hardly had she entered the room than she would run straight to the window . . . then tear open the casements with eager hands, almost as if she were suffocating, and remain for a little while at the window even in the coldest weather, breathing deeply. (p. 22)

In fact, Grete truly is trying hard to take care of the monstrous creature in the next room, but her goodness is overshadowed in the narration by the way her behaviour impacts Gregor, whose vulnerability, naiveté and good-heartedness are highlighted. This is a formerly pampered sixteen-year-old girl who has voluntarily taken upon herself the care of a horrifying, languageless creature, to whose humanity she has no access; yet, by the way this passage is narrated, the nausea that the close atmosphere in the creature's room causes her takes on the aspect of insensitivity towards Gregor.[4]

The way the story is told, thus, highlights the impression of Gregor as a gentle, suffering thing, and even, as the apparent allusion to the passion of Christ in the description of his final moments indicates, a sacrificial victim. This and other hints of symbolism have spawned a host of allegorizing readings that take his story with the utmost seriousness, and for which the slimy tracks Gregor's feet leave on the walls and ceiling, his taste for rotten food, the sudden, automatic, activation of his jaws or feet by external stimuli – in a way that shows his new insect-body gradually taking over his human consciousness – are vaguely understood as stigmata of sorts, signs of the disfigurement and devaluation of a human being by others, and, consequently, in his own experience of himself.

But consider in context some of these purportedly symbolic elements. Critics take for granted that the apple that Gregor's father throws at him at the end of Chapter 2, and which lodges painfully in his back, is an allusion to the forbidden fruit eaten by Adam and Eve; yet the story puts in play not just one apple but a bowl full of them, 'little' apples that Gregor's father has taken from a distinctly petit-bourgeois 'fruit bowl on the buffet' and with which he has 'filled his pockets', and which, after being 'lightly' thrown, seem to roll around on the floor like cartoon animations, 'as if electrified, clicking into each other'. The diminutive size and multiplicity of the apples and the whimsical depiction of their motion on the floor draw attention – even Gregor's – away from the supposed pathos of his persecution by the father; and the fact that the pursuit is said to be slow, and that at this slow-motion pace they circle the room several times before Gregor finally gets through his bedroom door, also throw the narration of this moment off-key from the tone that symbolic reading requires. Any allusion to the fruit of the Fall here would have to be parodic, on the same plane of the story as the bony maid with the feathered hat. Yet none of this has deterred readers from taking the fatal apple in its most tragic-existential resonance.

Another purportedly symbolic element is the father who hisses 'like a hundred fathers' as he pursues Gregor at the end of Chapter 1 (the same terrible father who, on entering the apartment at the end of Chapter 2, first, almost jauntily, throws his cap across the room onto the couch, and then throws *little* apples *softly* at Gregor). This figure is deflated when we remember that the perception of this hissing is focalized through Gregor, a fact the significance of which becomes apparent, when we learn that Gregor's senses become preternaturally heightened at times, to the point of being assaulted by perfectly normal household noises. He becomes overwhelmed by the 'coming and going' of his mother and sister from his room as they remove his furniture, their 'little calls to each other' and the scraping of the furniture on the floor having the effect on him 'of a great turmoil swelling on all sides' (p. 26). Recall too, in this connection, the truly very funny reflection by Gregor on the 'gigantic size' of the soles of his father's boots when Mr Samsa first approaches him in the second persecution scene, a reflection that reminds us of Gregor's physical point of view as a bug, his head very low to the floor.

What has Gregor, in fact, become, considered apart from the sentimental framing of him as innocent victim? Has he become, as Mark Anderson in one of the most brilliant allegorical readings of *The Metamorphosis* has it, 'an unself-conscious child-animal', such that the new motions that drive his bug-body represent 'an almost musical rhythm'? Does Gregor become a figure of the artist, one whose body itself has been transformed into 'the vehicle of his art?'.[5] On this interpretation, Gregor's pleasure in freely running around the walls and ceiling shows his impulse to aesthetic play, while his refusal of food and the drying and thinning of his body represent its etherealization and spiritualization.

In fact, this reading too is an artifact of the sentimental framing, made viable only by ignoring or minimizing the insistently comic-grotesque elements of the story and the off-key use of the narratorial voice. To describe what Gregor becomes as a 'child-animal', innocent, playful and creative, is to ignore what we are told in the very first sentence of the story, that he has become an *ungeheuren Ungeziefer*, a 'monstrous vermin' in Corngold's translation. Gregor descends not towards innocent animality like that of a young mammal but towards an instinctual automaticity like that of an insect, one that bypasses Gregor's subjectivity and increasingly determines it. When he first feels his legs on the floor under him, we are told that 'they obeyed him completely', but this appears to be an overstatement, perhaps expressing Gregor's misperception, because the autonomy of instinctual mechanism is indicated immediately afterward by the way 'he could not resist snapping his jaws several times in the air' at the sight of the coffee his mother has spilled (p. 14). And the real nature of his physical activity becomes increasingly manifest when at the end of Chapter 2 he pointlessly runs around the walls and ceiling in distress at his mother's fainting fit, and then plops down onto the middle of the dining table, where he lies until his father's return (one of the most grotesquely comic moments in the story), or when in Chapter 3 the bony cleaning woman suddenly opens his door, taking Gregor by surprise, and he begins, cockroach-like, 'to race back and forth although no one was chasing him' (p. 33). Gregor may enjoy it, but it is as an instinct-driven *Ungeziefer*, not as a child-animal, that he does so.

The 'bugginess' of his body gradually invades his interiority, expressing itself not only as his pleasure in its muscular motions but as his increasingly aggressive urges towards the other family members. This tendency can be seen in his readiness, near the end of Chapter 2, when he climbs onto the wall to protect with his body the picture of the lady in furs, to fly in his sister's face if she should try to remove it; and when, in Chapter 3, he becomes angry and resentful at his family and contemplates raiding the pantry to 'take what is his' even though he has no desire for food. Seen coldly, from the outside, the outbursts of violence from his father are a normal response on the part of someone who has no window onto Gregor's subjectivity, who sees only the monstrous vermin, to Gregor's attempts to invade the living space of the family; and the aggressive intention that the father sees in these attempts is one that becomes increasingly real, culminating in Gregor's incestuous fantasy in Chapter 3.

The judgment

All of this is narrated by a voice that isn't what on the surface it seems to be, the generic 'omniscient narrator' of realist fiction. Everything about this story tells us that this narration is crafted, not to create the illusion of a narrating human voice in the standard realist way, but to be subtly, disquietingly, off, to be missing something we're accustomed to hearing in a fully human voice.

The narrating voice of *The Metamorphosis*, which is almost entirely put at the service of Gregor's consciousness for the first two chapters of the story, makes itself prominently visible only once, a few pages into Chapter 3, but it does so in a way that, for this strangest of narratives, is truly remarkable: by momentarily performing the classic function of the intrusive realist narrator, that of moral arbiter who invokes an objective moral standard. 'Who in this overworked and exhausted family had time to worry about Gregor more than was absolutely necessary?' the narrative voice rhetorically asks. With this question, the narrator for the first and only time explicitly invokes an extratextual moral norm, explicitly taking the side of the family – and just when Gregor is starting to become resentful of his treatment. The narrating instance here raises itself out of the flow of Gregor's experience, appealing directly to the reader in a way that assumes a fixed framework of moral judgment common to narrator, audience, and family. This framework is even given a name at the beginning of Chapter 3; it is 'the commandment of family duty' of which the family is said to have been reminded by the wound the apple has inflicted on Gregor. The narrator's rhetorical question implies narratorial awareness that the reader might blame the family for its growing neglect of Gregor, as the spinning of the narration in his favour has invited us to do, and that therefore the family's treatment of him requires explanation and justification: the family is doing only the 'absolutely necessary', because it is 'overworked and exhausted'. A long account follows, detailing the travails of the other three family members, which are summarized as follows:

> What the world demands of poor people, they did to the utmost of their ability; his father brought breakfast for the minor officials at the bank, his mother sacrificed herself to the underwear of strangers, his sister ran back and forth behind the counter at the request of customers; but for anything more than this they did not have the strength. (p. 31)

This is the point at which the question of the moral authority of the voice that is speaking becomes important. Is it truly the narrator who is defending the family, or is the narratorial voice once again coloured by Gregor's sentimental view of them? In the earlier passage about Grete's motives in locking Gregor's door, as we saw, there were no stylistic marks indicating focalization through Gregor, yet the narratorial voice was infected with his consciousness. At this point, however, Gregor is losing patience with the family, and the lack of consonance between his present mood and the narrator's moral judgment suggests that the narratorial consciousness is indeed exerting moral authority.

For whatever that is worth.

For the thorough conventionality of the moral standard invoked – one which, conventional or not, would seem acceptable to all but the most cynical of readers – masks the resolute tone-deafness of the narrating instance's implied judgment, as well as the impoverished character of its moral purview, which reduces the moral world to its barest domestic outlines as the question of the care and feeding of Gregor, while blandly taking for granted the bizarre notion (at this point still shared by Gregor and his family) that Gregor is *still a member of the family* in the usual sense, and that therefore the normal moral rules apply. There is no awareness here of the monstrousness of the situation, of the extremity of the change that has overtaken Gregor, of the isolation that being unable to speak is causing him, or of the agony of the family over his transformation – and certainly no sense of the questions regarding larger social forces, or of the tragic-existential dimension of human existence, in which critics have been so interested. What we have in the narrator's rhetorical question is an astonishing parody of the realist narrator, the narratorial voice ploughing stolidly ahead, blinkered against circumstances to which its moralism is radically inadequate.

Structurally, the narrator's question marks the beginning of the story's turn towards its denouement, in which Gregor is dead and the family looks towards a new beginning – a strictly *comic* ending in the bluntest generic sense of the term, according to which comedy is above all deaf to the tragic-existential pathos of the individual. While this story does not end in a marriage, as the traditional rules of the comic genre dictate, it ends in the strong prospect of one. At the structural level, thus, the narrator's question is carried in the underlying comic-grotesque current of the story's flow. It invites us to begin shifting our sympathies from Gregor to the family (which in fact becomes the exclusive focus of attention after his death), to begin attuning ourselves to the 'upward' movement of comedy that will issue in a happy ending for the family.

It also for the first time fully lays bare the artifice of the story's design, making starkly apparent the split between the narratorial voice and the design-cunning behind it, which does not show itself as a voice at all, and which clearly has ends that have nothing to do with the narrator's conventional moralism.

The unknown nourishment

We need to be fully aware of this split in order to understand the extraordinary, and perhaps unprecedented, art of the story's climax in

Chapter 3, when the three bearded boarders ask for Grete to play the violin where they can properly hear it, and Gregor creeps out of his room to join the audience. Here is where the question 'who is speaking?' assumes critical importance for the reading of this narrative, the point at which its use of narrated interior monologue becomes most consequential.

The boarders very quickly become unhappy with the quality of Grete's playing and openly display their dissatisfaction. Gregor, by contrast, is enchanted with the music, by which he feels himself raised to a previously unknown level of sublimity; consequently, he becomes angry at the boarders for their negative reaction, and fantasizes that he will carry Grete off to his room and guard her there in perpetuity, protecting her against all comers.

At the climax of his musical rapture, we read this:

> Was he an animal, that music could move him so? He felt as though the way to the unknown nourishment he longed for were coming to light. (p. 36)

These astonishing lines attain a level of sublimity not previously glimpsed in the story, and are the strongest evidence for the reading of Gregor as figure of the artist, or at least of the impulse to art – but only if we read them out of context. In that case, the 'unknown nourishment' can be understood as some spiritual or intellectual sustenance of the kind that beautiful music can supply. But everything turns on the question of *how well his sister is actually playing*, and there is strong reason to believe that Gregor's exaltation is in response to bad, or at best mediocre, violin playing.

The indications are subtle but decisive. We have learned very early in the narrative that Gregor is not a music-lover; the three boarders, by contrast, clearly are attracted to music, and not only are they attracted, but we know that they are musically trained from the fact that all three situate themselves immediately behind her in order to follow the score as she plays. When they begin to show their dissatisfaction with the music, the narratorial voice says 'And yet his sister was playing so beautifully', and here is where the question 'who is speaking?' becomes acute, because if it's the narrator, Grete is definitely playing well, but if it's Gregor, then maybe not. And if this is narrated interior monologue, as indeed it is, then it's Gregor who thinks it – Gregor who we've been informed is not a music lover (p. 20). Anderson says that the boarders' lack of appreciation of the music shows them to be philistines, but he has it backwards. It's clearly the Samsas, Gregor included, who are the philistines, as we know from the fact that the only 'art' on their walls is a framed magazine photograph (probably an ad), and the only expression of their aesthetic taste in the story is Mrs. Samsa's comment to Gregor's boss about how pretty the frame is that Gregor has made for that photograph. Gregor's lack of appreciation of music is another index of the family's cultural level, and there is no indication that Grete's violin playing itself somehow transcends this level, other than the reaction of a bug whose musical taste we have no reason to trust. The boarders may be comical, cardboard cutout, figures, but they have to know quite a bit about music – more than most people know, certainly – to be able to enhance their enjoyment of it by following the score while Grete plays. There is no other reason for Kafka to have included this surprising detail other than to contrast their interest in music, and their knowledge of it, with Gregor's lack of same.

At this moment, then, the abject, grimy, cockroach-man, the one whose idea of art is a framed magazine picture, and who is spiralling towards ignominious death, followed by burial in the garbage bin, is listening to violin playing of dubious quality, and hearing it as sublimely beautiful, full of indignation towards the boarders for their lack of appreciation. Because this amazing scene is the setting of Gregor's climactic self-interrogation, the question 'Was he an animal, that music could move him so?' is endlessly mordant in its irony. At the formal level, one notices that it's a redo of the only other question he asks about the effect his metamorphosis is having on his humanity, when, near the beginning of Chapter 2, he first discovers his enjoyment of rotting food and asks himself (in narrated monologue) 'Was he becoming less sensitive?' There is nothing to parse about that first question; but it sets up the strangeness of the second question, which suggests that the original descent towards subhuman animality has been reversed by starvation into an ascent to sublime spirituality: 'He felt as though the way to the unknown nourishment he longed for were coming to light.'

But the sublimity of the key lines is mercilessly undermined by the irony of the narrative design. If we take these lines at face value, if we accept Gregor's own testimony that his sister is playing beautifully, and that he is having a genuinely sublime experience – that what he has attained is not merely a grotesque bug-sublimity, his 'unknown nourishment' not merely more bad art – then the immediate transition to his incestuous fantasy about his sister becomes jarring, unmotivated. Whereas, understood at their full parodic value, these lines come in the flow of events, bridging the transition from his crawling out where the boarders can see him, in full awareness that he is dust-covered and carries about 'on his back and along his sides fluff and hairs and scraps of food' and knowing how little consideration he is showing to the others, to the astonishing fantasy itself. Immediately after his musical epiphany we find out what the emotions are to which the music, which moves him so, has moved him. He will, he thinks (in narrated monologue), crawl to Grete, pluck at her skirt, and ask her to bring her violin with her to his room:

> He would never again let her out of his room – at least not for as long as he lived; for once, his nightmarish looks would be of use to him; he would be at all the doors of his room at once, hissing and spitting at the aggressors; his sister, however, would not be forced to stay with him, but would do so of her own free will; she should sit next to him on the couch,

> bending her ear down to him, and then he would confide to her that he had had the firm intention of sending her to the Conservatory . . . After this declaration, his sister would break into tears of emotion, and Gregor would raise himself up to her shoulder and kiss her on the neck, which ever since she went out to work she kept bare, without a ribbon or collar. (p. 36)

In this sequence, which is both pathetic and grotesquely humorous, the art of the story's design creates its maximum effects, effects that I can only describe as musical. Kafka-designer has here created new expressive tonalities, never sounded before in quite this way. The harmonious tones of the central lines ('Was he an animal?'), placed between the jarring dissonances of the lines that precede and follow, produce new, savagely dissonant harmonies of the type that at least since Baudelaire we think of as characteristically modernist.

The crux is the relation between Gregor's spiritual exaltation at this moment and the subtly carnal fantasy in which it issues. The inseparability of the high and the low, of the *highest* and the *lowest*: this is the phenomenon of human reality that transfixes the imagination of modernism. Sometimes, as in Rilke's 'Archaic Torso of Apollo', this phenomenon is merely grazed, in a modality that remains sublime, merely hinting at the tension between poles. Thus Rilke archly refers to the genitalia (the 'center of procreation') of the god-torso, suggesting that the sublime shining of the mutilated statue ('shimmering like the coat of some wild animal') in some mysterious way forms a harmonious unity with an underlying animal-being, or might form such a unity if we were only adequate to the task. Hence the concluding line, 'You must change your life!' – an admonition that implies hope and faith – the belief that it is indeed possible to change one's life, and so bring it into closer accord with the divine, but genitalia-equipped, shining of the torso. Sometimes, as often in T. S. Eliot, we veer to something like the opposite extreme, in which it seems that the blending is merely a defilement of sublimity, as in the ending of 'Sweeney among the Nightingales', in which the nightingales 'let their liquid siftings fall/To stain the stiff, dishonored shroud' of Agamemnon. But in the musical animal passage of *The Metamorphosis* the blending seems neither and both of the above.

Strictly speaking, 'Was he an animal, that music could move him so?' is ambiguous. It could mean what it is generally taken to mean, that if music can move him so, he cannot be an animal, he must have somehow transcended animality. But it can also mean, 'If music can move me so, does this mean that I am indeed an animal?' – that he finally acknowledges the animal-being that he has always been, whether as human or as bug. It is, after all, less plausible that music reflects a sphere of transcendence than that it's a product of evolution (here I refer the reader once again to Greg Tomlinson's superb book on the evolution of the music faculty, *One Million Years of Music*). The latter is the more difficult meaning, but also the one that best reflects the most characteristic impulse of modernism, which is *naturalistic* in the most radical philosophical sense. The urge to transcend animality, to escape entrapment in the biological flesh, is Christian-Cartesian, and modernism is best understood as a struggle to break the grip of this urge. This struggle runs into perplexities of many kinds, and in the grip of these perplexities, modernism strains in both directions at once – towards release from all sordid limitation of a materiality that is intrinsically alien and even hostile to aesthetic experience, and towards embrace of this same materiality as the real and unique source of all form and beauty. But there are various backdoor exits from these perplexities, such as the reduction of animality to its most acceptable traits, innocence and instinctual grace. Examples from Rilke, again, come to mind, 'The Gazelle', and 'The Panther'. That is why it is so important to stress that Gregor is not an animal in *that* sense, that he is an *ungeheurem Ungeziefer*, animality in its most reductive sense, the sense most unassimilable by the dualist consciousness – as the action of disgusting natural processes of motility, nutrition, secretion, excretion, at an extreme remove from anything like human subjectivity – but from which human subjectivity is inextricable. Kafka's bug is no empirically specifiable creature but a compendium of such maximally subhuman traits, and can be identified with, if at all, only as a figure for one's own worst feelings of worthlessness and experiences of isolation from humanity. But, while *The Metamorphosis* is carefully crafted to arouse such feelings, the arousing of these feelings is not the endgame; they are aroused in order to be used as component elements of a larger design. Gregor's abjection becomes the subject of a cartoon, the romantic monster who, dragon-like, keeps a maiden in his cave.

The contrast with 'Archaic Torso of Apollo' is stark: here there is no moral to be gleaned, only an experience to be had of violently dissonant emotional tonalities held together by the design of the story, which systematically, with grotesque good humour, drives Gregor down and down and finally to his death. The high-spirited sadism with which the story does this cannot be attributed to the narrating instance, which is too characterless to produce such effects. Our sense of the *designing* instance, the one that doesn't speak at all but that has constructed every aspect of this text, must be gleaned from the design itself; and this designing instance is very nearly merciless. It has constructed this entire story so far in order to bring Gregor to this final humiliation, which unlike that of the Crucifixion has no point beyond the delectation of the audience.

The 'unknown nouristhment' incident is the climax of the narrative, the point at which it attains its maximum effects, like a full orchestra swelling to the climax of a symphony. But Gregor's drama is not quite over; there remains one final turn, at which the narrative at last allows Gregor some dignity – immense dignity, in fact. If it weren't for this turn *The Metamorphosis* would be all humiliation and no catharsis. But before the narrative voice devotes itself entirely to the family, we read Gregor's return to sobriety, his acceptance of his fate and the remarkable narration of his final moments, in three paragraphs from which, remarkably, irony is banished , at least to the degree that, given the context, this is possible. Kafka's prose becomes gentle, even caressing, in these moving, hard-earned paragraphs. The final lines, which rightly remind readers of John 19:30, are a kind of prose *pietá*, a momentary verbal lap on which the pitiable dead body of Gregor can come to rest. But only for a moment, because in the next paragraph, perhaps the funniest in the entire narrative, the bony cleaning woman comes bustling in to poke at his dead body with a broom handle, slamming doors *hard* as she goes, 'although she had often been asked not to' (p. 39).

NOTES

1 See Émile Zola, *The Experimental Novel and other essays*, trans. Belle M. Sherman (New York: Cassell Pub. Co., 1893).

2 Franz Kafka, *The Metamorphosis*, trans. Stanley Corngold (New York: W. W. Norton, 1972).

3 Dorritt Coohn, *Transparent Minds: Narrative Modes for Presenting Consciousness in Fiction* (Princeton, NJ: Princeton University Press, 1978).

4 Her response to his change, by the way, is almost as unrealistic as Gregor's, but it manifests the naturalizing pull of the realist plot matrix.

5 Mark M. Anderson, 'Sliding Down the Evolutionary Ladder? Aesthetic Autonomy in *The Metamorphosis*', in Corngold, pp. 154–72, esp. 167–8.

PART FIVE

Techne Metatheory

CHAPTER TWELVE

Universal design space and the lines of force

There is a single, unified Design Space in which the processes of both biological and human creativity make their tracks, using similar methods.
– Daniel Dennett

The main focus of this book has been on the practicalities of techne. Now, in a more speculative mood, I want to place techne theory within a larger theoretical framework, based on the concept of universal design space (UDS) developed by Daniel Dennett in his book *Darwin's Dangerous Idea*. UDS, the 'logical space' that can be imaginatively projected as containing all the possible combinations of all existing design elements, whether biological or cultural, provides us with a conceptual grid on which we can picture all evolutionary movement towards new forms, and gives us a completely non-psychological (or 'post-human') way of envisioning the artisan's relation to forms that have not yet come into existence.[1]

Up to this point, our only theoretical light has been from the sketchy associationist account of Hadamard, which provides a plausible picture of how the mind operates with a techne-combinatory, but gives no insight into the dynamics of such a combinatory beyond the essential fact that its 'atoms' have an independent energy of their own, and a tendency to be pulled 'magnetically' into combinations. Dennett's model allows us to probe much deeper into the structure and above all the *evolutionary dynamics* of an abstract 'design space', within which all design, biological or cultural, can be conceived to develop. Biological evolution happens independently of the human mind, and cultural or *technosocial* evolution – which is the continuation of biological evolution by different means (as Aristotle almost said) – in a very important sense does too.

Once one has in mind how a design process can happen without the intervention of a planning intelligence, it becomes possible to conceive even the human activities of inventing, designing, and making in a way that is not tethered to what Derrida called 'present' consciousness. We can treat the design of human productions as I have in this book, as emerging out of cognitive processes that are distributed, according to circumstances, over time, space, and multiple individuals, processes in which design grows by accretion of design modifications occasioned by the friction of human purposiveness directed at some practical goal – a purposiveness itself inwardly structured by the system-dynamics of a historically evolved techne that the individual artisan inherits – with the materiality against which it bumps, always open to the contingencies of interaction with the world.

The deep analogy between this process and biological evolution is in the *retrospective* nature of its constructive logic. Darwinian logic knows only the past perfect tense: what *has succeeded*. A good design, in Darwinian terms, is not one that follows from a well-formed, pre-existent template but one that works, for whatever it happens to work – which might not be what it originally evolved to do but a function of lucky circumstance, and whose value can only be known retrospectively. If it works, it must be *preserved* and *repeated* in order to serve as the basis of progressive refinement of design. And once a functional design is in place, it can be, as Dennett says, 'reverse engineered', taken apart to see how it works. But reverse engineering, whether in electronics or poetry or biology, depends on the presupposition that what we are taking apart is, indeed, something *designed* to perform a *function*. To approach something in this way is to see it from what Dennett calls the 'design standpoint'. The design standpoint, of course, does not require us to posit a designer. That is the fundamental lesson of Darwin's theory of evolution.

Emergent design

Dennett presents the idea of a universal design space as an expansion of Borges's imaginary Library of Babel, which contains all the books that could ever be formed from all the possible permutations of an alphabet with a restricted set of characters; UDS contains, in addition to the Library of Babel, all possible cultural products, and all possible permutations of the component elements of DNA, thus all the possible organisms. UDS, thus, like Borges's library, is a logical 'possibility space', a sort of virtual reality, produced by a combinatory not unlike those imagined by Poincaré or the structuralists: a limited ensemble of elements that can then be put through all the permutations allowable by whatever set of principles or rules is in place. Even with a quite restricted 'alphabet' or set of combinatory elements, the number of possible combinations, while not infinite, is so large that Dennett has proposed to call such a number *Vast* (with a capital 'V'). The number of books in the Library of Babel, for instance, has been calculated to be so large as to exceed the number of particles in the visible universe. But most of these combinations will not form coherent, functioning ensembles; only a Vanishingly (i.e. Vastly tiny) small number of functional ensembles is dispersed among the Vast number of possible combinations. And, since evolutionary systems are in a perpetual state of mutation, the elementary ensembles of the biological and cultural combinatories will differ at any given time from themselves at any subsequent time, so the possibility spaces projectable from them will also differ.

Biological evolution is the process that, over vast spans of time, mindlessly winnows out the immense number of mutations that don't function as well, preserves the ones that work better, and accumulates them to make more efficient survival mechanisms, thereby achieving the same kinds of results that human beings (much more efficiently) achieve by intentionally designing things. Since there is no designer involved in the production of Darwinian design, there is no designing activity, either. The only actions we can even figuratively attribute to nature are overproduction of offspring, constant production of mutations and killing off of excess offspring. Given enough time, if nature keeps doing this, design 'emerges' from this process, without need of any kind of form-making impulse in nature.

Not everyone is comfortable with calling the results of this mechanical, or 'algorithmic', process, 'design', a notion that is hard to dissociate from the idea of a designing intelligence. But dissociate it we must, because the posited process definitely works, and it is definitely mind-free, and it definitely produces beautifully functioning organisms, according to a process that, despite not being mind-directed, can only be understood in teleological terms. This is because, as Dennett stresses, we cannot discern the evolutionary design process except in terms of *function* – Socrates's *ergon* or *dynamis* – and function is an intrinsically teleological concept. A function is defined in relation to its telos or 'final cause', its 'that for the sake of which'. Lungs are *for* breathing, wings are *for* flying. They would never have evolved except for the function that they successfully perform, and we must posit this function as the adaptation's cause – not because some designing intelligence aimed at it, but as the reason the bearers of the adaptation achieved a higher survival rate than their competitors. The steady occurrence of mutations generates new designs, most of which are non-functional, but by trying out new things (through the profligate overproduction of offspring that mutate in a variety of directions) species comb through the 'search space' of possible designs, and the evolutionary winnowing process mechanically or (as Dennett says) 'algorithmically' accumulates design improvements in a way that very slowly optimizes function. A species may thus be conceived as a gigantic, distributed, search engine, and evolution as a kind of mindless engineering intelligence, whose evolved designs can be reverse engineered to discover the steps by which they evolved (pp. 128–33).

Dennett suggests that the kind of teleology involved in evolution is that of *practical reasoning*, reasoning that guides action without necessarily involving intellectual activity (p. 132). If action did require thinking, no animal would be able to instantly bolt from a predator. Practical reasoning is knowing what to do when a need arises, and acting on instinct is a perfectly good form of it. The imperative of practical reason, which is expressed in action appropriate to a need or desire, can be expressed verbally as: in order to achieve goal X, you must do Y. This is simple enough when we speak of the action, whether instinctually or intellectually worked out, of an individual or group, but consider what it means when translated into the following practical evolutionary imperative: to fly, you must have wings. Here the 'agent' of the required action is not a discrete being but that necessary construct of biology, a species, and the goal is not one that can be aimed at in any sense, conscious or instinctive. Flying is not a goal for a species, nor is evolving wings. The concrete aims of individual organisms are things like finding food, copulating, defending against attackers – in aggregate, survival. And as a statistical result of the differential survival of populations of individuals, certain species eventually develop wings. Practical reasoning, concretized by evolution as (e.g.) the 'fight or flight instinct', says, 'to escape predators, move away as fast as you can'; and in response (according to one scenario of how it happened) individuals belonging to some species run, jump, wave their arms to get a bit of air support – not because they're trying to grow wings, but because it makes them go a bit faster, and bit by tiny bit mutations that make the flapping more effective are accumulated by natural selection, so that eventually wings develop. So the teleology of evolutionary design is, at base, nothing more than this – the practical necessity, woven into the nature of things in the way I just explained, of doing X if Y is to be the result. Every organism has to be a practical reasoner in this sense, and so must a species – or rather, the mechanism of evolution only becomes intelligible to us by conceiving species in this way, as a kind of agent.

Techne is humanity's own special way of reasoning in and through praxis, but every organism, including us, has the imperatives of praxis woven into its body by evolution – into its instincts and into the structure of nerve, muscle, tendon and bone – and it is these imperatives, woven into the 'co-evolution' of biology and culture, that eventually develop into our technai.[2]

Dennett emphasizes that, even though the evolutionary search process is itself algorithmic, mechanical, mindless, evolution itself is far from random. A machine or algorithm is exhaustively characterized by its structure as it exists at a given moment. It is a 'synchronic' entity. But when the search algorithms of evolution go to work they immediately begin to build up a historical residue of their operation. They build simple forms randomly, then modify and add on to them, and as they accumulate design in this way the evolutionary process lays down constraints on the form of future design developments, pointing them in one direction or another. The algorithms no longer function at random because the context of accumulated structure in a sense 'guides' them in specific directions. That's the beauty of evolution. I have argued in this book that a similar kind of design cunning is encoded in our technai.

The accumulation of structure is itself constrained and, in a very general sense, *guided by* the structure of the affordances that material reality makes available, affordances that vary in each case with the specific problems that evolution has to solve. These structuring constraints Dennett, in a wonderfully evocative figure, calls 'invisible maze walls in design space' (p. 261). That these are walls means that they define the limits of functional form, but that they are invisible means that the boundary they define is one that only becomes manifest in the dialectic between animal or human action and the body of nature, and which keeps shifting in response to changes in the way we probe them.[3] Good design, we might now say, is design that hugs the invisible maze walls of design space as tightly as possible.

Adjacency in design space

Let's call the region of UDS occupied by human-made forms *technosocial design space* (TDS). The Barthesian literary combinatory would be one little corner of TDS, which is itself the tiny human region of UDS. Taking his cue from Borges, Dennett calls the design space opened out by the alphabet 'The Library of Babel', and the design space of DNA 'The Library of Mendel'. Even though it is only a tiny fraction of UDS, the Library of Babel is, although not technically infinite, more than astronomically vast, and since there are no rules restricting the kinds of combinations into which the library's alphabet can enter, most of its volumes are, like UDS in general, almost entirely nonsense. Only a 'Vanishingly small' number of the volumes contain even one coherent sentence. The Library of Mendel is conceived by analogy with that of Babel, with some differences that we can ignore. For present purposes, let's say the Library of Mendel contains all the possible genomes constructible out of the four basic nucleotides of which DNA is made.

The reason most of the forms in the Library of Babel are nonsense is that Borges's combinatory has been cut loose from friction with any worldly context. Like Plato's Forms, the volumes of Babel are a timeless array, a closed totality that by definition can do no *design work*. So the Library of Mendel, which is conceived on the same principle, cannot, by itself, do any design work either. The structure of the two libraries – we might call it 'Borges World' – transparently reflects the mechanical operation, in a pure conceptual vacuum, of their generative algorithms, and Dennett uses it as a backdrop against which to show how, without any magic tricks, the teleology of evolutionary design work can emerge when the same algorithms are embedded in the temporality of natural process. In Borges World, there is no *cost* to the generation of nonsense, because everything survives, permanently shelved somewhere in the library (Dennett, p. 203). Because there is no penalty for poor form, there are neither 'correct' nor 'incorrect' ways of forming sentences and books. In the biosphere, by contrast, the penalty for poor form is extinction of the hereditary line, and a cutting off of all the future possibilities of form that the line would have opened up (and which notionally 'exist' in the abstract Library of Mendel); and this pruning of the non-functional and suboptimal is what drives the evolution of design, which is just the piling up across vast spans of time of solutions to the practical problems of survival.

The near-Platonic abstraction of universal design space allows us to conceptualize the relation between what is actual and what isn't actual *yet*, but could be – the new that hasn't yet emerged, but which is potential in the sense that the empirical conditions are present for its emergence. Before a new form emerges, imagine it as 'hidden' as a possibility in the Vast nonsense of abstractly possible, mostly non-functional, forms. This kind of potential is fundamentally different from either Aristotle's or Seamus Heaney's. It is, in fact, an important new conception of potentiality, one that enables us to think past the tired opposition of the merely mechanical and the 'creative'. Aristotle's *dynamis* is an ideal essence that fully predetermines the form of the actuality it potentiates; Romanticism like Heaney's, which follows in the tracks laid down by Schelling, is merely a vague version of idealist teleologism.[4] By posing the work of design against the background of the profligate generativity of UDS, Dennett conceives a space of open, yet not unconstrained, potentiality. The algorithms of evolution carry on a mechanical search of this logical space, actualizing forms that were merely potential in it, pruning out the forms that are not viable, preserving and repeating those that are, accumulating design.

In bioevolution, there's no actual selection, only pruning, while in technosocial design there is selection also; but both kinds of evolution proceed by the same 'engineering' logic of optimization (Dennett, p. 144). Because the logic of evolution turns out to be an engineering logic, we can reverse engineer both biological and cultural design in terms of optimality considerations. Reverse engineering involves asking the reasons something came to be the way it is, 'why' questions, where 'why' means 'what function does this feature serve?' (p. 213); and functional analysis requires the specification of a 'building path' – the beginning state of the feature, the steps by which it got to its end state, and the order in which they were executed or occurred (p. 220).

Reverse engineering is, thus, as Dennett emphasizes, historical in nature. In order to study the 'why' of design, we must be immersed in the specificity of historical location, in the constraint of what has already happened. Out of the practically infinite space of possible forms, *this* and only *this* radically delimited subset of forms has in fact been historically actualized. Out of all the biological forms that might have evolved, we have at a certain moment in evolutionary history this subset; out of all the poems that could have been written in English, we have this corpus, and so forth across all the technai. And at any given moment, only those new forms are possible that are at that moment *adjacent* in design space to the set of forms that already exists, and which is the context for new combinations (pp. 118–20). This apparently rather modest concept of adjacency gives its value specifically for techne theory to the 'design space' model, because it provides a formal model for how invention happens. Any location in design space will be adjacent to a limited number of new possibles, and an artisan who incorporates the know-how of a techne gains access to the area of adjacent possibles, and only to it. Adjacency here is conceived very flexibly; the more capable the artisan, the greater the field of forms to which she gains access; but even the greatest genius has a horizon of adjacency that is not overleapable.

On this model, to specify the historical techne-context of design is to place one's analysis on the imaginary grid of design space. The notion of design space gives us a formal model in terms of which to conceptualize, for example, what happened when Picasso and Braque walked into the great Cézanne retrospective in 1907. Their own work had developed up to the point of adjacency in design space to a whole new field of possibilities of form, which with a boost from Cézanne they unlocked for a whole generation of painters who were themselves adjacent to Picasso and Braque's design locus, and who then developed these possibilities along their own lines.

The virtual forms of UDS are, like Aristotelian forms, in a sense already there before we look for them, but unlike Aristotelian forms they are merely a logical projection, a way of conceptualizing the dynamis of existing forms, and the Vast majority of them will never be actualized. Thus there are two degrees of possible: the notionally possible, most of which is not viable, and the actually possible, which nevertheless might or might not become actual. The actually possible can meaningfully be labelled *potential*, in a sense descended from Aristotle's *dynamis*. But unlike Aristotelian potential, Dennettian potential is *incomplete* in its specification of form, which 'emerges' out of a complex confluence of processes, involving serendipity and friction with a real-world context. (It isn't, by the way, just biological evolution, or Art, that works this way; even the egg that contains the form of the future chicken turns out to do so.)[5]

UDS projects as a closed timeless array at any given moment of historical time; but, considered in a diachronic, evolutionary perspective, it morphs into new shapes at each successive moment, as a consequence of both its own internal dynamics and the influence of external factors. As new forms are actualized, lines of development that were formerly possible cease to be so, and new possibilities of form open up. Thus, for example, in the tradition of Western easel painting as it became more and more realistic it became impossible to develop further the static Byzantine elements of Medieval representations of the Virgin. The stunning Hall 2 of the Uffizi, with the three Madonnas by Duccio, Cimabue and Giotto, shows the inexorable movement of Western painting into a 'search space' that excludes old elements and includes new ones, and therefore lights up a new array of possible constellations of elements and switches off the lights on old arrays. Something analogous happens, within the tradition of the blues, when it begins to utilize electric instruments, and a whole new galaxy of possible forms (such as the music of Captain Beefheart) opens out to be explored, while the possibilities of development of the acoustic Delta Blues, out of which electric Chicago Blues grew, become severely limited.

As Dennett says, there isn't just one way to skin a cat; yet all the ways in which it would be possible to skin it are necessarily vectors or pathways along the maze walls of design space. The productive potential of any techne is indefinitely various and subject to historical contingency, yet any of the actualizations of its potential may be conceptualized as belonging to the logical field of possibility of its productive dynamis.

Lines of force

Design work, according to this model, accumulates design developments along a line that is constrained by the structure of the accumulated design as it exists to that point, and which flexes according to the unfolding changes in the design context. Design space contains a near-infinity of bad moves that lead to nonsense forms, and a Vanishing number of good moves that, threaded together in the right sequence – one that tracks the 'invisible maze walls' of the meta-engineering constraints on good design – create viable forms. Nothing dictates that a good move will be actualized, or that a viable form, once actualized, will survive and thrive; this is an entirely contingent matter. An asteroid can always hit the earth and cut off a multitude of beautiful evolutionary lines. But for even the *possibility* of actualization of a form to exist, there needs to have been just the right sequence of design developments leading up to its threshold. We don't know what lies just over the conceptual horizon, but we know it has to be adjacent to what we see on the horizon, because there's no way to get to design that's farther away, unprepared for.

A constellation of good moves is functional because its elements are linked in a way that actualizes the *ergon* 'work-power' that the evolution of this lineage of forms has designed into each element. This ergon is itself a function of the 'organic' relation among elements, a relation that exists not because they are held together by some principle analogous to that of the life of an organism, but because the ergon of each of these elements has evolved in reciprocal relation to that of the others. I call the pathways of connectivity that link the elements of a potential constellation of elements (one that would be functional if actualized), *lines of force*. Out of the Vast array of nonsense volumes on the shelves of the library of Babel, the lines of force define only potentially existent ones that would make sense. UDS contains all the logically possible forms; history contains the forms that have so far become actual; the lines of force define the subset of logically possible forms that *would be* viable *if* they were to become actual.

Think of the timeless quasi-Platonic array of algorithmically generated virtual forms of UDS as almost entirely dark, and of lines of force as lighted-up dotted lines outlining the pathways through the invisible maze walls of design space that constitute viable constellations of good moves – constellations that, if the historical development of a species or a techne should be headed in their direction, could begin to be actualized as they become adjacent to forms that this historical process has already actualized. The lighted lines represent a tendency, in the system of relations of the entire ensemble of elements, to constellate in certain ways as a consequence of what Dennett calls 'overall good fit' conditions; collections of elements that do not constellate in this way will be inert or will quickly decay and fall apart.

In some design lineages most such forms, at some design junctures all, will be actualized if some contingency does not intervene, because the lines of force that delineate them correspond to what Dennett calls 'forced moves' in design space. Calculus, or eyes, are solutions to design problems that are highly likely, or, under the right circumstances, certain, to be found because there is no other remotely competitive way to skin these cats. The same is true of many moves in practical fields like carpentry or engineering. In Art, by contrast, there is a much larger set of potential forms that will never be actualized, for no reason other than that the search space of painting or music is too large, offering lines of force leading in too many directions, for any one design to force itself into actuality.

An artisan is a historically and culturally determinate subject located by training in a techne at a given point in the matrix of cultural design space, such that a given array of configurations of possible good moves, Vanishingly small subset of the configurations of abstractly possible moves, is open to this subject as a set of real possibilities, the ones defined by the lines of force. Lines of force are neither full positivities in a positive order or mere abstractions in a system of possibility. As adjacent to a present, already actualized moment in the historical development of a culture, they are located at the threshold of being. Out of the many actually possible constellations of force or form available in a given culture at a given moment, only a tiny subset can be realized, and *only* those which inhabit this threshold are capable of being realized. These threshold constellations are not only impressed with the potential for significant form by their relation to the forms that precede them and of which they are mutations or permutations, they are also pregnant with the force accumulated from the history of the culture that has brought it to this moment. They are, as it were, trembling with the potential for actualization. The *act* of the subject is to bring about this actualization, by applying the necessary quantum of energy, in the necessarily cunning way, to bring a given constellation across the threshold of possibility into the full light of being.

Finding 'join'

The cunning encoded in techne is the knowledge accumulated in it of the structure of the maze walls in design space. The constraints of this structure are what we feel for when we are trying to achieve good join in our work. Apprenticeship is practice running our fingers over the set of maze walls that has been explored by a given techne, until we become accustomed to their characteristic contours and can perceive the correctness or incorrectness of a move. But the maze walls of design space are not fixed channels, they are multidimensional possibility spaces, and what I'm calling their 'contours' are not like the contours of ordinary walls. These contours may be extremely variable and subject to 'mutation', as when a piece of wood turns out to have an irregularity that affects how the carpenter can use it, or when the necessity of making a rhyme at line 3 forces a rewriting of the first two lines; and learning to flex with this variability is a crucial part of mastering a techne.

To approach Art in this framework is to bring it down to earth, to treat it as fundamentally a matter of fitting together physical components, in a way related to the work of the practical crafts, or the way that the the atoms of DNA had to physically fit together in the right helical pattern in Watson and Crick's physical model. Poetry and music, which have since the Greeks been treated as Something Higher, are, like other technai, subject to the constraints of simple materiality, a constraint the elementary model of which is 'you can't put a square peg into a round hole'. Let's call this principle, which represents perhaps the most fundamental invisible maze wall in cultural design space, the principle of *fit* or *join*. Any system of design elements is going to have a set of possibilities and constraints that belongs to it as a consequence of what can be thought of as the 'shape' (loosely speaking) of the elements, the ways in which those shapes are capable of being combined (think of Greek atomism), and the geometry of the design space in which they are being combined. Making music or poetry is fundamentally fitting together a series of vibratory patterns in air, and other technai that join series of symbols (numerals, words, machine code) also make arrays of physical tokens using a kind of techne-cunning that is fundamentally akin to laying mosaics or doing a jigsaw puzzle. The significance or combinatorial potential of a symbol or representation's physical 'shape', of course, is not intrinsic to its materiality (as, to a considerable degree, that of a piece of wood or a mosaic is), but is determined by the conventional system within which this shape plays its specific function. Rhyme, for instance, is a historical, entirely contingent convention of English poetry. But, given the convention, it is the case that certain words will rhyme and others won't, as a function of more or less physical properties.[6]

Finding fit in this way is just the first stage of form-finding, however; and it isn't characteristic of plastic arts like sculpture, pottery-making, and painting, which work with actual physical materials, but materials that are initially formless (unlike mosaics, two-by-fours, or words). Yet the way form is found in these technai provides a model for understanding the second phase of form-finding in the symbolic arts themselves. Say I'm writing a sonnet. I concatenate words in ways that are attentive to the 'music' of their combination, and also to the rhythm of the syntax and the meter of the line, looking for proper join. But all of this local work is controlled at a higher level by the evolving shape of the poem as a whole, in which every element will ideally spark the function of every other element, all of this activity contained within a well-designed overall form, with local climaxes, minor and major 'turns', and a resonant closure. We push materials of one sort or another around, forming larger and larger shaped masses out of them until we find an overall shape that achieves rightness, or comes as close as we think we can.

This is even truer of prose than it is of poetry, because prose can, in the initial phase of drafting, form globs of words that are as far from the well-trimmed form of the finished essay as a piece of freshly quarried marble is from the finished statue. At this level – the level of the form of the whole – there's no fundamental difference between writing an essay or a poem, on the one hand, and moulding a clay pot, on the other. Nor is there any fundamental difference between these moulding activities and those of bees making their hives out of wax or wasps their nests out of paper pulp, or birds 'warbling their woodnotes wild'. In the end, the Romantics were right about the naturalness of creation; they simply didn't know about the evolutionary dynamics by means of which nature works.

Situated subjects in technosocial design space

Techne, then, is the *form of forms* in technosocial design space, in a sense of 'form' that is immensely more abstract than that of a physical object or pattern. It is, rather, the evolving logic or *logos* that holds together a practice dispersed over time, space, and individual practitioners whose individual appropriations of it might differ in ways large and small, and which enables them to track given lines of force. Yet techne is also real, in the homeliest sense of 'real'. Technai manifest themselves continually in everyday practice, and most illuminatingly in everyday scenes of teaching and learning. When we get to scenes of techne-practice, and above all, in scenes of techne-instruction, we reach rock bottom in our inquiry. There we see techne 'laid bare' for the apprentice, and for us: the young guitarist learning how to finger-pick, the kindergartner learning to write. As the utterances of native speakers are the raw material with which the linguist must begin, and beyond which there is no appeal, so skilled and apprentice artisans doing what they do, or teaching and learning how to do it, are the raw material of techne theory – that which must be taken for granted and to which all explanations must be referred as a basis. Of course the 'how' of this doing is not so easily revealed; that's where long apprenticeship comes in for the artisan, and why techne theory is necessary. But in a single scene we nevertheless see the thing itself, not the whole techne all at once – there *is* no 'all at once' of a techne – but a synecdoche for it.

Because technai are evolved phenomena, they have themselves been 'designed' by the same kind of process that hones the form of the things technai make. The elements, instruments or 'organs' of a techne evolve as an ensemble, such that the ergon or dynamis of each element exists only in relation to the ensemble. The creation of new forms, then, comes not from the depths of human interiority but from the system-dynamics of established techne-ensembles as embodied in the psyche-somas of individual artisans, and also, in a way that has scarcely begun to be understood, in the techne-community as a whole, which itself may draw from encompassing energies in the larger community. It's clear from the evidence of history that the dynamics of a system like that of English poetry operate at the communal level as well as the individual level, and that the former set the limits – or expand the limits – of creativity of the latter. Entire communities, such as classical Athens, Renaissance Florence, Shakespeare's London, or Harlem in the 20s, explode with creativity, and it is within such milieus that a great deal of the most revolutionary creative activity of individuals takes place.[7]

In the realm of literature as in the realm of life an emerging form must be conceived as possessing a certain autonomy and as exercising formative constraint over the elements out of which it is composed. An emerging form – an actually possible form, and one that conforms to good design principles – at a certain point becomes, it is said, *self-organizing*. At a certain point, the form begins to crystallize, and at that point its own dynamics become the leading factor in the process (what artists refer to as the work's acquiring life of its own). The art of the most illustrious artisan is the ability to feel and move with this dynamics.

Within social design space new forms in order to be actualized have to be 'tapped' into being (as a tap on a beaker catalyses a salt solution into crystallizing) by a human agent's bringing to bear, skilfully, along the relevant lines of force, the requisite quantum of energy. This force is always applied at a determinate historical moment at a determinate locus in technosocial design space, and will therefore never be the blind activation of an arbitrary form but an action that follows in the channels that technosocial history has grooved into the techne involved, and which thus observes the principles of good design intrinsic to the relationality of the elements of the combinatory in question. The solution to the problem of how the privileged forms are selected out of design space is therefore nothing but the poststructuralist notion of the historically situated subject, which articulates quite naturally with Dennett's account. Or, applying the theory I am elaborating to its own elaboration, we could say that the notions of UDS and that of the situated subject are good moves in conceptual design space that fit well together according to the principles of meta-engineering, and which have been brought together by the lines of force that are accessible at this time and place in history from the specific locus in social design space that I occupy as I write this book.

A human agent is, on this account, an essential and intrinsic factor in the functioning and evolution of technai; not as a geistig originator of form, but as the absolutely unique particularity of a specific organic body organized as a social actor and occupying a unique location in technosocial design space, with an effective, organically based quantum of energy that can be socially amplified or diminished, primarily through apprenticeship in a techne but also by a variety of other factors, social and economic.

To conceive Shakespeare's agency in this way is not at all to eliminate Shakespeare *an sich* from the picture. It is to reduce him to his absolute singularity as a particular, socially and historically located, organic body. The subject is, in the first instance, a particular body located in a space and time that are articulated as social space and social time; and social space-time is the matrix of design space with which each living human body must interact in order to become endowed with creative agency. What we think of as creativity and originality are, on the model I am sketching here, *primarily*, not exclusively, the product of the fact that different subjects occupy different locations in design space, and from each location a different set of lines of force in design space becomes available. Shakespeare produced works that were available from his precise location in social-historical design space; he could not have produced anything faintly resembling them had he occupied a radically different location. He might have been able to produce impressive work of some quite different kind, had he found himself in some other design locus; and then again he might not. This is not something we can test, but nothing we know supports the idea that 'genius' is a portable essence, stashed in the organism, that can be located anywhere in social-historical design space and still yield cascades of creativity.

No doubt there was something special about Shakespeare's organic endowment that enabled him to perceive greater possibilities of form generation from his design locus than someone else would have perceived, even if this someone else had been born in Shakespeare's place to Shakespeare's mother and father. But this something special does not have to be conceived as a creative, form-originating power. On the present model it shows up primarily as an unusually great techne-formed quantum of energy, partly but not entirely expressed as a capacity for great amounts of techne-labour, a quantum that, beginning from a specific location in design space was able to push farther and farther into the matrix of potential forms that successively opened up as he worked. But even energetic quantum is given in a highly indeterminate form in the physical organism, and must be socially formed and augmented if it is to become capable of great cultural achievement.

Self-organizing forms

We end with the deepest puzzle of techne theory, that of self-organizing form. If techne-forms evolve in ways fundamentally like the ways organisms evolve, then we can, at least up to a point, understand our own form creation in a way that involves no pre-positing of the forms to be achieved. Genuinely new forms 'emerge' from system-dynamics that, as they reach given levels of complexity, develop spontaneous powers of 'self-organization'. Here again, however, the bug of Romanticism easily sneaks back into our account. Self-organization sounds like an intrinsic power, some sort of mysterious nisus towards form, a new version of Schelling's rude matter striving towards 'something stereometeric'. Terrence Deacon has recently exposed the conceptual muddles to which the existing accounts of self-organization are liable, and proposed to replace the term 'self-organization' with the more precise notion of *morphodynamics*. As Deacon cautions, the 'self' in 'self-organization' is misleading, since it suggests something that first exists in some unspecified way as a unified holistic system-dynamics and then organizes its elements by exercising a 'top-down causality' on them. Self-organization also suggests that the holistic dynamics of the system guide its elements away from a disorganization that is their spontaneous state; whereas, Deacon shows, it is the spontaneous 'interaction dynamics' arising out of the intrinsic features of the component elements themselves that produces the new organization. The term self-organization thus obscures the fact that the features of the 'global wholeness of the system' are 'emergent consequences' rather than the prior cause (p. 244). Strikingly, this means that morphodynamics is more spontaneous, more intrinsic to the systems involved, than the notion of self-organization suggests, and yet in a way that involves *no nisus towards form*.

On Deacon's account, the deep spontaneity of nature is, ultimately, nothing other than the regularities described by the laws of physics, which turn out, on his account, to be something much more interesting than the banging of particle on particle as which the Romantic fear of physics conceives them. These 'laws' describe what physical reality will automatically do, if some countervailing force doesn't interfere, as for example a particle in motion will continue in motion in a straight line unless some force pushes it in another direction, or a mass will fall towards the centre of gravity of the earth if nothing gets in its way. Deacon usefully groups together all these spontaneous tendencies of nature as 'orthograde' tendencies. The most profound and pervasive spontaneity or orthograde tendency of all is entropy, the universal tendency of matter in motion to, so to speak, 'relax' into the most even distribution of energy that spreads the highs and lows in the system equally around its entire extent. We usually think of entropy as the ultimate destroyer of all order, and of life as an anti-entropic system – which it is. But Deacon shows how anti-entropy, order, emerges out of entropy itself. This happens because orthograde forces are constantly interfering with each other's spontaneity, disturbing each other's natural tendency to do what they do, thus creating the interactions that under certain conditions 'self-organize' into the kinds of forms we recognize as anti-entropic, symmetrical or otherwise well-organized forms such as Fibonacci sequences in plants and mineral nodules, frost polygons caused by the freezing and thawing of water in the soil of arctic regions, vortices and convection cells in fluids, and snow crystals. These are all processes that 'generate regularity not in response to the extrinsic imposition of regularity, or by being shaped by any template structure, but rather by virtue of regularities that are amplified internally via interaction dynamics alone under the influence of external perturbations' (p. 242).[8]

The most striking of Deacon's examples of how these kinds of shapings happen is his description of how Raleigh-Bénard convection works on 'convection cells' in a thin layer of heated liquid. Heated from the bottom, such a cell often forms a regular pattern of hexagonally shaped surface dimples as the heat dissipates out the top. This happens because the spontaneous tendency of the liquid is for the hotter molecules at the bottom to transfer their momentum to the cooler molecules at the top, from where it gets dissipated into the air. As the temperature gradient is increased, the lighter molecules from below move upward in masses, while the cooler regions descend; and the most efficient geometry according to which the masses can be arranged for the fastest transfer of heat is for the regions of hot and cold molecules to form into hexagonal columns – hexagon shapes being 'the most densely packed way to fill a surface with similar-size subdivisions'. 'Subdividing the plane of liquid into hexagonal subregions thus most evenly distributes the inversely moving columns of flowing liquid, and represents the most evenly distributed pattern of heat dissipation that can occur via fluid movement' (p. 252). In this way, then, under the right conditions, fundamentally involving the disturbance of one orthograde force (the liquid's equilibrium dynamics) by another (the heat that disturbs this equilibrium), the entropic tendency of energy, by doing what it does, results in geometric form.

The upshot of Deacon's reconception of self-organization as morphodynamics is that the emergence of form is now explained not as matter 'rising' towards form, as the idealist and Romantic notions have it, but as *falling* towards it (p. 245), in obedience to the orthograde spontaneity that drives nature to 'relax' into what we see as disorder.[9] Entropy is not the only force involved in form production, but it is the most fundamental and universal, the most apparently antithetical to order, and therefore the most revelatory of the fundamental tendency of Deacon's radical revision of our notions of self-organization. To have entropy revealed as the ultimate source of order is stunning, and deeply satisfying to the naturalistically inclined humanist mind, because it reveals the deepest sense in which it is true that, in Wallace Stevens's resonant phrase, *death is the mother of beauty*.

NOTES

1 Daniel Dennett, *Darwin's Dangerous Idea* (New York: Simon and Schuster, 1995).

2 Gary Tomlinson presents a wonderfully lucid overview of the process of co-evolution in his latest book, *Culture and the Course of Human Evolution* (Chicago: University of Chicago Press, 2018).

3 Here once again I refer the reader to Ludwig Fleck, *Genesis and Evolution of a Scientific Fact*, ed. Thadeuss J. Trenn and Robert K. Merton, trans. Fred Bradly and Thadeuss J. Trenn, with introduction by T. S. Kuhn (Chicago: University of Chicago Press, 1979).

4 Schelling writes that 'rude matter strives, as it were, blindly, after regular shape, and unknowingly assumes pure stereometric forms, which belong, nevertheless, to the realm of ideas, and are something spiritual in the material'. F. W. von Schelling, 'On the Relation of the Plastic Arts to Nature', in *Critical Theory Since Plato*, rev. edn, ed. Hazard Adams (Fort Worth: Harcourt, Brace, Jovanovich, 1992), pp. 457–67, quotation from pp. 458–9.

5 There is a kind of programming in the DNA that ensures the species will 'breed true', but, as Terrence Deacon explains, while there is a kind of 'preformation' contained in the DNA code, the 'vast majority' of the 'structural information' that determines the development of the embryo 'is generated anew in each organism as an emergent consequence of a kind of ecology of developing cells' (*Incomplete Nature*, [New York: W. W. Norton, 2012] 69).

6 These properties change over the course of history, and sometimes words that used to rhyme no longer do; but more commonly, the entire system of pronunciation changes in such a way that words continue to rhyme, because their sounds all change together. Thus Shakespeare's plays are pronounced very differently today than they were in Shakespeare's time, and differently in Britain than in the United States, and yet most of the rhymes still work. This shows that the power of rhyme is not a direct result of the individual physical sounds as such but of a given language's *system* of sounds.

7 In this connection, see the astonishingly comprehensive investigation of the history of intellectual communities across the world by Randall Collins, *The Sociology of Philosophies: A Global Theory of Intellectual Change* (Cambridge, MA: Belknap Press of Harvard University Press, 1998). Collins comments that

> intellectual groups, master-pupil chains, and contemporaneous rivalries together make up a structured field of forces within which intellectual activity takes place. And there is a pathway from such social structures into the inner experience of the individual's mind. The group is present

> in consciousness even when the individual is alone; for individuals who are the creators of historically significant ideas, it is this *intellectual* community which is paramount precisely when he or she is alone. (p. 7)

8 More elaborate forms like snowflakes are explained along similar lines. The key to the explanation of the more complex forms is the hierarchical layering of morphodynamic processes.

9 I wonder what Hegel would say about this. One is tempted to think that, on Deacon's account, entropy is *aufgehoben* into a producer of form; but it isn't, because the form is only temporary, and entropy will in the end reassert its identity as Shiva the destroyer.

INDEX